* 1,000,000 *

Free E-Books
@
www.ForgottenBooks.org

* Alchemy *

The Secret is Revealed
@
www.TheBookofAquarius.com

English

Composition and Literature

By

William Franklin Webster

Published by Forgotten Books 2012

PIBN 1000151196

Copyright © 2012 Forgotten Books
www.forgottenbooks.org

ENGLISH:

COMPOSITION AND LITERATURE

BY

W. F. WEBSTER

PRINCIPAL OF THE EAST HIGH SCHOOL
MINNEAPOLIS, MINNESOTA

BOSTON, NEW YORK, AND CHICAGO
HOUGHTON, MIFFLIN AND COMPANY
The Riverside Press, Cambridge

COPYRIGHT, 1900, BY W. F. WEBSTER
ALL RIGHTS RESERVED

D

PREFACE

IN July, 1898, I presented at the National Educational Association, convened in Washington, a Course of Study in English. At Los Angeles, in 1899, the Association indorsed the principles [1] of this course, and made it the basis of the Course in English for High Schools. At the request of friends, I have prepared this short text-book, outlining the method of carrying forward the course, and emphasizing the principles necessary for the intelligent communication of ideas.

It has not been the purpose to write a rhetoric. The many fine distinctions and divisions, the rarefied examples of very beautiful forms of language which a young pupil cannot possibly reproduce, or even appreciate, have been omitted. To teach the methods of simple, direct, and accurate expression has been the purpose; and this is all that can be expected of a high school course in English.

The teaching of composition differs from the teaching of Latin or mathematics in this point: whereas pupils can be compelled to solve a definite number of problems or to read a given number of lines, it is not possible to compel expression of the full thought. The full thought is made of an intellectual and an emotional element. Whatever is intellectual may be compelled

[1] See pp. 13, 14, of the Report of Committee on College Entrance Requirements.

by dint of sheer purpose; whatever is emotional must spring undriven by outside authority, and uncompelled by inside determination. A boy saws a cord of wood because he has been commanded by his father; but he cannot really laugh or cry because directed to by the same authority. There must be the conditions which call forth smiles or tears. So there must be the conditions which call forth the full expression of thought, both what is intellectual and what is emotional. This means that the subject shall be one of which the writer knows something, and in which he is interested; that the demands in the composition shall not be made a discouragement; and that the teacher shall be competent and enthusiastic, inspiring in each pupil a desire to say truly and adequately the best he thinks and feels.

These conditions cannot be realized while working with dead fragments of language; but they are realized while constructing living wholes of composition. It is not two decades ago when the pupil in drawing was compelled to make straight lines until he made them all crooked. The pupil in manual training began by drawing intersecting lines on two sides of a board; then he drove nails into the intersections on one side, hoping that they would hit the corresponding points on the other. Now no single line or exercise is an end in itself; it contributes to some whole. Under the old method the pupil did not care or try to draw a straight line, or to drive a nail straight; but now, in order that he may realize the idea that lies in his mind, he does care and he does try: so lines are drawn better and nails are driven straighter than before. In all training that combines intellect and hand, the principle has been recognized that the best work is done when the pupil's interest has been enlisted by making each exercise contribute directly to the construction of some whole. Only in the range of the spiritual are we twenty years behind time, trying to get the best construction by compulsion. It is quite time that we recognized that the best work in composition can be done, not while the pupil is correcting errors in the use of language which he never dreamed of, nor while he is writing ten similes or ten periodic sentences, but when both intellect and feeling combine and work together to produce some whole. Then into the construction of this whole the pupil will throw all his strength, — using the most apt comparisons, choosing the best words, framing adequate sentences, — in order that the outward form may worthily present to others what to himself has appeared worthy of expression.

There are some persons who say that other languages are taught by the word and sentence method; then why not English? These persons overlook the fact that we are leaving that method as rapidly as possible, and adopting a more rational method which at once uses a language to communicate thought. And they overlook another fact of even greater importance: the pupil entering the high school is by no means a beginner in English. He has been using the language ten or twelve years, and has a fluency of expression in English which he cannot attain in German throughout a high school and college course. The conditions under which a pupil begins the study of German in a high school and the study of English composition are entirely dissimilar; and a conclusion based upon a fancied analogy is worthless.

It is preferable, then, to practice the construction of wholes rather than the making of exercises; and it is best at the beginning to study the different kinds of wholes, one at a time, rather than all together. No one would attempt to teach elimination by addition and subtraction, by comparison and by substitution, all together; nor would an instructor take up heat, light, and electricity together. In algebra, or physics, certain great principles underlie the whole subject; and these appear and reappear as the study progresses through its allied parts. Still the best results are obtained by taking up these several divisions of the whole one after another. And in English the most certain and definite results are secured by studying the forms of discourse separately, learning the method of applying to each the great principles that underlie all composition.

If the forms of discourse are to be studied one after another, which shall be taken up first? In general, all composition may be separated into two divisions: composition which deals with things, including narration and description; and composition which deals with ideas, comprising exposition and argument. It needs no argument to justify the position that an essay which deals with things seen and heard is easier for a beginner to construct than an essay which deals with ideas invisible and unheard. Whether narration or description should precede appears yet to be undetermined;

for many text-books treat one first, and perhaps as many the other. I have thought it wiser to begin with the short story, because it is easier to gain free, spontaneous expression with narration than with description. To write a whole page of description is a task for a master, and very few attempt it; but for the uninitiated amateur about three sentences of description mark the limit of his ability to see and describe. To get started, to gain confidence in one's ability to say something, to acquire freedom and spontaneity of expression, — this is the first step in the practice of composition. Afterward, when the pupil has discovered that he really has something to say, — enough indeed to cover three or four pages of his tablet paper, — then it may be time to begin the study of description, and to acquire more careful and accurate forms of expression. Spontaneity should be acquired first, — crude and unformed it may be, but spontaneity first; and this spontaneity is best gained while studying narration.

There can be but little question about the order of the other forms. Description, still dealing with the concrete, offers an admirable opportunity for shaping and forming the spontaneous expression gained in narration. Following description, in order of difficulty, come exposition and argument.

I should be quite misunderstood, did any one gather from this that during the time in which wholes are being studied, no attention is to be given to parts; that is, to paragraphs, sentences, and words. All things cannot be learned at once and thoroughly; there must be some order of succession. In the beginning the primary object to be aimed at is the construction of wholes; yet during their construction, parts can also be incidentally studied. During this time many errors which annoy and exasperate must be passed over with but a word, in order that the weight of the criticism may be concentrated on the point then under consideration. As a pupil advances, he is more and more competent to appreciate and to form good paragraphs and well-turned sentences, and to single out from the multitude of verbal signs the word that exactly presents his thought. The appreciation and the use of the stronger as well as the finer and more delicate forms of language come only with much reading and writing; and to demand everything at the very beginning is little less than sheer madness.

Moreover there never comes a time when the construction of a paragraph, the shaping of a phrase, or the choice of a word becomes an end in itself. Paragraphs, sentences, and words are well chosen when they serve best the whole composition. He who becomes enamored of one form of paragraph, who always uses periodic sentences, who chooses only common words, has not yet recognized that the beauty of a phrase or a word is determined by its fitness, and that it is most beautiful because it exactly suits the place it fills. The graceful sweep of a line by Praxiteles or the glorious radiancy of a color by Angelico is most beautiful in the place it took from the master's hand. So Lowell's wealth of figurative language and Stevenson's unerring choice of delicate words are most beautiful, not when torn from their original setting to serve as examples in rhetorics, but when fulfilling their part in a well-planned whole. And it is only as the beauties of literature are born of the thought that they ever succeed. No one can say to himself, "I will now make a good simile," and straightway fulfill his promise. If, however, the thought of a writer takes fire, and instead of the cold, unimpassioned phraseology of the logician, glowing images crowd up, and phrases tipped with fire, then figurative language best suits the thought, — indeed, it is the thought. But imagery upon compulsion, — never. So that at no time should one attempt to mould fine phrases for the sake of the phrases themselves, but he should spare no pains with them when they spring from the whole, when they harmonize with the whole, and when they give to the whole added beauty and strength.

It is quite unnecessary at this day to urge the study of literature. It is in the course of study for every secondary school. Yet a word may be said of the value of this study to the practice of composition. There are two classes of artists: geniuses and men of talent. Of geniuses in literature, one can count the names on his fingers; most authors are simply men of talent. Talent learns to do by doing, and by observing how others have done. When Brunelleschi left Rome for Florence, he had closely observed and had drawn every arch of the stupendous architecture in that ancient city; and so he was adjudged by his fellow citizens to be the only man competent to lift the dome of their Duomo. His observation discovered the secret of Rome's architectural grandeur; and it is the accumulation of such secrets which is the development of every art and science. Milton had his method of writing prose, Macaulay his, and Arnold his, — all different and all excellent. And just as the architect stands before the cathedrals of Cologne, Milan, and Salisbury to learn the secret of each; as the painter searches out the secret of Raphael, Murillo, and Rembrandt; so the author analyzes the masterpieces of literature to discover the secret of Irving, of Eliot, and of Burke. Not that an author is to be a servile imitator of any man's manner; but that, having knowledge of all the secrets of composition, he shall so be enabled to set forth for others his own thought in all the beauty and perfection in which he himself conceives it.

One thing further. A landscape painter would not make a primary study of Angelo's anatomical drawings; a composer of lyric forms of music would not study Sousa's marches; nor would a person writing a story look for much assistance in the arguments of Burke. The most direct benefit is derived from studying the very thing one wishes to know about, not from studying something else. That the literature may give the greatest possible assistance to the composition, the course has been so arranged that narration shall be taught by Hawthorne and Irving, description by Ruskin and Stevenson, exposition by Macaulay and Newman, and argument by Webster and Burke. Literature, arranged in this manner, is not only a stimulus to renewed effort, by showing what others have done; it is also the most skillful instructor in the art of composition, by showing how others have done.

It would be quite impossible for any one at the present time to write a text-book in English that would not repeat what has already been said by many others. Nor have I tried to. My purpose has been rather to select from the whole literature of the subject just those principles which every author of a book on composition or rhetoric has thought essential, and to omit minor matters and all those about which there is a difference of opinion. This limits the contents to topics already familiar to every teacher. It also makes it necessary to repeat what has been written before many times. Certain books, however, have treated special divisions of the whole subject in a thorough and exhaustive manner. There is nothing new to say of Unity, Mass, and Coherence; Mr. Wendell said all concerning these in his book entitled "English Composition." So in paragraph development, Scott and Denney hold the field. Other books which I have frequently used in the classroom are "Talks on Writing English," by Arlo Bates, and Genung's "Practical Rhetoric." These books I have found very helpful in teaching, and I have drawn upon them often while writing this text-book.

If the field has been covered, then why write a book at all? The answer is that the principles which are here treated have not been put into one book. They may be found in several. These essentials I have repeated many times with the hope that they will be fixed by this frequent repetition. The purpose has been to focus the attention upon these, to apply them in the construction of the different forms of discourse, paragraphs, and sentences, and to repeat them until it is impossible for a student to forget them. If the book fulfils this purpose, it was worth writing.

Acknowledgments are due to Messrs. Charles Scribner's Sons for their kind permission to use the selections from the writings of Robert Louis Stevenson contained in this book; also, to Messrs. D. Appleton & Co., The Century Co., and Doubleday & McClure Co. for selections from the writings of Rudyard Kipling.

W F. WEBSTER.

MINNEAPOLIS, 1900.

CONTENTS

Chapter I. — Forms of Discourse

	Page
Composition	1
English Composition	1
Composition, Written and Oral	2
Conventions of Composition	2
Five Forms of Discourse	3
Definitions	4
Difficulty in distinguishing	4
Purpose of the Author	6

Chapter II. — Choice of Subject

Form and Material	8
Author's Individuality	8
Knowledge of Subject	9
Common Subjects	10
Interest	11
The Familiar	11
Human Life	12
The Strange	12

Chapter III. — Narration

Material of Narration	13
In Action	14
The Commonest Form of Discourse	14
Language as a Means of Expression	15
Without Plot	15
Plot	16
Unity, Mass, and Coherence	20
Main Incident	20
Its Importance	21
Unity	21
Introductions and Conclusions	23
Tedious Enumerations	23
What to include	24

Consistency	25
An Actor as the Story-teller	26
The Omniscience of an Author	27
The Climax	28
Who? Where? When? Why?	29
In what Order?	29
An Outline	32
Movement	32
Rapidity	32
Slowness	33
Description and Narration	34
Characters few, Time short	35
Simple Plot	36
Suggestive Questions and Exercises	38

Chapter IV. — Description

Difficulties of Language for making Pictures	49
Painting and Sculpture	50
Advantages of Language	50
Enumeration and Suggestion	52
Enumerative Description	54
Suggestive Description	55
Value of Observation	55
The Point of View	56
Moving Point of View	58
The Point of View should be stated	58
Mental Point of View	59
Length of Descriptions	63
Arrangement of Details in Description	64
The End of a Description	70
Proportion	73
Arrangement must be natural	74
Use Familiar Images	75
Simile, Metaphor, Personification	77
Choice of Words. Adjectives and Nouns	78
Use of Verbs	79
Suggestive Questions and Exercises	81

Chapter V. — Exposition

General Terms difficult	89
Definition	91
Exposition and Description distinguished	91

Logical Definition	91
Genus and Differentia	92
Requisites of a Good Definition	93
How do Men explain? First, by Repetition	94
Second, by telling the obverse	95
Third, by Details	96
Fourth, by Illustrations	97
Fifth, by Comparisons	98
The Subject	99
The Subject should allow Concrete Treatment	100
The Theme	100
The Title	102
Selection of Material	102
Scale of Treatment	104
Arrangement	108
Use Cards for Subdivisions	108
An Outline	109
Mass the End	110
The Beginning	112
Proportion in Treatment	114
Emphasis of Emotion	115
Phrases indicating Emphasis	116
Coherence	116
Transition Phrases	118
Summary and Transition	119
Suggestive Questions and Exercises	121

CHAPTER VI. — ARGUMENT

Induction and Deduction	129
Syllogism Premises	129
Terms	129
Enthymeme	130
Definition of Terms	130
Undistributed Middle	131
False Premises	131
Method of Induction	132
Arguments from Cause	133
Arguments from Sign	134
Sequence and Cause	135
Arguments from Example	137
Selection of Material	138
Plan called The Brief	138

Climax 139
Inductive precedes Deductive 140
Cause precedes Sign 140
Example follows Sign 141
Refutation 141
Analysis of Burke's Oration 142
Suggestive Questions 148

CHAPTER VII. — PARAGRAPHS

Definition 151
Long and Short Paragraphs 151
Topic Sentence 157
No Topic Sentence 161
The Plan 162
Kinds of Paragraphs 163
Details 163
Comparisons 165
Repetition 167
Obverse 169
Examples 171
Combines Two or More Forms 173
Unity 173
Need of Outline 174
Mass 174
What begins and what ends a Paragraph ? . . . 175
Length of opening and closing Sentences . . . 178
Proportion 179
Coherence and Clearness 180
Two Arrangements of Sentences in a Paragraph . . 181
Definite References 187
Use of Pronouns 188
Of Conjunctions 190
Parallel Constructions 192
Summary 195
Suggestive Questions 196

CHAPTER VIII. — SENTENCES

Definition and Classification. Simple Sentences . . 200
Compound Sentences 200
Short Sentences 204
Long Sentences 204
Unity 205

CONTENTS

Mass	207
End of a Sentence	208
Effect of Anti-climax	210
Use of Climax	211
Loose and Periodic	212
The Period	212
Periodic and Loose combined	214
Which shall be used?	215
Emphasis by Change of Order	217
Subdue Unimportant Elements	219
The Dynamic Point of a Sentence	221
Good Use	223
Clearness gained by Coherence	224
Parallel Construction	226
Balanced Sentences	227
Use of Connectives	228
Suggestive Questions	231

CHAPTER IX. — WORDS

Need of a Large Vocabulary	236
Dictionary	237
Study of Literature	238
Vulgarisms are not reputable	240
Slang is not reputable	240
Words must be National. Provincialisms	242
Technical and Bookish Words	242
Foreign Words	243
Words in Present Use	244
Words in their Present Meaning	245
Words of Latin and Saxon Origin	245
General and Specific	248
Use Words that suggest most	249
Synecdoche, Metonymy	250
Care in Choice of Specific Words	250
Avoid Hackneyed Phrases	253
"Fine Writing"	253
In Prose avoid Poetical Words	254

APPENDIX

A. Suggestions to Teachers	257
B. The Form of a Composition	260
C. Marks for Correction of Compositions	264
D. Punctuation	265
E. Supplementary List of Literature	275

A COURSE OF STUDY

IN LITERATURE AND COMPOSITION

THE Course of Study which follows is presented not because it is the only one, nor because it is better than many others which might be made. For the purposes of the book it was necessary that some course be adopted as the basis of the text. The principles which guided in arranging this course I believe are sound; but the preferences of teachers and the peculiarities of environment might make it wise to use other selections of literature. Of this a large "supplementary list" is given at the back of the book.

It has been recommended that the time devoted to the whole course in English shall be four years. If such an amount be given, during the first year Narration should be the subject for study. During the second, Description and Paragraphs should be taken up; and some teachers think it wise to add here the study of Sentences. This arrangement throws into the third year the study of the more difficult chapters on Exposition and Argument; to which should be added the chapter on Words, and that on Sentences if not already taken. The last year should be devoted to a review of principles, and to the study of the more difficult selections now on the list for College Requirements. The whole course should be closed by the study of a History of English Literature. If, however, the time for the study be less than four years, the order of progression should not be changed, but the amount of literature to be studied may be decreased.

COMPOSITION.

NARRATION.

To give Spontaneity.

I. EXTERNAL FORM OF COMPOSITION (p. 260).
   a. Heading.
   b. Margin.
   c. Indention of Paragraphs.
   d. Folding and Indorsement.
II. MARKS FOR THE CORRECTION OF ESSAYS (p. 264).
III. SIMPLE RULES FOR PUNCTUATION (p. 265).
IV. FORMS OF DISCOURSE. DEFINITIONS (pp. 1–7).
V. CHOICE OF SUBJECT (pp. 8–12).
VI. STUDY OF NARRATION (pp. 13–48).
   a. Definition and General Discussion.
   b. Narration without Plot.
      Interest the essential Feature.
   c. Narration with Plot.
      1. Selection of Main Incident of first Importance.
         _{It gives to the story}
         Unity, ridding it of
            Long Introductions and Conclusions,
            Tedious Enumerations, and
            Irrelevant Details.
      2. Arrangement of Material.
         Close of Story contains Main Incident.
         Opening of Story contains Characters, Place, and Time.
         Incidents generally follow in Order of Time.
      3. Movement.
      4. Use of Description in Narration.
      5. Some General Considerations.

LITERATURE.

NARRATION.

The Great Stone Face, The Gentle Boy, The Gray Champion, Roger Malvin's Burial, and other Stories. *Hawthorne.*
Tales of a Wayside Inn. *Longfellow.*
The Gold-Bug. *Poe.*
Marmion, or The Lady of the Lake. *Scott.*
A Christmas Carol, or The Cricket on the Hearth. *Dickens.*
The Vision of Sir Launfal, and other Narrative Poems. *Lowell.*
An Incident of the French Camp, Hervé Riel, The Pied Piper, How they brought the good News from Ghent to Aix. *Browning.*
Poems selected from Palgrave's Golden Treasury.

Meaning of the Author, calling for
  A Study of Words.
  Outline of Story.
  Turning Points in the Story.
  Central Idea or Purpose of the Story.
Method of the Author.
  Is there a Main Incident?
  Do all other Incidents converge to it?
  Is the Order a Sequence of Time alone?
  Is the Interest centred in Characters or Plot?
Style of the Author.
  Compare the Works of the Authors.

Home Reading.

The Last of the Mohicans. *Cooper.*
The Jungle Books. *Kipling.*
Treasure Island. *Stevenson.*
Tom Brown at Rugby. *Arnold.*
Nicholas Nickleby. *Dickens.*

(*For list of available texts see advertising pages at the end of the book.*)

COMPOSITION.

DESCRIPTION.

To secure Accuracy of Expression (pp. 49–88).

I. DEFINITION AND GENERAL DISCUSSION.
   Difficulties in Language as a means of Picturing.
   Value of Observation.

II. STRUCTURE OF WHOLE.
   a. To secure Unity.
      Select a Point of View.
         Physical.
         Mental.
   b. To secure Coherence.
      Arrange Details in Natural Order.
   c. To secure Emphasis.
      Arrange and proportion Treatment to effect your Purpose.

III. PARAGRAPH STRUCTURE (pp. 151–199).
   Definition.
   Length of Paragraphs.
   Development of Paragraphs.
   Principles of Structure.
      Unity.
      Mass.
      Coherence.

IV. WORDS.
   Specific rather than General.
   Adjectives, Nouns, and Verbs.

LITERATURE.

DESCRIPTION.

The Old Manse, The Old Apple Dealer. *Hawthorne.*
An Indian-Summer Reverie, The Dandelion, The Birch, The Oak, and other Descriptive Poems. *Lowell.*
The Fall of the House of Usher. *Poe.*
The Legend of Sleepy Hollow, Selections from the Sketch Book. *Irving.*
Selections from Childe Harold. *Byron.*
Silas Marner. *Eliot.*
The Deserted Village. *Goldsmith.*
Julius Cæsar. *Shakespeare.*
The Merchant of Venice. *Shakespeare.*
Poems selected from Palgrave's Golden Treasury.

Meaning of the Author (as under Narration)..
Method of the Author.
    Does the Author keep his Point of View?
    Are the Details arranged in a Natural Order?
    Has any Detail a supreme Importance?
    Are the Details treated in Proper Proportion?
    Has the Whole a Unity of Effect? Do you see the Picture distinctly?
    For what Purpose has the Author used Description?
    Does the Author employ Figures?
Style of the Author.

Home Reading.

Tales of a Traveller, Sketch Book. *Irving.*
Lorna Doone. *Blackmore.*
Ivanhoe, or The Talisman. *Scott.*
The Princess. *Tennyson.*
Pepacton, or Sharp Eyes. *Burroughs.*

(*For list of available texts see advertising pages at the end of the book.*)

COMPOSITION.

EXPOSITION AND ARGUMENT.

To encourage Logical Thinking and Adequate Expression (pp. 89–150).

Exposition.

I. DEFINITION AND GENERAL CONSIDERATIONS.
II. EXPOSITION OF TERMS. DEFINITION.
III. EXPOSITION OF PROPOSITIONS.
   a. Clear Statement of the Proposition in a "Key-Sentence."
      <small>This will limit</small>
   b. The Discussion.
      1. What shall be included?
      2. What shall be excluded?
      3. How shall important matters be emphasized?
         Mass and Proportion.
         Expansion and Condensation.
         To effect these ends use an
      4. Outline.

Argument.

I. KINDS OF ARGUMENTS.
   Deduction and Induction.
   Cause, Sign, and Example.
II. ORDER OF ARGUMENTS.
   Inductive precede Deductive.
   Cause, Sign, and Example.
   Mass to produce Climax.

Sentences (pp. 200–234).

Words (pp. 235–256).

LITERATURE.

Exposition and Argument.

L'Allegro, Il Penseroso, Comus, and Lycidas. *Milton.*
Essay on Milton. *Macaulay.*
Commemoration Ode. *Lowell.*
Bunker Hill Oration or Adams and Jefferson. *Webster.*
Intimations of Immortality, and other Poems. *Wordsworth.*
Of Kings' Treasuries. *Ruskin.*
Conciliation with the Colonies. *Burke.*

Meaning of the Author.
  Outline showing the Main Thesis with the Dependence of Subordinate Propositions.

Method of the Author.
  Does he hold to his Point and so gain Unity?
  Does he arrange his Material so as to secure Emphasis?
  Does one Paragraph grow out of another?
  Does each Paragraph treat a Single Topic?
  Are the Sentences dovetailed together?
  Does the Author use Figures?
  Are the Figures Effective?
  Are his Words General or Specific?

Style of the Author.
  Is it Clear?
  Has it Force?
  Is the Diction Elegant?
  How has he gained these Ends?

Home Reading.

De Coverley Papers. *Addison.*
Essay on Addison. *Macaulay.*
Backlog Studies. *Warner.*
Prue and I. *Curtis.*
Lincoln. *Schurz.*

(*For list of available texts see advertising pages at the end of the book.*)

COMPOSITION.

The compositions should be such as will test the maturer powers of the pupil. They should be written under the careful supervision of the teacher. They should be of all forms of discourse, and the subjects should be drawn from the subjects of study in the high school, especially from the literature.

LITERATURE.

Difficult Selections.

Paradise Lost. Two Books. *Milton.*
Selected Poems. *Burns.*
Essay on Burns. *Carlyle.*
In Memoriam, and other Poems. *Tennyson.*
The Lost Leader, Rabbi Ben Ezra, A Grammarian's Funeral. *Browning.*
Friendship, Self-Reliance. *Emerson.*
Short History of English Literature.

Home Reading.

The Autocrat of the Breakfast-Table. *Holmes.*
Our Old Home. *Hawthorne.*
How the Other Half Lives. *Riis.*
Walden. *Thoreau.*
On a Certain Condescension in Foreigners, Cambridge Thirty Years Ago, Emerson, Keats, Don Quixote. *Lowell.*
Lantern Bearers, A Humble Remonstrance, Gossip about Romance. *Stevenson.*
The Choice of Books. *Harrison.*
On the Threshold. *Munger.*

(*For list of available texts see advertising pages at the end of the book.*)

ENGLISH:
COMPOSITION AND LITERATURE

CHAPTER I

FORMS OF DISCOURSE

COMPOSITION, from the Latin words *con*, meaning together, and *ponere*, to place, signifies a grouping or arrangement of materials, generally with a definite end in view. *[Composition.]* We speak of the "composition of forces," and mean the combining of different forces acting along different lines to produce a single, definite resultant acting along a single line. In music, an author composes, whether songs or operas, by uniting musical phrases so that they produce a desired result. So in painting, composition has to do with the arrangement of the objects, combining them so as to produce a unity, a picture. In literature, too, the composition is, strictly speaking, the grouping of materials to produce a definite result.

In practice, however, English composition has come to include not only the arrangement of materials, objects or ideas, as the case may be, to produce this single impression; the term has *[English Composition.]* been extended to include the means by which the speaker or writer seeks to convey this single impression to other persons. As the painter is compelled to understand line drawing, the values of lights and shades, and the mixing of colors before he can successfully reproduce for others the idea he has to express, so the artist in literature needs a knowledge of elementary grammar and the elementary usages of language in order clearly to represent to others the idea which lies in his own mind. *English composition* may be defined as *the art of communicating ideas by means of the English language;* and the study of English composition is a study of the means by which this communication of ideas may be made to approach completeness.

<small>Composition and Oral.</small>

The term "English composition" is now generally understood to mean written composition, and not oral composition. At first thought they seem to be the same thing. So far as grouping is concerned, they are the same; but the means employed for expression is very different. Both use words; both employ sentences; but here the likeness ends. If sentences were put upon paper exactly as they were spoken, in most instances they would not convey the same thought to the readers as they did to the listeners. It is much more exacting to express the truth one wishes to convey by silent, featureless symbols than by that wonderful organ of communication, the human voice. If to the human voice be added eyes, features, gestures, and pose, we easily understand the great advantage the speaker has over the writer.

<small>Conventional Composition.</small>

Moreover, there are imposed upon a writer certain arbitrary conventions which are a source of annoyance. He must spell correctly, and he must know the general rules of punctuation. These things need not be considered by the speaker; yet they are conditions which must be obeyed by the writer. The man who eats with a knife succeeds in getting the food to his mouth, yet certain conventionalities exclude such a person from polite society. So in composition, it is possible for a person to make himself understood, though he write "labratory" and never use a semicolon; still, such a person would hardly be considered a cultured gentleman. To be able to say in an easy, effective way with pen and ink what one wishes to say requires a thorough knowledge of the conventions of composition; and in written composition, more than in oral, it demands implicit obedience to the conventions of literature.

The study of composition includes, then, the careful selection of materials and their effective arrangement. It presupposes a knowledge of the simpler usages of the language, its common idioms and the elements of its grammar. Already spelling and the commonest uses of the marks of punctuation — of the period, question mark, exclamation point, colon, semicolon, and comma — have been learned. From the beginning of the high school course, the theme, the paragraph, the sentence, the word, is to be studied with special attention to the effective use of each in adequately communicating ideas.

All literature has been separated into five groups, — narration, description, exposition, argument, and persuasion. These divisions are spoken of as if they could be readily distinguished, and it is true that every person has an idea of the characteristics which distinguish them. Narration and description are alike in this, — they deal with things and actual occurrences. In this respect they differ from exposition, argument, and persuasion, which deal with ideas. Narration tells what things do; description tells how things look. Narration deals with occurrences; description deals with appearances. Of those forms which deal with ideas, exposition defines a term or explains a proposition; argument establishes the truth

Forms of Discourse.

or falsity of a proposition; persuasion urges to action upon a proposition. Exposition explains; argument convinces; persuasion arouses. These, then, are the broad lines of distinction which separate the forms of discourse.

Narration is that form of discourse which recounts events in a sequence. It includes stories, novels, romances, biographies, some books of travel, and some histories.

<small>Definitions.</small>

Description is that form of discourse which aims to present a picture. It seldom occurs alone, but it is found in combination with the other forms of discourse.

Exposition is that form of discourse which seeks to explain a term or a proposition. Text-books, books of information, theses, most histories, many magazine articles, and newspaper leaders are of this class of literature.

Argument is that form of discourse which has for its object the proof of the truth or falsity of a proposition.

Persuasion is that form of discourse the purpose of which is to influence the will.

Though these definitions seem to set apart the great classes of literature, and to insure against any danger of confusion, it is not at all easy to place individual pieces of literature in any of these divisions. Whittier's "Barbara Frietchie" and Stevenson's "Treasure Island" are narrative beyond any peradventure; but what about "Snow-Bound" and "Travels with a Donkey" by the same authors? In these the narrative and descriptive portions are so nearly equal that one hesitates to set them down to either class; the reader is constantly called from beautiful pictures to delightful stories. The combination

<small>Difficulty in distinguishing.</small>

of narration and description is, however, only a mixture. And as it is easy to tell salt from pepper when they are mixed together, so it is not difficult to separate the narrative from the descriptive portions of any piece of literature. Yet when the narrative has been separated from the descriptive portion, has it been decided whether the whole piece is narration or description? When, however, one takes up the other forms of discourse, the difficulty increases. They resemble a real compound. As in water the oxygen and hydrogen are so intimately combined that it is hard, almost impossible, to separate them, so it is extremely difficult to pick out the descriptive and narrative portions of exposition, and to tell just where exposition passes over into argument and persuasion. Newman in the beginning of one of his essays gives a wonderful description of "bright and beautiful Athens," but only for the purpose of showing that for a university "the site should be a liberal and noble one." So a text-book in physics might describe a steam engine; in a text-book, however, the purpose is to present a type of all engines, and so explain their working. In both cases description is the servant of exposition. Again, when Dickens wrote his account of "Dotheboys Hall," he was not alone detailing the abuses which were the peculiar regime in Squeers's school, but by this single instance he placed before the English people the horrible conditions existing in many boarding schools at that time. His purpose was to show conditions; a study of conditions is usually exposition. Still, "Nicholas Nickleby" is a novel. Narration has been employed to explain conditions. And once more, exposition easily passes over into argument and persuasion. In many cases all ground for argument is removed as soon as the terms are defined and the proposition explained. The explanation alone is convincing. Is it exposition or is it argument? Exposition stands at the opening of every argument; indeed, the argument cannot proceed until the terms and the proposition have been explained. A lecturer might explain the effects resulting from the intemperate use of spirituous liquors. The very exposition would be an argument to a wise man, convincing him that he should abstain from their use. Again, the will of a rational man is influenced when reasons for action have been given; that is, when he has been convinced. Only ignorant people are thrown into a fury by the tricky art of a demagogue. Following up the former illustration, when a man has been convinced by the exposition of the results of intemperance, he may find himself persuaded to become a temperate man. So exposition has become a persuasive argument. Exposition and argument are the foundation of any discourse that influences reasonable men to action. Exposition, argument, and persuasion all employ narration and description to effect their purposes. Exposition alone may convince, and therefore be the strongest kind of proof. Conviction is followed by action, so that either exposition or argument may serve to persuade. Rarely does any form of discourse appear without an admixture of other forms, and it is with extreme difficulty that we can classify every bit of literature we read.

How, then, shall we make an approach to a classification? In most cases by ascertaining the purpose of the author.[1] If the purpose is merely to place a picture before the reader's mind, it is description; if to explain conditions without bias, it is exposition; if to convince the reason of the truth or falsity of a proposition, it is argument;

Purpose of the author.

---

[1] See *Specimens of Narration*: Henry Holt & Co.

while if the writer addresses himself to the emotions and the will, no matter whether he tells anecdotes, paints lurid pictures, explains conditions, or convinces of the danger of the present policy, — if he does all this to urge the reader to do something, the composition belongs in the literature of persuasion. These four forms of discourse are most easily distinguished by discovering the purpose of the author.

In narration the case is somewhat different. The novelist with a purpose has been at work, and all too few have been satisfied with telling a good story. " Baa, Baa, Black Sheep," though Kipling has here shown the imperative necessity of the sympathetic knowledge of children which springs from the sensitive love of " a real, live, lovely mamma ; " " Quo Vadis," though Sienkiewicz has before all given the reader a picture of dissolute Rome, very much heightened in color by his genius ; and " Looking Backward," though Bellamy has with great skill set forth the advantages of living in socialistic communities, hoping by this means to persuade his many readers to adopt his belief ; — yet these, and the hundreds of their kind, whatever the purpose of the author when writing them, belong to the " story " or " novel " class. His purpose *in telling* the story is secondary to his purpose *to tell* a story. Each of this class of novels recounts events in a sequence, whatever it may be done for, and is, by its form, to be classified as narration.

English composition, then, is a study of the methods of using the English language in communicating ideas. All composition is generally divided into five classes. These classes have broad lines of distinction, which are most easily applied by determining the purpose of the author.

CHAPTER II

CHOICE OF SUBJECT

Form and Material. FROM the considerations in the preceding chapter may be derived several principles regarding the choice of theme. If the composition is to be narrative, it should be upon a theme that readily lends itself to narrative form. One can tell a story about " A Day's Hunt " or " What We did Hallowe'en; " but it would try one's powers of imagination to write a story of " A Tree " or " A Chair." The latter subjects do not lend themselves to narration, but they may be described. Josiah P. Cooke has written a brilliant exposition of " Fire " in " The New Chemistry; " yet a young person would be foolish to take " Fire " as a subject for exposition, though he might easily write a good description of " How the Fire looked from My Window," or narrate " How a Fireman rescued My Sister." So in all work in composition, *select a theme that readily lends itself to the form of discourse demanded; or, conversely, select the form of discourse suitable for presenting most effectively your material.*

Author's Individuality. If an author is writing for other purposes than for conscious practice, he should choose the form of discourse in which he can best work, and to which he can best shape his material. Some men tell stories well; others are debaters; while yet others are wonderfully gifted with eloquence. Canon Farrar made good sermons; " Darkness and Dawn," however, can scarcely be called a good story. Emerson understood life thoroughly. He knew man's feelings, his motives, his hopes, his strength, his weakness; yet one cannot imagine Emerson shaping this material into a novel. But just a little way down the road lived a wizard who could transmute the commonest events of this workaday world to the most beautiful shapes; no one wishes that Hawthorne had written essays. The second principle guiding in the choice of a theme is this: *Select a theme which is suited to your peculiar ability as an author.*

The form, then, should suit the matter, and it should be the form in which the author can work. There is a third principle that should guide in the choice of a theme. *It should be a theme of which the author knows something.* Pupils often exclaim, "What can I write about!" as if they were expected to find something new to write. An exercise in composition has not for its object the exploiting of any new and unheard-of thing, any more than an exercise in music. It is an exercise in the expression of things already known. Even when the subject is known, the treatment offers difficulties enough. It is not true that what is thoroughly understood is easily explained. Many excellent scholars have written very poor text-books because they had not learned the art of expression. A necessary antecedent of all good composition is an accurate knowledge of the subject; and even with this essential condition of effective writing, the exercise offers many difficulties.

To demand accurate knowledge of the subject before an author begins work upon it narrows the field from which themes may be drawn. Burroughs is an authority on all the tenants of our groves; "Wake-Robin," "Pepacton," and his other books all show the master's certain hand. So Stedman is an authority in matters relating to literature. But Burroughs and Stedman alike would find difficulty in writing an essay on "Electricity in the Treatment of Nervous Diseases." They do not know about it. A boy in school probably knows something of fishing; of this he can write. A girl can tell of "The Last Parlor Concert." Both could write very entertainingly of their "First Algebra Recitation;" neither could write a convincing essay on "The Advantages of Free Trade."

This will seem to limit the list of subjects to the commonplace. The fact is that in a composition exercise the purpose is not to startle the world with some new thing; it is to learn the art of expression. And here in the region of common things, things thoroughly understood, every bit of effort can be given to the manner of expression. The truth is, it does not require much art to make a book containing new and interesting material popular; the matter in the book carries it in spite of poor composition. Popular it may be, but popularity is not immortality. Columns of poorly written articles upon "Dewey" and "The Philippines" have been eagerly read by thousands of Americans; it would require a literary artist of great power to write a one-column article on "Pigs" so that it would be eagerly read by thousands. Real art in composition is much more manifest when an author takes a common subject and treats it in such a way that it glows with new life. Richard Le Gallienne has written about a drove of pigs so beautifully that one forgets all the traditions about these common animals.[1] Choose common subjects, then, — subjects that allow every particle of your strength to go into the manner of saying what you already know.

The requirement that the subject shall be common

[1] See the first essay in *Prose Fancies*.

does not mean that the subject shall be trivial. "Sliding to First," "How Billy won the Game," with all of this class of subjects, at once put the writer into a trifling, careless attitude toward his work. The subjects themselves seem to call forth a cheap, slangy vocabulary and the vulgar phrases of sporting life. An equally common subject could be selected which would call forth serious, earnest effort. If a boy knew nothing except about ball games, it might be advisable for him to write upon this subject. Such a condition is hardly possible in a high school. *Choose common subjects, but subjects that call for earnest thinking and dignified expression.*

Interest is the last consideration in the choice of a subject. It applies equally to writer and reader. *Choose subjects that are interesting.* Not only must an author know about the subject; he must be interested in it. A pupil may have accurate knowledge of the uses of a semicolon; but he would not be likely to succeed in a paragraph about semicolons, largely because he is not much interested in semicolons. This matter of interest is so important that it is well to know what things all persons, authors and readers alike, are interested in. What, then, is generally interesting?

<small>Interest.</small>

First, *the familiar is interesting.* When reading a newspaper each one instinctively turns to the local column, or glances down the general news columns to see if there is anything from his home town. To a former resident, Jim Benson's fence in Annandale is more interesting than the bronze doors of the Congressional Library in Washington. For the same reason a physician lights upon "a new cure for consumption," a lawyer devours Supreme Court decisions, while the dealer in silks is absorbed in the pro-

<small>The Familiar.</small>

cess of making silk without the aid of the silkworm. Each is interested in that which to him is most familiar.

Second, *human life in all its phases is interesting.*
Human Life. The account of a fire or of a railroad accident takes on a new interest when, in addition to the loss of property, there has been a loss of life. War is horribly fascinating, not so much because there is a wanton destruction of property, as because it involves the slaughter of men. Stories about trees and animals are usually failures, unless handled by artists who breathe into them the life of man. Andersen's "Tannenbaum" and Kipling's "Jungle Books" are intensely interesting because in them trees and animals feel and act just as men do.

Third, *the romantic, the unique, and the impossible are interesting.*
The Strange. All men are more or less like those dwellers in Athens in the days of Paul who were always seeking some new thing. A new discovery, a new invention, a people of which little is known, — anything new is interesting. The stories of Rider Haggard and Jules Verne have been popular because they deal with things which eye hath not seen. This peculiar trait of man allows him to relish a good fish story, or the latest news from the sea-serpent. Just for the same reason, children love to hear of Little Red Riding Hood and Cinderella. Children and their parents are equally interested in those things which are entirely outside of their own experience.

These, then, are the general conditions which govern the choice of a subject. It shall easily lend itself to the form of discourse chosen; it shall be suited to the peculiar ability of the author; it shall be thoroughly understood by the author, — common, but not trivial; it shall be interesting to both reader and author.

CHAPTER III

NARRATION

NARRATION has been defined as the form of discourse which recounts events in sequence. It includes not only letters, journals, memoirs, biographies, and many histories, but, in addition, that great body of literature which people generally include in the comprehensive term of "stories." If this body of literature be examined, it will be found that it deals with things as opposed to ideas; incidents as opposed to propositions. Sometimes, it is true, the author of a story is in reality dealing with spiritual ideas; yet even in this case he embodies the idea in a character, incarnates the passion in a person, so that the reader may the better grasp the thought. It is one thing for an essayist to write of the destruction which follows inordinate ambition of power; but for most readers it is a much more effective thing to present those dangers as we see them in the story of Macbeth. Lowell's "Sir Launfal," Hawthorne's "Feathertop," George Eliot's "Silas Marner," stand for deep spiritual ideas which we better understand for this method of presentation. In an allegory like "Pilgrim's Progress," the passions and emotions, the sins and weaknesses of men are treated as real persons. However delicate the handling, it still is an incarnation of the idea in a character, a living, breathing person; and we may say that the narrative deals, not with ideas, but, for want of a better word, with things.

[margin: Material of Narration.]

Not only does narration deal with things, but with things doing something. Things inactive might be written of, but this would be description. It is necessary in narration that the things be in an active mood; that something be doing. "John struck James," then, is a narrative sentence; it tells that John has been doing something. Still, this one sentence would not ordinarily be accepted as narration. For narration there must be a series, a sequence of individual actions. *Recounting events in a sequence is narration.*

<small>In Action.</small>

Narration is the most popular form of discourse. Between one fourth and one third of all books published are stories; and more than one half of the books issued by public libraries belong to the narrative class. Such a computation does not include the large number of stories read in our papers and magazines. In addition to being the most popular form of discourse, it is the most natural. It is the first form of connected discourse of the child; it is the form employed by the uncultured in giving his impressions; it is the form most used in conversation. Moreover, narration is the first form found in great literatures: the Iliad and the Odyssey, the songs of the troubadours in France, and the minnesingers in Germany, the chronicles and ballads of England, — all are narrative.

<small>Commonest of Discourse.</small>

Narration is especially suited to the conditions imposed by language. Men do not think in single words, but in groups of words, — phrases, clauses, and sentences. In hearing, too, men do not consider the individual words; the mind waits until a group of words, — a phrase, or a simple sentence perhaps, — which expresses a unit of thought, has been uttered. In narration these groups of words follow in

<small>Language of Expression.</small>

a sequence exactly as the actions which they represent do. Take this rather lurid bit from Stevenson: —

"He dropped his cutlass as he jumped, and when he felt the pistol, whipped straight round and laid hold of me, roaring out an oath; and at the same time either my courage came again, or I grew so much afraid as came to the same thing; for I gave a shriek and shot him in the midst of the body."

Each phrase or clause here is a unit of thought, and each follows the others in the same order as the events they tell of occurred. On the other hand, when one attempts description, and exposition too in many cases, he realizes the great difficulties imposed by the language itself; for in these forms of discourse the author not infrequently wishes to put the whole picture before the reader at once, or to set out several propositions at the same time, as belonging to one general truth. In order that the reader may get the complete picture or the complete thought, he must hold in mind often a whole paragraph before he unites it into the one conception the author intended. In narration one action is completed; it can be dropped. Then another follows, which can also be dropped. They need not be held in mind until the paragraph is finished. Narration is exactly suited to the means of its communication. The events which are recorded, and the sentences which record them, both follow in a sequence.

The sequence of events in narration may be a simple sequence of time, in which case the narrative is without plot. This is the form of narration employed in newspapers in giving the events of the day. It is used in journals, memoirs, biographies, and many elementary histories. It makes little demand upon an author further than that he shall

Without Plot.

say clearly something that is interesting. Interesting it must be, if the author wishes it to be read; readers will not stay over dull material. Newspapers and magazines look out for interesting material, and it is for the matter in them that they are read. So memoirs and biographies are read, not to find out what happens at last, — that is known, — but to pick up information concerning an interesting subject.

Or the sequence may be a more subtle and binding relation of cause and effect. This is the sequence employed in stories. One thing happens because another thing has happened. Generally the sequence of time and the sequence of cause and effect correspond; for effects come after causes. When, however, more than one cause is introduced, or when some cause is at work which the author hides until he can most advantageously produce it, or when an effect is held back for purposes of creating interest, the events may not be related exactly in the order in which they occurred. When any sequence is introduced in addition to the simple sequence of time, or when the time sequence is disturbed for the purpose of heightening interest, there is an arrangement of the parts which is generally termed plot.

Plot.

Plot is a term difficult to define. We feel, however, that Grant's "Memoirs" have no plot, and we feel just as sure that "King Lear" has a plot. So, too, we say that "Robinson Crusoe" has little, almost no plot; that the plot is simple in "Treasure Island," and that "Les Miserables" has an intricate plot. A plot seems to demand more than a mere succession of events. *Any arrangement of the parts of a narrative so that the reader's interest is aroused concerning the result of the series of events detailed is a plot.*

It often occurs that a book which, as a whole, is

without a plot, contains incidents which have a plot. In "Travels with a Donkey," by Stevenson, no one cares for the plot of the whole book, — in fact there is none; yet the reader is interested in the purchase of the "neat and high bred" Modestine up to the "last interview with Father Adam in a billiard-room at the witching hour of dawn, when I administered the brandy." This incident has a plot. The following is a paragraph from "An Autumn Effect" by Mr. Stevenson. The simple events are perfectly ordered, and there is a delightful surprise at the end. This paragraph has a plot. Yet the thirty pages of "An Autumn Effect" could not be said to have a plot.

"Bidding good-morning to my fellow-traveler, I left the road and struck across country. It was rather a revelation to pass from between the hedgerows and find quite a bustle on the other side, a great coming and going of school-children upon by-paths, and, in every second field, lusty horses and stout country-folk a-ploughing. The way I followed took me through many fields thus occupied, and through many strips of plantation, and then over a little space of smooth turf, very pleasant to the feet, set with tall fir-trees and clamorous with rooks, making ready for the winter, and so back again into the quiet road. I was now not far from the end of my day's journey. A few hundred yards farther, and, passing through a gap in the hedge, I began to go down hill through a pretty extensive tract of young beeches. I was soon in shadow myself, but the afternoon sun still colored the upmost boughs of the wood, and made a fire over my head in the autumnal foliage. A little faint vapor lay among the slim tree-stems in the bottom of the hollow ; and from farther up I heard from time to time an outburst of gross laughter, as though clowns were making merry in the bush. There was something about the atmosphere that brought all sights and sounds home to one with a singular purity, so that I felt as if my senses had been washed with water. After I had crossed the little zone of mist, the path began to remount the hill; and just as I, mounting along with it, had got back again from the head downwards, into the thin golden sunshine, I saw in front of me a donkey tied to a tree. Now, I have a certain liking for donkeys, principally, I believe, because of the delightful things that Sterne has written of them. But this was not after the pattern of the ass at Lyons. He was of a white color, that seemed to fit him rather for rare festal occasions than for constant drudgery. Besides, he was very small, and of the daintiest proportions you can imagine in a donkey. And so, sure enough, you had only to look at him to see he had never worked. There was something too roguish and wanton in his face, a look too like that of a schoolboy or a street Arab, to have survived much cudgeling. It was plain that these feet had kicked off sportive children oftener than they had plodded with freight through miry lanes. He was altogether a fine-weather, holiday sort of a donkey; and though he was just then somewhat solemnized and rueful, he still gave proof of the levity of his disposition by impudently wagging his ears at me as I drew near. I say he was somewhat solemnized just then; for with the admirable instinct of all men and animals under restraint, he had so wound and wound the halter about the tree that he could go neither back nor forwards, nor so much as put his head down to browse. There he stood, poor rogue, part puzzled, part angry, part, I believe, amused. He had not given up hope, and dully revolved the problem in his head, giving ever and again another jerk at the few inches of free rope that still remained unwound. A humorous sort of sympathy for the creature took hold upon me. I went up, and, not without some trouble on my part, and much distrust and resistance on the part of Neddy, got him forced backwards until the whole length of the halter was set loose, and he was once more as free a donkey as I dared to make him. I was pleased (as people are) with this friendly action to a fellow-creature in tribulation, and glanced back over my shoulder to see how he was profiting by his freedom. The brute was looking after me; and no sooner did he catch my eye than he put up his long white face into the air, pulled an impudent mouth at me, and began to bray derisively. If ever any one person made a grimace at another, that donkey made a grimace at me. The hardened ingratitude of his behavior, and the impertinence that inspired his whole face as he curled up his lip, and showed his teeth and began to bray, so tickled me and was so much in keeping with what I had imagined to myself of his character, that I could not find it in my heart to be angry, and burst into a peal of hearty laughter. This seemed to strike the ass as a repartee, so he brayed at me again by way of rejoinder; and we went on for awhile, braying and laughing, until I began to grow a-weary of it, and shouting a derisive farewell, turned to pursue my way. In so doing — it was like going suddenly into cold water — I found myself face to face with a prim, little old maid. She was all in a flutter, the poor old dear! She had concluded beyond question that this must be a lunatic who stood laughing aloud at a white donkey in the placid beech-woods. I was sure, by her face, that she had already recommended her spirit most religiously to Heaven, and prepared herself for the worst. And so, to reassure her, I uncovered and besought her, after a very staid fashion, to put me on my way to Great Missenden. Her voice trembled a little, to be sure, but I think her mind was set at rest; and she told me, very explicitly, to follow the path until I came to the end of the wood, and then I should see the village below me in the bottom of the valley. And, with mutual courtesies, the little old maid and I went on our respective ways."

Books of travel, memoirs, and biographies, as whole books, are generally without any arrangement serious enough to be termed a plot; yet a large part of the interest in such books would be lost were the incidents there collected not well told, with a conscious attempt to set them out in the very best fashion; indeed, if each incident did not have a plot. In " Vanity Fair " with its six hundred pages, in "Silas Marner" with its two hundred pages, in the short stories of our best magazines, in the spicy little anecdotes in the "Youth's Companion," — in the least bit of a good story as well as the three-volume novel, the authors have used the means best suited to retain the interest to the end. They have constructed plots.

In the construction of any piece of composition there are three principles of primary im-
<small>Unity, Mass, and Coherence.</small> portance: they are Unity, which is concerned with the material itself; and Mass and Coherence, which are concerned with the arrangement of the material. A composition has unity when all the material has been so sifted and selected that each part contributes its share to the central thought of the whole. Whether of a sentence, a paragraph, or a whole composition, all those parts must be excluded which do not bring something of value to the whole; and everything must be included which is necessary to give a clear understanding of the whole. Mass, the second principle of structure, demands that those parts of a composition, paragraph, or sentence which are of most importance shall be so placed that they will arrest the attention. By coherence is meant that principle of structure which, in sentences, paragraphs, and whole compositions, places those parts related in thought near together, and keeps separate those parts which are separated in thought.

For the construction of a story that will retain the
<small>Main Incident.</small> reader's interest to the end, for the selection of such material as will contribute to a central thought, for the arrangement of this material so that the most important matter shall occupy the most important position in the theme, one simple rule is of value. It is this: *First choose the main incident*

towards which all the other incidents converge, and for the accomplishment of which the preceding incidents are necessary. A few pages will be given to the application of this rule, and to the results of its application.

There should be in each story, however slight the plot, some incident that is more important than the others, and toward which all the others converge. *Its Importance.* A reader is disappointed if, after reading a story through, he finds that there is no worthy ending, that all the preparation was made for no purpose. If, in "Wee Willie Winkie," Kipling had stopped just before Miss Allardyce started across the river, it would have been a poor story. It would have had no ending. It is because a story gets somewhere that we like it. Yet not just somewhere; it must arrive at a place worthy of all the preparation that has preceded. A very common fault with the compositions of young persons is that they begin big and end little. It is not infrequent that the first paragraph promises well; the second is not quite so good; and the rest gradually fall off until the end is worthless. The order should be changed. Have the first paragraph promise well, make the second better, and the last best of all. The main incident should be more important than each incident that precedes it. Get the main incident in mind before beginning; be sure it is the main incident; then bend all your energies to make it the most important incident toward which all the other incidents converge.

The choice of a main incident will determine what incidents to exclude. The world is full of incidents — enough to make volumes more than we now have. *Unity.* A phonograph and a camera could gather enough any day at a busy corner in a city to fill a volume; yet these pictures and these bits of conversation, interesting as each in itself might be, would not be a unit, — not one story, but many. Few persons, indeed, would write anything so disjointed as the report made by this phonograph; yet good writers are often led astray by the brilliancy of their own ideas. They have so many good stories on hand which they would like to tell, that they force some of them into their present story, and so spoil two stories. In the very popular "David Harum," it would puzzle any one to know why the author has introduced the ladies from the city and the musical party at the lake. The episode is good enough in itself; but in this story it has not a shadow of excuse. There is a phrase of Kipling's that should ring in every story-teller's ears. Not once only, but a number of times, this prince of modern story-tellers catches himself — almost too late sometimes — and writes, "But that is another story." One incident calls up another; paragraph follows paragraph naturally. It is easy enough to look back and trace the road by which the writer arrived at his present position; yet it would be very hard to tell why he came hither, or to see how the journey up to this point will at all put him toward his destination. He has digressed; he has left the road. And he must get back to the road. By this digression he has wasted just as much time as it has taken to come from the direct road to this point added to the time it will take to go back. Do not digress; tell one story at a time; let no incident into your story which cannot answer the question, "Why are you here?" by "I help;" keep your eye on the main incident; things which do not unquestionably contribute something to the main incident should be excluded.

The choice of the main incident towards which all

other incidents converge will rid compositions of worthless introductions and trailing conclusions. A story should get under way at once; and any explanations at the beginning, the introduction of long descriptions or tedious paragraphs of "fine writing," will be headed off if the pupil keeps constantly in mind that it must all lead directly toward the main incident. Again, if everything converges to the main incident, when that has been told the story is finished. After that there must be no explanations, no moralizing, nothing. When the story has been told it is a good rule to stop. *Introductions and Conclusions.*

An excellent example of a short story well told is "An Incident of the French Camp," by Robert Browning. Only the absolutely necessary has been introduced. The incidents flash before the reader. Nothing can be said after the last line. "Herve Riel" is a vivid piece of narrative too. Such an exhibition of manliness appeals to all. Was it necessary to attach the last stanza? If this poem needed it, why not the other? If the story has no moral in it, no man can tie it on; if there is one, the reader should be accounted intelligent enough to find it without any help.

Making all the incidents converge to one main incident will avoid tiresome enumerations of inconsequential events, which frequently fill up the compositions of young pupils. Such essays generally start with "a bright, clear morning," and "a party of four of us." After recounting a dozen events of no consequence whatever, "we came home to a late supper, well repaid for our day's outing." These compositions may be quite correct in the choice of words, sentences, and paragraphs, and with it all be flat. There is nothing to them; they get the reader nowhere. Pick out one of the many incidents. *Tedious Enumerations.*

Work it up. Turn back to the paragraph from Stevenson and notice how little there is to it when reduced to bare outline. He has worked it up so that it is good. Always remember that a short anecdote well told is worth pages of aimless enumeration.

The selection of the main incident will guide in determining what to include; for every detail must be included that is necessary to make the main incident possible. A young pupil wrote of a party in the woods. The girls had found pleasant seats in a car and were chatting about their friends, when they felt a sudden lurch, and soon one of the party was besmeared by slippery, sticky whites of eggs. Now, if eggs were in the habit of clinging to the roofs of cars and breaking at unfortunate moments, there would be no need of any explanation; but as the cook forgot to boil the eggs and the girl had put them up into the rack herself, some of this should have been told. Enough at least should be told to make the main incident a possibility. Stories are full of surprises, but they can be understood easily from the preceding incidents; or else the new element is one that happens frequently, and of itself is nothing new. In the paragraph from Stevenson, the entrance of the "prim, little old maid" is a surprise, but it is a very common thing for ladies to walk upon a public highway. Any surprise must be natural, — the result of causes at work in the story, or of circumstances which are always occurring and by themselves no surprises. If the story be a tangled web of incidents culminating in some horror, as the death of the beautiful young wife in Hawthorne's "Birthmark," all the events must be told that are necessary to carry the reader from the first time he beholds her beauty until he sees her again, her life ebbing away as the fairy hand

What to include.

fades from her cheek. In "Baa, Baa, Black Sheep" it would be impossible to pass directly from the sweet boy of the first chapter to the little liar of the last; something must be told of those miserable days that intervene, and their telling effect on the little fellow. So a reader could not harmonize his idea of old Scrooge gained in the first chapter with generous Mr. Scrooge of the last without the intermediate chapters. Keeping the main incident in mind, include all that is necessary to make it possible.

This same rule more than any other will make a story consistent. If incidents are chosen with relation to the one main incident, they will all have a common quality; they can scarcely be inconsistent. It is much more essential that a story be consistent than that it be a fact. Indeed, facts are not necessary in stories, and they are dangerous. Ian Maclaren says that the only part of his stories that has been severely criticised is a drowning episode, which was a fact, and the only one he ever used. Yet to those who have read "The Bonnie Brier Bush," the old doctor is as well known as any person who lives across the street; he is real to us, though he never lived. "Old Scrooge" and "Brom Bones" are better known than John Adams is. A good character or a good story need not be drawn from facts. Indeed, in literature as in actual life, facts are stubborn things, and will not accommodate themselves to new surroundings. Make the story consistent; be not too careful about the facts.

Consistency.

A story may be good and be entirely contrary to all known facts. "The Ugly Duckling" is as true as Fiske's "History of the United States," and every whit as consistent. "Alice in Wonderland" is an excellent story; yet it contains no facts. The introduction of a single fact would ruin the story; for between the realm of fact and the region of fancy is a great gulf fixed, and no man has successfully crossed it. Whatever conditions of life and action are assumed in one part of a story must be continued throughout. If walruses talk and hens are reasonable in one part of the story, to reduce them to every-day animals would be ruinous. Consistency, that the parts stand together, that the story seem probable, — this is more essential than facts. And to gain this consistency the surest rule is to test the material by its relation to the main incident.

The choice of the main incident, then, will determine to a great degree what to exclude and what to include; it will assist in ridding compositions of countless enumerations, aimless wanderings, and flat endings; it will help the writer to get started, and insure a stop when the story is told; and it will give to the story the quality most essential for its success, consistency.

There is yet another condition that enters into the selection of materials: it makes a difference who tells the story. If the story be told in the first person, that is, if one of the actors tell the story, he cannot be supposed to know all that the other persons do when out of sight and hearing, nor can he know what they think. To take an illustration from a pupil's essay. A girl took her baby sister out upon the lake in a rowboat. A violent storm arose, lashing the lake into a fury. The oars were wrenched from her hands. Helpless on the water, how was she to be saved? Here the essayist recited an infinite amount of detail about the distress at home, giving the conversation and the actions. These things she could not have known in the character she had assumed at the beginning, that of the chief actor. All

<small>An Actor the Storyteller.</small>

of that should have been excluded. When Stevenson tells of the fight in the round house, though he knew what those old salts were doing outside, matters of great interest to the reader, he does not let David say anything except what he could see or hear, and a very little of what he "learned afterwards." Stevenson knew well who was telling the story; David is too good a story-teller to tell what he could not know. In the pupil's essay and in "Kidnapped," all such matters would have a direct bearing on the main incident; they could be included without destroying the unity of the story. But they cannot be included when the story is told by one of the actors.

Many stories, probably most stories, are told in the third person. In this case the author assumes the position of an omniscient power who knows everything that is done, said, or thought by the characters in his story. Not only what happens in the next room, but what is thought at the other side of the world, is comprehended in his omniscience. This is the position assumed by Irving in "The Legend of Sleepy Hollow," by Kipling in the series of stories included with "Wee Willie Winkie," by Scott in "Marmion," and by most great novelists. Omniscience is, however, a dangerous prerogative for a young person. The power is so great that the person who has but recently come into possession of it becomes dizzy with it and uncertain in his movements. A young person knows what he would do under certain conditions; but to be able to know what some other person would do and think under a certain set of circumstances requires a sure knowledge of character, and the capability of assuming entirely different and unaccustomed points of view. It is much safer for the beginner to take the point of view of one of the

The Omniscience of an author.

actors, and tell the story in the first person. Then when the grasp has become sure from this standpoint, he may assume the more difficult role of the omniscient third person.

To sum up what has been said about the selection of materials: only those materials should be admitted to a story which contribute to its main incident, which are consistent with one another, and which could have been known by the narrator.

When the materials for a story have been selected, the next consideration is their arrangement. If the materials have been selected to contribute to the main incident and converge toward it, it will follow that *the main incident* will come last in the story; it *will be the climax* towards which the several parts of the story are directed. Moreover, it should be last, in order to retain the interest of the reader up to that time. This is in accordance with the demands of the second great principle of structure, Mass. An essay is well massed if the parts are so arranged that things of importance will arrest the attention. In literature to be read, to arrest the attention is almost equivalent to catching the eye. The positions that catch the eye, whether in sentence, paragraph, or essay, are the beginning and the end. Were it not for another element which enters into the calculation, these positions would be of nearly equal importance. Since, however, the mind retains the most vivid impression of the thing it received last, the impression of the end of the sentence, paragraph, or essay is stronger than the impression made by its beginning. The climax of a story should come at the end, both because it is the result of preceding incidents, and because by this position it receives the additional emphasis due to its position.

The Climax.

The beginning is the position of second importance. What, then, shall stand in this place? A story resembles a puzzle. The solution of the puzzle is given at the end; the thing of next importance is the conditions of the puzzle. In "Baa, Baa, Black Sheep" the story culminates in the surprise of a devoted mo- Who?
Where?
When?
Why? ther when she discovers that her boy is a secretive little liar, who now deserves to be called "Black Sheep." This is the end; what was the beginning, — the conditions necessary to bring about this deplorable result? First, they were *the persons;* second, *the place;* third, *the time.* In many stories there is introduced the reason for telling the story. These conditions, answering the questions Who? Where? When? and Why? are all, or some of them, introduced at the beginning of any narrative, and as soon as it can be done, they ought all to be given. In a short essay, they are in the first paragraph; in a novel, in the first chapters. In "Marmion" the time, the place, and the principal character are introduced into the first canto. So Irving begins "The Legend of Sleepy Hollow" with the place and time, then follow the characters. In all stories the beginning is occupied in giving the conditions of the story; that is, the principal characters, the time, and the place.

Having the end and the beginning clearly in mind, the next question is how best to get from one In what
Order? to the other. Shall the incidents be arranged in order of time? or shall other considerations govern? If it be any narrative of the journal form, whether a diary or a biography, the chronological arrangement will direct the sequence of events. Again, if it be a simple story with a single series of events, the time order will prevail. If, however, it be a narrative which contains several series of events, as a history or a novel, it may be wise, even necessary, to deviate from the time sequence. It would have been unwise for Scott to hold strictly to the order of time in "Marmion;" after introducing the principal character, giving the time and the setting, it was necessary for him to bring in another element of the plot, Constance, and to go backward in time to pick up this thread of the story. The really essential order in any narrative is the order of cause and effect. As causes precede effects, the causal order and the time order generally coincide. In a single series of events, that is, where one cause alone produces an effect, which in turn becomes the cause of another effect, the time order is the causal order. In a novel, or a short story frequently, where there are more than one series of incidents contributing to and converging towards the main incident, these causes must all be introduced before the effect, and may break the chronological order of the story. In "Roger Malvin's Burial," it would be impossible to tell what the stricken father was doing and what the joyous mother was thinking at the same time. Hawthorne must leave one and go to the other until they meet in their awful desolation. The only rule that can be given is, introduce causes before effects. In all stories, short or long, this will result in an approximation to the order of time; in a simple story it will invariably give a time sequence.

There is one exception to this rule which should be noted. It is necessary at the very beginning to have some incident that will arrest the attention. This does not mean that persons, place, and time shall not come first. They shall come first, but they shall be so introduced as to make an interesting opening to the story. The novels of some decades ago did not sufficiently recognize the principle. One can frequently hear it said of Scott's stories, "I can't get started with them; they are too dry." The introductory chapters are often uninteresting. So much history is introduced, so much scenery is described before the author sets out his characters; and all this is done before he begins the story. Novelists of to-day realize that they must interest the reader at the beginning; when they have caught him, they are quite certain that he will bear with them while they bring up the other divisions of the story, which now have become interesting because they throw light on what has already been told. Even more than novelists, dramatists recognize this principle. When the curtain rises on the first act, something interesting is going on. The action frequently begins far along in the time covered by the story; then by cleverly arranged conversation all circumstances before the time of the opening that are necessary to the development of the plot are introduced. The audience receives these minor yet essential details with no impatience, since they explain in part a situation already interesting. The time order may be broken in order to introduce at the beginning of the story some interesting situation which will immediately engage the reader's attention.

In arranging the materials of a story, the main considerations are Mass and Coherence. Mass demands important matters at the beginning and at the end of a story. Coherence demands that events closely related shall stand close together: that an effect shall immediately follow its cause. Beginning with some interesting situation that will also introduce the principal characters, the time, and the setting, the story follows in the main the order of time, and concludes with the main incident.

One practical suggestion will assist in arranging the

parts of a story. Use an outline. It will guard against the omission of any detail that may afterward be found necessary, and against the necessity of offering the apology, inexcusable in prepared work, of "forgetting to say;" it will help the writer to see the best arrangement of the parts, to know that causes have preceded effects. The outline in narration should not be too much in detail, nor should it be followed if, as the story progresses, new light comes and the writer sees a better way to proceed. The writer should be above the outline, not its slave; but the outline is a most valuable servant of the writer.

Movement is an essential quality of narrative; a story must advance. This does not mean that the story shall always go at the same rate, though it does mean that it shall always go. If a story always had the rapidity and intensity of a climax, it would be intolerable. Music that is all rushing climaxes is unbearable; a picture must not be a glare of high lights. The quiet passages in music, the grays and low tones in the background of the picture, the slow chapters in a story, are as necessary as their opposites; indeed, climaxes are dependent on contrasts in order to be climaxes.

The question of movement resolves itself into these two: how is rapidity of movement obtained, and how can the writer delay the movement. Rapidity is gained by the omission of all unnecessary details, and the use of the shortest, tersest sentences to express the absolutely essential. Dependent clauses disappear; either the sentences are simple, just one sharp statement, or they are made of coordinate clauses with no connectives. Every weight that could clog the story is thrown away, and it runs with the swiftness of the thought. At such a time it would be a waste of good material to introduce beautiful descriptions or profound philosophy. Such things would be skipped by the reader. Everything must clear the way for the story.

What has been said of rapidity will indicate the answer to the second question. Slowness of movement is obtained by introducing long descriptions, analyses of characters, and information regarding the history or customs of the time. Sentences become long and involved; dependent clauses abound; connective words and phrases are frequent. Needless details may be introduced until the story becomes wearisome; it has almost no movement. *Slowness.*

Very closely connected with what has been said above is another fact concerning movement. Strip the sentences as you may, there are still the verbs remaining. Verbs and derivatives from verbs are the words which denote action. If other classes of words be taken out, the ratio of verbs to the other words in the sentence is larger. Shorter sentences and an increased ratio of verbs mark the passages in which the movement is more rapid. In "Baa, Baa, Black Sheep" the sentences average twenty-five words in the slower parts; in the intenser paragraphs the sentences have an average of fifteen words. Poe's "Gold-Bug" changes from thirty-eight to twenty-one. Again, Stevenson's essays have a verb to eight words, while the fight at the round house has a verb to about five and a half words. One of Kipling's stories starts in with a verb to eight and a half words, and the climax has a verb in every four words. These figures mean that as the sentences are shortened, adjectives, adverbs, phrases, connectives, disappear. Everything not absolutely necessary is thrown away when the passage is to express rapid movement.

No person should think that, by eliminating all dependent clauses, cutting away all unnecessary matters, and putting in a verb to every four words, he can gain intensity of expression. These are only accompanying circumstances. Climaxes are in the thought. When the thought moves rapidly, when things are being done with a rush, when the climax has been reached, then the writer will find that he can approach the movement of the thought most nearly by using these means.

A valuable accessory to narration is description; in truth, description for its own sake is not frequently found. The story must be somewhere; and it is more real when we know in what kind of a place it occurs. Still it is not wise to do as Scott so often has done, — give chapters of description at the beginning of the story. Rather the setting should be scattered through the story so that it is hardly perceptible. At no time should the reader halt and realize that he is being treated to a description. Even in the beautiful descriptions by Stevenson quoted in the next chapter, the work is so intimately blended with the story that the reader unfortunately might pass over it. A large part of the pleasure derived from the best stories is supplied by good descriptions, giving a vivid picture of the setting of the story.

Description and Narrat on.

Description has another use in narration beside giving the setting of the story; it is often used to accent the mood of the action. In "The Fall of the House of Usher" by Poe, much of the gloomy foreboding is caused by the weird descriptions. Hawthorne understood well the harmony between man's feelings and his surroundings. The Sylvan Dance in "The Marble Faun" is wonderfully handled. Irving, in "The Legend of Sleepy Hollow," throws about the story a "witching influence," and long before the Headless Horseman appears, the reader is quite sure that the region abounds in "ghosts and goblins," dwelling in its "haunted fields, and haunted brooks, and haunted bridges, and haunted houses." The danger in the use of description for this purpose is in overdoing it. The fact is, as Arlo Bates says, "the villains no longer steal through smiling gardens whose snowy lilies, all abloom, and sending up perfume like incense from censers of silver, seem to rebuke the wicked." Yet when handled as Stevenson and Irving handled it, description assists in accenting the mood of the action.

The number of characters should be few and the time of the action short. Pupils are not able to handle a large number of persons. There is, however, a stronger reason for it than incapacity. A young person would have great trouble in remembering the large number of persons introduced into "Little Dorrit." Many of them would always remain entire strangers. Such a scattering of attention is unfavorable to a story. To focus the interest upon a few, to have the action centred in these few, increases the movement and intensity of the narrative. The writers of short stories in France (perhaps the best story-tellers of the present), Kipling, Davis, Miss Wilkins, and some others of our best authors, find few characters all that are necessary, and they gain in intensity by limiting the number of characters.

<small>Characters few, Time short.</small>

For the same reason *the time should be short.* If all the incidents chosen are crowded into a short period of time, the action must be more rapid. The reader does not like to know five years have elapsed between one event and the next, even if the story-teller does not try to fill up the interim with matters of no consequence to the narrative. One exception must be made to this rule. In stories whose purpose is to portray a change of character, a long time is necessary; for the transformation is not usually the result of a day's experience, but a gradual process of years. "Silas Marner" and "Baa, Baa, Black Sheep" demand time to make naturally the great changes recounted. In general, however, the time should be short.

Moreover, *the plot should be simple.* This is not saying that the plot should be evident. No one is quite satisfied if he knows just how the story will turn out. There are, however, so many conditions in a story that the accentuation of one or the subordination of another may bring about something quite unexpected, yet perfectly natural. Complicated plots have had their day; simple plots are now in vogue. They are as natural as life, and quite as unfathomable. In Davis's "Gallegher" there is nothing complicated; one thing follows another in a perfectly natural way; yet there are many questions in the reader's mind as to how the little rascal will turn out, and whether he will accomplish his mission. Much more cleverness is shown by the sleight-of-hand trickster, who, unassisted and in the open, with no accessories, dupes his staring assembly, than by him who, on the stage, with the aid of mirrors, lights, machines, and a crowd of assistants, manages to deceive your eyes. A story that by its frank simplicity takes the reader into its confidence, and brings him to a conclusion that is so natural that it should have been foreseen from the beginning, has a good plot. The conclusion of a story must be natural, — the result of the causes at work in the story. It must be an expected surprise. If it cannot be accounted for by the causes at work in the story, the construction is faulty. In the world of fiction there is not the liberty one experiences in the world of fact. There things unexpected and un-

[margin: Simple Plot.]

explainable occur. But the story-teller has no such privilege. Truth is stranger than fiction dare be. A simple, natural story, with few characters and covering but a short period of time, has three elements of success.

Paragraph structure, sentence structure, and choice of words are taken up in subsequent chapters. Of paragraphs it may be wise to say that there will be as many as there are divisions in the outline; and sometimes, by reason of the length of topic, a subdivision may be necessary. The paragraph most common in narration is the paragraph of details, the first form presented in the chapter on paragraphs. What needs to be said of sentences has already been said when treating of movement. Of words one thing may be suggested. Choose live words, specific words, words that have "go" in them.

It should be remembered that everything cannot be learned at once. The study of the whole is the principal occupation just now. Select the main incident; choose other incidents to be consistent with it; start out at once giving the conditions of the story; proceed now fast, now slow, as the thought demands, arriving at a conclusion that is an expected surprise, the result of forces at work in the story.

SUGGESTIVE QUESTIONS AND EXERCISES

THE questions are only suggestive. They indicate how literature can be made to teach composition. Some questions may seem hard, and will provoke discussion. To have even a false opinion, backed by only a few facts, is better than an entire absence of thought. Encourage discussion. The answers to the questions have not been suggested in the questions themselves. The object has been to throw the pupil upon his own thinking.

These questions upon the "Method of the Author" should not be considered until the far more important work of deriving the "Meaning of the Author" has been finished. Only after the whole piece has been carefully studied can the relation of the parts to the whole be understood. Reserve the questions for the review.

QUESTIONS.

THE GREAT STONE FACE.

(Riverside Literature Series, No. 40.)

In what paragraphs is the main incident?

Can you find one sentence on the second page of the story that foreshadows the result?

How many incidents or episodes contribute to the story?

Do these help in the development of Ernest's character? If not, what is the use of them?

Why are they arranged in this order?

Introduce into its proper place an incident of a scientist. Write it up.

Do you think one of the incidents could be omitted? Which one?

Are the incidents related in the order in which they occurred? Is one the cause of another?

Has the story a plot? Why do you think so? What is a plot?

Where are introduced the time, place, and the principal character?

What is the use of the description of "the great stone face"?

Why does the author tell only what "was reported" of the interior of Mr. Gathergold's palace? Is it better so?

Are the descriptions to accent the mood of the story? or are they primarily to make concrete and real the persons and places?

Is there any place where the movement of the story is rapid?

Does the author begin at once, and close when the story is told?

Did you find any use of comparisons in the piece? (See top of p. 6, top of p. 19, middle of p. 23.)[1]

Of what value are they in composition?

THE GENTLE BOY.

(Riverside Literature Series, No. 145.)

What is the main incident?

In relation to the whole story, in what place does it stand?

Do the other incidents serve to develop the character of "the gentle boy"? or are they introduced to open up to the reader that character? (Compare with "Wee Willie Winkie.")

Do you consider all the incidents necessary?

Why has the author introduced the fact that Ilbrahim gently cared for the little boy who fell from the tree?

What is the use of the first two pages of the story?

Where does the story really begin?

---

[1] Unless otherwise stated, all page references are to the Riverside Literature Series.

How could you know the time, if the first page were not there? Is it a delicate way of telling "when"?

Notice that time, place, and principal characters all are introduced into the first paragraph of the real story.

Why does the author note the change in Tobias's circumstances? Does it add to the interest of the story? Would you omit it?

Do you think this plot more complicated than that of "The Great Stone Face"?

What is the use of the description on p. 31?

What do you note as the difference between

(*a*) second line of p. 19, sixth line of p. 27, sixteenth line of p. 29, and (*b*) fourth line of p. 25, the figure in the complete paragraph on p. 40?

THE GRAY CHAMPION.

(Riverside Literature Series, No. 145.)

Note the successive stages by which the time is approached. (Compare with the beginning of "Silas Marner.")

Can you feel any difference between the movement of this story and the movement in "The Gentle Boy"?

Is there any difference in the length of the sentences? (Remember that the independent clauses of a compound sentence are very nearly the same as simple sentences.)

Is there any difference in the proportion of verbs and verbals? What parts of speech have almost disappeared?

ROGER MALVIN'S BURIAL.

(Riverside Literature Series, No. 145.)

Why is the first paragraph needed?

Why could the incident in the first paragraph on p. 50 not be omitted? Do you find it later?

How many chapters could you divide the story into? What is the basis of division?

Why did not Hawthorne tell the result of the shot at once?

A plot is usually made by introducing more than one cause, by hiding one of the causes, or by holding back an effect. Which in this story?

Is there a change of movement between the beginning and the end of the story? Look at the last two pages carefully. How has the author expressed the intensity of the situation?

Does the story end when it is finished?

THE WEDDING KNELL.

(Riverside Literature Series, No. 145.)

Of the three common ways of giving uncertainty to a plot, which has been used?

Do you call this plot more complicated than those of the other tales studied?

Why does the author say, at the top of p. 72, "necessary preface"? Could it not be omitted? If not, what principle of narrative construction would be violated by its omission?

Why has he introduced the last paragraph on p. 74 reaching over to p. 75?

THE AMBITIOUS GUEST.

(Riverside Literature Series, No. 40.)

In what order are the elements of the story introduced?

Pick out phrases which prepare you for the catastrophe.

Can you detect any difference in the movement of the different parts of the story? What aids its expression?

THE GOLD-BUG.

(Riverside Literature Series, No. 120.)

Would you have been satisfied if the story had stopped when the treasure was discovered? What more do you want to know?

What, then, is the main incident? Was the main incident the last to occur in order of time? Why did Poe delay telling it until the end?

Do you see how relating the story in the first person helped him to throw the main incident last? Why could he not tell it before?

Does Poe tell any other stories in the first person?

In what person are "Treasure Island" and "Kidnapped" told? Are they interesting?

If a friend is telling you a story, do you care more for it if it is about a third party or about himself? Why?

What, then, is the advantage of making an actor the narrator? What are some of the disadvantages?

Do you think this plot as good as those of Hawthorne's stories?

Why was it necessary to have "a day of remarkable chilliness" (p. 3), and a Newfoundland dog rushing into the room (p. 6)?

What principle would it violate to omit these little matters? (Text-book, p. 24.)

What of the rapidity of movement when they are digging? How has rapidity been gained?

What form of wit does Poe attempt? Does he succeed?

Do you think the conversation is natural? If not, what is the matter with it?

Are negroes usually profane? Does Jupiter's general character lead you to expect profanity from him? Is anything gained by his oaths? Is anything sacrificed? In this story is profanity artistic? (To know what is meant by "artistic," read the last line of "L'Envoi" on p. 253 of the text-book.)

THE VISION OF SIR LAUNFAL.

(Riverside Literature Series, No. 30.)

What is the purpose of the first stanza?

What connection in thought is there between the second, third, and fourth stanzas? What have these stanzas to do with the story? If they have nothing to do with it, what principle of structure do they violate? Would Lowell be likely to do this?

What is the use of the description beginning " And what is so rare as a day in June " ?

Would the story be complete without the preludes? Would the teaching be understood without them ?

Are time and place definitely stated in the poem ? Why should they be, or not be ?

Why does so much time elapse between Part I. and Part II. of the story ?

In what lines do you find the main incident ?

In the first prelude is Lowell describing a landscape of New England or Old England? Where is the story laid? What comment have you to make upon these facts ?

Pick out the figures. Are they useful?

Can you find passages of exposition and description in this narrative ? Why do you call it narration ?

What is Lowell's criticism upon himself ? (See " Fable for Critics.")

A CHRISTMAS CAROL.

(Riverside Literature Series, No. 57.)

Is the opening such as to catch the attention ?

What is the essential idea in the description of Scrooge ? Do all details enforce this idea ? Do you know Scrooge?

In what paragraph does Dickens tell where the story occurs ?

Find places on p. 19 and p. 96 where Dickens has used " in " for " into."

What advantage to the story is the appearance in Scrooge's office of his nephew and the two gentlemen ? Do they come into the story again ?

Are the details in the description of the apparition on p. 41 in the order in which they would be noted ? Which is the most important detail ? Where is it in the description ?

Is the description of Mrs. Fezziwig on p. 52 successful?

What helps express rapidity of movement in the paragraph at the bottom of p. 53 ? (See also paragraph on p. 85.)

Examining the words used by Dickens and Hawthorne, which are longer? Which are most effectual? Are you sure? Rewrite one of Hawthorne's paragraphs with a Dickens vocabulary. What is the result?

What word is the topic of the last paragraph on p. 73?

Recast the first sentence of the last paragraph on p. 77.

Does Dickens use slang? (Do not consider conversation in the answer to this question.)

What is the main incident? Is there one of the minor incidents that could be omitted?

Which one could you most easily spare?

What is the need of the last chapter?

MARMION.

(Rolfe's Student's Series, Vol. 2.)

How do you know the time of "Marmion"?

Do you see any reason why stanza vi. of Canto I. would better precede stanza v.?

Where is the first mention of De Wilton? the first intimation of Clara de Clare? of Constance?

What form of discourse in stanza vii. of Canto II.?

What part in the development of the narrative does Fitz-Eustace's song make?

Does the tale related by the host break the unity of the whole? Is it "another story"? What value has it?

Why does Scott not tell of Marmion's encounter with the Elfin Knight in Canto III.? Where is it told? Why there?

Why is Canto II. put after Canto I.? Did the events related in II. occur after those related in I.?

How many of the descriptions of persons in "Marmion" begin with the face? How many times are they of the face only?

Try to write the incident related in stanzas xix., xx., xxi., and xxii. of Canto III. in fewer words than Scott has done it without sacrificing any detail.

Are you satisfied with the description of King James in stanza viii. Canto V.? Do you see him?

Write an outline of the plot of "Marmion" in two hundred words.

Why is the story of Lady Clare reserved until Canto V.?

What cantos contain the main incident?

Were all that precedes omitted, would "The Battle" be as interesting?

Do you think the plot good? Is it complicated?

What of the number of figures used in the last canto compared with those used in any other canto? Do you find more in narrative or descriptive passages? Why?

Read stanza viii. Canto III. Can you describe a voice without using comparison?

Do the introductions to the several cantos form any part of the story? Would they be just as good anywhere else? Would the story be better with them, or without them? What principle of structure do they violate?

EXERCISES.

The subjects for composition given below are not intended as a course to be followed, but only to suggest a plan for the work. The individual topics for essays may not be the best for all cases. Long lists of topics can be found in rhetorics. Bare subjects, however, are usually unsuggestive. They should be adapted to the class. Put the subjects in such shape that there is something to get hold of. Give the pupils a fair start.

1–4. In order to place before the pupils good models for constructing stories, read one like "A Piece of String" in "Number Thirteen," by Maupassant. Stories for this purpose should not be long. Talk the story over with the pupils, bringing out clearly the main incident and the several episodes which contribute to it. Have them notice how characters, time, and place are introduced; and how each succeeding event is possible and natural. Then have it rewritten. This will fix the idea of plan. For this purpose some of Miss Wilkins's stories are excellent; Kenneth Grahame's

"Golden Days," and Miss Jewett's short stories are good material. Some of the short stories in current magazines serve well.

5, 6. Read the first of a story and its close, — enough to indicate the main incident and the setting of the story. Have the pupils write it complete.

7. Read the close of a story. The pupils will then write the whole.

8. Read the opening of a story. Have the pupils complete it.

9. Finish "The Circus-Man's Story" (Text-book, p. 261.)

10. My First Algebra Lesson. Remember that in composition a good story is worth more than a true one. The basis may be a fact. Do not hesitate to fix it up.

11. A delivery horse runs away. No persons are in the wagon. Tell about it.

12. Write about a runaway in which you and your little sister are injured. (I have found it very helpful to use the same subject, but having the relation of the narrator to the incident very different. It serves to bring out a whole new vocabulary in order to express the difference in the feelings of the narrator.)

13. Write the story suggested to your mind by these words: Digging in the sand I found a board much worn by the waves, on which were cut, in characters scarcely traceable, these words: " Dec. —— 18 9,   N. J."

14. A humorous incident in a street car, in which the joke was on the other fellow.

15. Another in which the joke was on me. The same incident may be used with good effect. The choice of new words to express the difference of feelings makes an excellent exercise.

16. Tell the story that Dorcas related to her neighbors about her husband's escape and her father's death.

17. To bring out the fact that the language must be varied to suit the character of the reader or listener, tell a fairy story to a sleepy five-year old so that he will not go

to sleep. Do not hesitate at exaggerations. Only remember it must be consistent.

18. Have "The Gentle Boy" tell one of the incidents in which he was cruelly treated. This may well be an incident of your own life adapted to its purpose.

19, 20. Jim was a mean boy. Meanness seemed to be in his blood. He was all mean. His hair was mean; his freckles were mean; his big, chapped hands were mean. And he was always mean. He was mean to his pets; he was meaner to small boys; and he was as mean as he dared to be to his equals in size.

Write one incident to show Jim's meanness.

Write another to show how Jim met his match, and learned a lesson.

21. Work up the following into a story. It all occurs in one day at the present time. Place, your own city. Characters, a poor sewing girl, her little sick brother, and a wealthy society lady. Incidents: a conversation between brother and sister about some fruit; a conversation between the sewing girl and the lady about money due for sewing; stealing apples; arrest; appearance of the lady. Subject: Who was the Criminal?

22. A story of a modern Sir Launfal.

23. The most thrilling moment of my life.

24. Tell the whole story suggested by the stanza of "A Nightingale in the Study," by Lowell, which begins, "Cloaked shapes, a twanging of guitars."

25. Write a story which teaches a lesson. Remember that the lesson is in the story, not at its end.

In the work at this time but little attention can be given to the teaching of paragraphs and sentences. The pupil should learn what a paragraph is, and should have his composition properly divided into paragraphs. But the form and massing of paragraphs cannot be taken up at this time. The same may be said of sentences. He should have no sentences broken in two by periods; nor should he have two sentences forced into one. Grammatical errors should be severely criticised. However, the present work is to get the pupils started; and they cannot get started if there is a teacher holding them back by discouraging criticisms. Mark all mistakes of whatever kind; but put the stress upon the whole composition: its unity, its coherence, its mass, and its movement. Everything cannot be done at once; many distressing faults will have to be passed over until later.

CHAPTER IV

DESCRIPTION

DESCRIPTION has been defined as the form of literature which presents a picture by means of language. In the preceding chapter, it has been pointed out that the sequence of language is perfectly adapted to detail the sequence of action in a narrative. For the purpose of constructing a picture, the means has serious drawbacks. The picture has to be presented in pieces; and the difficulties are much as would be experienced if "dissected maps and animals" used for children's amusement were to be put together in the head. It would not be easy to arrange the map of the United States from blocks, each containing a small part of it, taken one at a time from a box. Yet this closely resembles the method language forces us to adopt in constructing a picture. Each phrase is like one of the blocks, and introduces a new element into the picture; from these phrases the reader must reconstruct the whole. This means not alone that he shall remember them all, but there is a more serious trouble: he must often rearrange them. For example, a description by Ruskin begins, "Nine years old." Either a boy or a girl, the reader thinks, as it may be in his own home. In the case of this reader it is a boy, rather tall of his age, with brown hair and dark eyes. But the next phrase reads, "Neither tall nor short for her age." Now the reader knows it is a girl of common stature.

Difficulties of Language making Pictures.

Later on he learns that her eyes are "deep blue;" her lips "perfectly lovely in profile;" and so on through the details of the whole sketch. Many times in the course of the description the reader makes up a new picture; he is continually reconstructing. Any one who will observe his own mind while reading a new description can prove that the picture is arranged and rearranged many times. This is due to the means by which it is presented. Language presents only a phrase at a time, — a fragment, not a whole, — and so fails in the instantaneous presentation of a complete picture.

Painting and Sculpture.
The painter or sculptor who upon canvas or in stone flashes the whole composition before us at the same instant of time, has great advantages over the worker in words. In these methods there is needed no reconstruction of previous images, no piecing together of a number of fragments. Without any danger of mistakes which will have to be corrected later, the spectator can take in the whole picture at once, — every relation, every color, every difference in values.

It is because pictures are the surest and quickest means of representing objects to the mind that books, especially text-books, and magazines are so profusely illustrated. No magazine can claim popularity to-day that does not use illustrations where possible; no text-book in science or history sells unless it contains pictures. And this is because all persons accurately and quickly get the idea from a picture.

Advantages of Language.
Whatever be the disadvantages of language, there are some advantages. Who could paint this from Hawthorne?

"Soon the smoke ascended among the trees, impregnated with *savory incense*, not *heavy, dull,* and *surfeiting*, like the steam of cookery indoors, but *sprightly* and *piquant*. The *smell* of our feast was akin to the woodland *odors* with which it mingled."

Or this from Lowell? —

"Under the yaller-pines I house,
  When sunshine makes 'em all *sweet-scented*,
An' *hear* among their furry boughs
  The *baskin'* west wind *purr contented*,
While 'way o'erhead, ez *sweet* an' *low*
  Ez distant bells thet ring for meetin',
The wedged wil' geese *their bugles blow*,
  Further an' further South retreatin'."

Or cut this from marble? —

"O mother Ida, many-fountained Ida,
Dear mother Ida, hearken ere I die.
For now the noonday quiet holds the hill;
The grasshopper is silent in the grass;
The lizard, with his shadow on the stone,
Rests like a shadow, and the winds are dead.
The purple flower droops; the golden bee
Is lily-cradled; I alone awake.
My eyes are full of tears, my heart of love,
My heart is breaking, and my eyes are dim,
And I am all aweary of my life."

The painter cannot put sounds upon a canvas, nor can the sculptor carve from marble an odor or a taste. We use the other senses in determining qualities of objects; and words which describe effects produced by other senses beside sight are valuable in description. As Lowell says, "we may shut our eyes, but we cannot help knowing" a large number of beautiful things. Moreover, language suggests hidden ideas that the representative arts cannot so well do. The following from a " Song " by Lowell has in it suggestions which the picture could not present.

> " Violet ! sweet violet !
>   Thine eyes are full of tears ;
>   Are they wet
>   Even yet
> With the thought of other years ?
> Or with gladness are they full,
> For the night so beautiful,
> And longing for those far-off spheres ?
>
> " Thy little heart, that hath with love
>   Grown colored like the sky above,
>   On which thou lookest ever, —
>   Can it know
>   All the woe
> Of hope for what returneth never,
> All the sorrow and the longing
> To these hearts of ours belonging ? "

Enumerated
Suggestion.

Description, like narration, has two large divisions: one simply to give information or instruction ; the other to present a vivid picture. One is *representative* or *enumerative;* the other, *suggestive*. One may be illustrated by guide-books; the other by the descriptions of Stevenson or Ruskin. And in the most artistic fashion the two have been made to supplement each other in the following picture of " bright and beautiful Athens " by Cardinal Newman. From the first, to the sentence beginning " But what he would not think of," there is simply an enumeration of features which a commercial agent might see ; the rest is what the artistic soul of the lover of beauty saw there. One is enumeration ; the other a gloriously suggestive picture.

"A confined triangle, perhaps fifty miles its greatest length, and thirty its greatest breadth; two elevated rocky barriers, meeting at an angle; three prominent mountains, commanding the plain, — Parnes, Pentelicus, and Hymettus; an unsatisfactory soil; some streams, not always full; — such is about the report which the agent of a London company would have made of Attica. He would report that the climate was mild; the hills were limestone; there was plenty of good marble; more pasture land than at first survey might have been expected, sufficient, certainly, for sheep and goats; fisheries productive; silver mines once, but long since worked out; figs fair; oil first-rate; olives in profusion. But what he would not think of noting down was that that olive-tree was so choice in nature and so noble in shape that it excited a religious veneration; and that it took so kindly to the light soil as to expand into woods upon the open plain, and to climb up and fringe the hills. He would not think of writing word to his employers, how that clear air, of which I have spoken, brought out, yet blended and subdued, the colors on the marble, till they had a softness and harmony, for all their richness, which in a picture looks exaggerated, yet is after all within the truth. He would not tell how that same delicate and brilliant atmosphere freshened up the pale olive, till the olive forgot its monotony, and its cheek glowed like the arbutus or beech of the Umbrian hills. He would say nothing of the thyme and the thousand fragrant herbs which carpeted Hymettus; he would hear nothing of the hum of its bees; nor take account of the rare flavor of its honey, since Gaza and Minorca were sufficient for the English demand. He would look over the Ægean from the height he had ascended; he would follow with his eyes the chain of islands, which, starting from the Sunian headland, seemed to offer the fabled divinities of Attica, when they would visit their Ionian cousins, a sort of viaduct thereto across the sea; but that fancy would not occur to him, nor any admiration of the dark violet billows with their white edges down below; nor of those graceful, fan-like jets of silver upon the rocks, which slowly rise aloft like water spirits from the deep, then shiver, and break, and spread, and shroud themselves, and disappear in a soft mist of foam; nor of the gentle, incessant heaving and panting of the whole liquid plain; nor of the long waves, keeping steady time, like a line of soldiery as they resound upon the hollow shore, — he would not deign to notice the restless living element at all except to bless his stars that he was not upon it. Nor the distinct details, nor the refined coloring, nor the graceful outline and roseate golden hue of the jutting crags, nor the bold shadows cast from Otus or Laurium by the declining sun; — our agent of a mercantile firm would not value these matters even at a low figure. Rather, we must turn for the sympathy we seek to yon pilgrim student, come from a semi-barbarous land to that small corner of the earth, as to a shrine, where he might take his fill of gazing on those emblems and coruscations of invisible unoriginate perfection. It was the stranger from a remote province, from Britain or from Mauritania, who in a scene so different from that of his chilly, woody swamps, or of his fiery, choking sands, learned at once what a real University must be, by coming to understand the sort of country which was its suitable home."

Enumerative Description.

Enumerative description has one point of great difference from suggestive description. In the former everything is told; in the latter the description is as fortunate in what it omits as in what it includes. Were an architect to give specifications for the building of a house, every detail would have to be included; but after all the pages of careful enumeration the reader would know less of how it looked than after these few words from Irving. "A large, rickety wooden building stood in its place, with great gaping windows, some of them broken and mended with old hats and petticoats, and over the door was painted 'The Union Hotel, by Jonathan Doolittle.'" So the manual training student uses five hundred words to describe in detail a box which would be thrown off with but a few words in a piece of literature. In enumerative description, one element is of as much importance as another; no special feature is made primary by the omission or subdual of other qualities. It has value in giving exact details of objects, as if for their construction, and in including an object in a class.

Suggestive description, description the aim of which is not information, but the reproduction of a picture, is the kind most employed in literature. To present a picture, not all the details should be given. *(Suggestive Description.)* The mind cannot carry them all, and, much worse, it cannot arrange them. Nor is there any need for a detailed enumeration. A room has walls, floor, and ceiling; a man naturally has ears, arms, and feet. These things may be taken for granted. It is not what is common to a class that describes; it is what is individual, what takes one object out of a class.

This leads to the suggestion that *good description depends largely on accurate observation.* A selection frequently quoted, but none the less valuable because often seen, is in point here. *(Value of Observation.)* It is the last word on the value of observation.

"Talent is long patience. It is a question of regarding whatever one desires to express long enough and with attention close enough to discover a side which no one has seen and which has been expressed by nobody. In everything there is something of the unexplored, because we are accustomed to use our eyes only with the thought of what has already been said concerning the thing we see. The smallest thing has in it a grain of the unknown. Discover it. In order to describe a fire that flames or a tree in the plain, we must remain face to face with that fire or that tree until for us they no longer resemble any other tree or any other fire. This is the way to become original.

"Having, moreover, impressed upon me the fact that there are not in the whole world two grains of sand, two insects, two hands, or two noses absolutely alike, he forced me to describe a being or an object in such a manner as to individualize it clearly, to distinguish it from all other objects of the same kind. 'When you pass,' he said to me, 'a grocer seated in his doorway, a concierge smoking his pipe, a row of cabs, show me this grocer and this concierge, their attitude, all their physical appearance; suggest by the skill of your image all their moral nature, so that I shall not confound them with any other grocer or any other concierge; make me see, by a single word, wherein a cab-horse differs from the fifty others that follow or precede him.' . . . Whatever may be the thing which one wishes to say, there is but one word for expressing it; only one verb to animate it, but one adjective to qualify it. It is essential to search for this verb, for this adjective, until they are discovered, and never to be satisfied with anything else." [1]

The Point of View. With the closest observation, an author gets into his own mind what he wishes to present to another; but with this essential step taken, he is only ready to begin the work of communication. For the successful communication of a picture there are some considerations of value. And first is *the point of view*. It has much the same relation to description as the main incident has to narration. In large measure it determines what to exclude and wh.t to include. When a writer has assumed his point f view, he must stay there, and tell not a thing more than he can see from there. It would hardly be possible for a man, telling only so much as he saw whi e gazing from Eiffel Tower into the streets below, to say that the people looked like Lilliputians and that their hands were dirty. To one lying on the bank of a

---

[1] *Pierre et Jean*, by Maupassant. Quoted from Bates's *Talks on Writing English*.

stream, it does not look like "a silver thread running through the landscape." Things do not look the same when they are near as when at a distance. This fact has been acted upon more by the modern school of painting than ever before in art. Verboeckhoven painted sheep in a marvelous way. The drawing is perfect, giving the animal to the life. Still, no matter how far away the artist was standing, there are the same marvelously painted tufts of wool, showing almost the individual fibres. Tufts of wool were on the sheep, and made of fibres; but no artist at twenty rods could see them. The new school gives only what actually can be seen. Its first law is that each "shall draw the thing as he sees it for the God of Things as They Are." Make no additions to what you can actually see because, as a result of experience, you know that there are some things not yet mentioned in your description; the hands may be dirty, but the man on the tower cannot see the dirt. Neither make an addition simply because it sounds well; the "silver thread through the landscape" is beautiful, but, unfortunately, it is not always true.

Not only does distance cut out details from a picture; the fact that man sees in a straight line and not around a corner eliminates some features. In describing a house, remember that as you stand across the street from it, the back porch cannot be seen, neither can the shrubbery in the back yard. A writer would not be justified in speaking of a man's necktie, if the man he was describing were walking in front of him. In enumerative description the inside of a box may be told of; a man may be turned around, as it were; but to present a picture, only one side can be described, just as it would be shown in a photograph. Any addition to what can actually be known from the point of view assumed by the author is a fault and a source of confusion. Choose your point of view; stay there; and tell only what is seen from that point.

It has been said that the point of view should not be changed. This requires one modification. It may be changed, if the reader is kept informed of the changes. If a person wished to describe an interior, he would be unable to see the whole from any one point of view. As he passed from room to room he should inform his reader of his change of position. Then the description, though a unit, is a combination of several descriptions; just as the house is one, though made of dining-room, sitting-rooms, bed-rooms, and attic. This kind of description is very common in books of travel, in which the author tells what he sees in passing. The thing to be remembered in writing this kind of description is to inform the reader where the author is when he writes the different parts of the description, — to give the points of view.

<small>Mo Point of View.</small>

The point of view, whether fixed or moving, should be made clear. Either it should be definitely stated, or it should be suggested by some phrase in the description. In the many examples which are quoted in this chapter, it would be well to see what it is that gives the point of view. The picture gains in distinctness when the point of view is known. The following sentences are from "The Old Manse;" there is no mistake here. The reader knows every move the author makes. It opens with: —

<small>The Point Vi should be stated.</small>

"Between two tall gateposts of rough-hewn stone (the gate itself having fallen from its hinges at some unknown epoch) we beheld the gray front of the old parsonage terminating the vista of an avenue of black ash-trees."

From the street the reader is taken to "the rear of the house," where there was "the most delightful little nook of a study that ever offered its snug seclusion to a scholar." Through its window the clergyman saw the opening of the "deadly struggle between two nations." He heard the rattle of musketry, and

"there needed but a gentle wind to sweep the battle smoke around this quiet house. Perhaps the reader, whom I cannot help considering as my guest in the Old Manse and entitled to all courtesy in the way of sight-showing, — perhaps he will choose to take a nearer view of the memorable spot. We stand now on the river's brink." . . . " Here we are, at the point where the river was crossed by the old bridge." . . . " The Old Manse! We had almost forgotten it, but will return thither through the orchard." . . . " What with the river, the battle-field, the orchard, and the garden, the reader begins to despair of finding his way back into the Old Manse. But in agreeable weather it is the truest hospitality to keep him out-of-doors. I never grew quite acquainted with my habitation till a long spell of sulky rain had confined me beneath its roof. There could not be a more sombre aspect of external nature than as then seen from the windows of my study."

And so Hawthorne continues through this long and beautiful description of "The Old Manse;" every change in the point of view is noted.

Closely connected with the physical point of view is the mood or purpose of the writer; this might be called *the mental point of view.* Not everything should be told which the author could know from his position, but only those things which at the time serve his purpose. In the description already quoted from Newman, the mercantile gentleman notes a large number of features which are the commercial advantages of Attica; of these but three are worthy of mention by "yon pilgrim student" in giving his impression of Athens as " a shrine where he might

<small>Mental Point of View.</small>

take his fill of gazing on those emblems and coruscations of invisible unoriginate perfection." The others — the soil, the streams, the climate, the limestone, the fisheries, and the silver mines — do not serve his purpose. Hawthorne in the long description already mentioned has retained those features which suggest quiet and peace. Such a profusion of " quiet," " half asleep," " peaceful," " unruffled," " unexcitable " words and phrases never " loitered " through forty pages of " dreamy " and " whispering " description.

In the following bit from " Lear," where Edgar tells his blinded father how high the cliff is, only those details are included which measure distance.

" How fearful
And dizzy 't is to cast one's eyes so low!
The crows and choughs that wing the midway air
Show scarce so gross as beetles; half way down
Hangs one that gathers samphire, — dreadful trade!
Methinks he seems no bigger than his head:
The fishermen, that walk upon the beach,
Appear like mice; and yond tall anchoring bark,
Diminished to her cock; her cock, a buoy
Almost too small for sight: the murmuring surge,
That on th' unnumbered idle pebbles chafes,
Cannot be heard so high. — I 'll look no more,
Lest my brain turn, and the deficient sight
Topple down headlong."

The following is from Kipling's " The Light that Failed : " —

" What do you think of a big, red, dead city built of red sandstone, with green aloes growing between the stones, lying out neglected on honey-colored sands? There are forty dead kings there, Maisie, each in a gorgeous tomb finer than all the others. You look at the palaces and streets and shops and tanks, and think that men must live there, till you find a wee gray squirrel rubbing its nose all alone in the marketplace, and a jeweled peacock struts out of a carved doorway and spreads its tail against a marble screen as fine pierced as point-lace. Then a monkey — a little black monkey — walks through the main square to get a drink from a tank forty feet deep. He slides down the creepers to the water's edge, and a friend holds him by the tail, in case he should fall in.

"Is all that true?

"I have been there and seen. Then evening comes and the lights change till it's just as though you stood in the heart of a king-opal. A little before sundown, as punctually as clockwork, a big bristly wild boar, with all his family following, trots through the city gate, churning the foam on his tusks. You climb on the shoulder of a big black stone god, and watch that pig choose himself a palace for the night and stump in wagging his tail. Then the night-wind gets up, and the sands move, and you hear the desert outside the city singing, 'Now I lay me down to sleep,' and everything is dark till the moon rises."

Note how every detail introduced serves to make the city dead. Dead kings, a wee gray squirrel, a little black monkey, a bristly wild boar, the night wind, and the desert singing, — these could not be seen or heard in a live city with street cars; but all serve to emphasize the fact that here is "a big, red, dead city."

At the risk of over-emphasizing this point that the purpose of the author, the mental point of view of the writer, the feeling which the object gives him and which he wishes to convey to the reader, the central thought in the description, is primary, and an element that cannot be overlooked in successful description, I give another example. This point really cannot be over-emphasized: a writer cannot be too careful in selecting materials. Careless grouping of incongruous matters cannot make a picture. Nor does the artistic author leave the reader in doubt as to the purpose of the description; its central thought is usually suggested in the first sentence. In the quotations from Shakespeare and Kipling, the opening sentences are the germ of what follows. Each detail seems to grow out of this sentence, and serves to emphasize it. In the following by Stevenson, the paragraphs spring from the opening sentence; they explain it, they elaborate it, and they accent it.

"Night is a dead monotonous period under a roof; but in the open world it passes lightly, with its stars and dews and perfumes, and the hours are marked by changes in the face of Nature. What seems a kind of temporal death to people choked between walls and curtains is only a light and living slumber to the man who sleeps afield. All night long he can hear Nature breathing deeply and freely; even as she takes her rest she turns and smiles; and there is one stirring hour unknown to those who dwell in houses, when a wakeful influence goes abroad over the sleeping hemisphere, and all the outdoor world are on their feet. It is then that the first cock crows, not this time to announce the dawn, but like a cheerful watchman speeding the course of the night. Cattle awake on the meadows; sheep break their fast on the dewy hillsides, and change to a new lair among the ferns; and houseless men, who have lain down with the fowls, open their dim eyes and behold the beauty of the night.

"At what inaudible summons, at what gentle touch of Nature, are all these sleepers thus recalled in the same hour to life? Do the stars rain down an influence, or do we share some thrill of mother earth below our resting bodies? Even shepherds and old country-folk, who are the deepest read in these arcana, have not a guess as to the means or purpose of this nightly resurrection. Towards two in the morning they declare the thing takes place; and neither know nor inquire further. And at least it is a pleasant incident. We are disturbed in our slumber only, like the luxurious Montaigne, 'that we may the better and more sensibly enjoy it.' We have a moment to look upon the stars. And there is a special pleasure for some minds in the reflection that we share the impulse with all outdoor creatures in our neighborhood, that we have escaped out of the Bastille of civilization, and are become, for the time being, a more kindly animal and a sheep of Nature's flock."

There is one more step in the exclusion of details. This considers neither the point of view nor the purpose of the writer, but it is what is due the reader. Stevenson says in one of his essays that a description which lasts longer than two minutes is never attempted in conversation. The listener cannot hold the details enumerated. The clearest statement regarding this comes from Jules Lemaitre in a criticism upon some descriptions by Emile Zola which the critic says are praised by persons who have never read them. He says: —

Descriptions.

"It has been one of the greatest literary blunders of the time to suppose that an enumeration of parts is a picture, to think that forever placing details side by side, however picturesque they may be, is able in the end to make a picture, to give us any conception of the vast spectacles in the physical universe. In reality, a written description arranges its parts in our mind only when the impression of the first features of which it is formed are remembered sufficiently, so that we can easily join the first to those which complete and end it. In short, a piece of description is ineffective if we cannot hold in mind all its details at one time. It is necessary that all the details coexist in our memory just as the parts of a painting coexist under our eye. This becomes next to impossible if the description of one definite object last over fifteen minutes of reading. The longer it is, the more obscure it becomes. The individual features fade away in proportion to the number which are presented; and for this reason one might say that we cannot see the forest for the trees. Every description which is over fifty lines ceases to be clear to a mind of ordinary vigor. After that there is only a succession of fragmentary pictures which fatigues and overwhelms the reader."

These, then, are the principles that guide in the choice of materials for a description. First, the point of view, whether fixed or movable, should be made clear to the reader; it should be retained throughout the description, or the change should be announced. By regard for it the writer will be guided to the exclusion of matters that could not be observed, and to the inclusion of such details as can be seen and are essential. Second, the writer will keep out matters that do not contribute to his purpose, and will select only those details which assist in producing the desired impression. Third, the limitations of the reader's powers advise a writer to be brief: five hundred words should be the outside; two hundred are enough for most writers. These principles will give to the whole that unity of materials and of structure which is the first requisite of an effective description.

The next matter for consideration is the arrangement of the materials. The arrangement depends on the principles that guided in narration, Mass and Coherence.

Arrangement of Details in Description.
After we have looked at any object long enough to be able to write about it, one feature comes to assume an importance that sets it far above all others. To a writer who has looked long at a man, he may shrink to a cringing piece of weakness, or he may grow to a strong, self-centred power whose presence alone inspires serenest trust. Hawthorne, standing in St. Peter's, saw only the gorgeous coloring; proportions, immensity, and sacredness were as nothing to the harmonious brilliancy of this expanded "jewel casket."[1] Stevenson, thinking of the

[1] *The Marble Faun*, by Nathaniel Hawthorne.

beast of burden best suited to carry his great sleeping sack, discarded the horse, for, as he says, "she is a fine lady among animals."[1] The description of a horse which follows this statement emphasizes the fact that a horse is not intended for carrying burdens. From the germinal impression of a description, all the details grow; to this primary impression they all contribute. In the case of buildings, or other things material, this impression is generally one of form, sometimes of the height of the object; if striking, it may be color. The strongest impression of persons is a quality of character which shows itself either in the face or in the pose of a man. An example of each may be found in the following paragraphs from "David Copperfield:" —

"At length we stopped before a very old house bulging out over the road; a house with long, low lattice-windows bulging out still farther, and beams with carved heads on the ends bulging out too, so that I fancied the whole house was leaning forward, trying to see who was passing on the narrow pavement below. It was quite spotless in its cleanliness. The old-fashioned brass knocker on the low-arched door, ornamented with carved garlands of fruits and flowers, twinkled like a star; the two stone steps descending to the door were as white as if they had been covered with fair linen; and all the angles and corners, and carvings and mouldings, and quaint little panes of glass, and quainter little windows, though as old as the hills, were as pure as any snow that ever fell upon the hills.

"When the pony-chaise stopped at the door, and my eyes were intent upon the house, I saw a cadaverous face appear at a small window on the ground floor (in a little round tower that formed one side of the house), and quickly disappear. The low arched door then opened, and the face came out. It was quite as cadaverous as it had looked in the window, though in the grain of it there was that tinge of red

---

[1] *Travels with a Donkey*, by R. L. Stevenson.

which is sometimes to be observed in the skins of red-haired people. It belonged to a red-haired person — a youth of fifteen, as I take it now, but looking much older — whose hair was cropped as close as the closest stubble; who had hardly any eyebrows, and no eyelashes, and eyes of a red-brown; so unsheltered and unshaded that I remember wondering how he went to sleep. He was high-shouldered and bony; dressed in decent black, with a white wisp of a neck cloth; buttoned up to the throat; and had a long, lank, skeleton hand, which particularly attracted my attention, as he stood at the pony's head, rubbing his chin with it, and looking up at us in the chaise."

Hawthorne thus begins his description of "The House of the Seven Gables:" —

"Maule's Lane, or Pyncheon Street, as it were now more decorous to call it, was thronged, at the appointed hour, as with a congregation on its way to church. All, as they approached, looked upward at the imposing edifice, which was henceforth to assume its rank among the habitations of mankind."

And in the same volume his description of "The Pyncheon of To-day" begins: —

"As the child went down the steps, a gentleman ascended them, and made his entrance into the shop. It was the portly, and, had it possessed the advantage of a little more height, would have been the stately figure of a man, considerably in the decline of life, dressed in a black suit of some thin stuff, resembling broadcloth as closely as possible."

If the description be long, and the object will lend itself to such a treatment, a definite, tangible, easily understood shape or form should be suggested at once. Notice Newman's first sentence describing Attica: "A confined triangle, perhaps fifty miles its greatest length, and thirty its greatest breadth." Like this is the beginning of the description of the battle of Waterloo by Victor Hugo.

"Those who would get a clear idea of the battle of Waterloo have only to lay down upon the ground in their mind a capital letter A. The left stroke of the A is the road to Nivelles, the right stroke is the road from Genappe, the cross of the A is the sunken road from Ohain to Braine l'Alleud. The top of the A is Mont Saint Jean, Wellington is there; the left-hand lower point is Hougomont, Reille is there with Jerome Bonaparte; the right-hand lower point is La Belle Alliance, Napoleon is there. A little below the point where the cross of the A meets and cuts the right stroke, is La Haie Sainte. At the middle of this cross is the precise point where the final battle word was spoken. There the lion is placed, the involuntary symbol of the supreme heroism of the Imperial Guard. The triangle contained at the top of the A, between the two strokes and the cross, is the plateau of Mont Saint Jean. The struggle for this plateau was the whole of the battle."

In "The Vision of Sir Launfal" Lowell opens his beautiful description with the words, "And what is so rare as a day in June?" From this general and comprehensive sentence follow all the details which make a June day perfect.

Hawthorne, after telling how he happened to write of him, begins his long description of "The Old Apple Dealer" with the following paragraph: —

"He is a small man, with gray hair and gray stubble beard, and is invariably clad in a shabby surtout of snuff color, closely buttoned, and half concealing a pair of gray pantaloons; the whole dress, though clean and entire, being evidently flimsy with much wear. His face, thin, withered, furrowed, and with features which even age has failed to render impressive, has a frost-bitten aspect. It is a moral frost which no physical warmth or comfortableness could counteract. The summer sunshine may fling its white heat upon him, or the good fire of the depot room may make him the focus of its blaze on a winter's day; but all in vain; for still the old man looks as if he were in a frosty atmosphere, with scarcely warmth enough to keep life in the region about his heart. It is a patient, long-suffering, quiet, hopeless, shivering aspect. He is not desperate, — that, though its etymology implies no more, would be too positive an expression, — but merely devoid of hope. As all his past life, probably, offers no spots of brightness to his memory, so he takes his present poverty and discomfort as entirely a matter of course; he thinks it the definition of existence, so far as himself is concerned, to be poor, cold, and uncomfortable. It may be added, that time has not thrown dignity as a mantle over the old man's figure: there is nothing venerable about him: you pity him without a scruple."

So this old apple dealer shivers all through this description of nine pages to the last sentences: —

"God be praised, were it only for your sake, that the present shapes of human existence are not cast in iron nor hewn in everlasting adamant, but moulded of the vapors that vanish away while the essence flits upward to the Infinite. There is a spiritual essence in this gray and lean old shape that shall flit upward too. Yes; doubtless there is a region where the lifelong shiver will pass away from his being, and that quiet sigh, which it has taken him so many years to breathe, will be brought to a close for good and all."

The prominent characteristic may be the feeling aroused by the object. It may be horror, as in a description of a haunted house or a murderer; it may be love, as in the picture of an old home or a sainted mother. The emotion occasioned is often mentioned or suggested at once, and the details are afterward given which have called forth the feeling. Poe uses this in the first paragraph of "The House of Usher."

"During the whole of a dull, dark, and soundless day in the autumn of the year, when the clouds hung oppressively low in the heavens, I had been passing alone, on horseback, through a singularly dreary tract of country, and at length found myself, as the shades of evening drew on, within view of the melancholy House of Usher. I know not how it was — but, with the first glimpse of the building, *a sense of insufferable gloom pervaded my spirit.* I say insufferable; for the feeling was unrelieved by any of that half-pleasurable, because poetic, sentiment with which the mind usually receives even the sternest natural images of the desolate or terrible. I looked upon the scene before me — upon the mere house, and the simple landscape features of the domain — upon the bleak walls — upon the vacant, eye-like windows — upon a few rank sedges — and upon a few white trunks of decayed trees — with an utter depression of soul which I can compare to no earthly sensation more properly than to the after-dream of a reveler upon opium — the bitter lapse into every-day life — the hideous dropping off of the veil. There was an iciness, a sinking, a sickening of the heart — an unredeemed dreariness of thought which no goading of the imagination could torture into aught of the sublime. . . . It was possible, I reflected, that a mere different arrangement of the particulars of the scene, of the details of the picture, would be sufficient to modify, or perhaps to annihilate, its capacity for sorrowful impression; and, acting upon this idea, I reined my horse to the precipitous brink of a black and lurid tarn that lay in unruffled lustre by the dwelling, and gazed down — but with a shudder even more thrilling than before — upon the remodeled and inverted images of the gray sedge, and the ghastly tree-stems, and the vacant and eye-like windows."

And one may see from looking back at the illustrations given that the dominant impression which gives the character to the whole description, this leading quality which is the essence of the whole, usually stands at the very beginning, and to it all the succeeding details cling.

The end of a description is equally as important as the opening. In most descriptions, whether short or long, the most important detail, the detail that emphasizes most the general feeling of the whole, stands at the end. If the description be short, the necessity of a comprehensive opening statement is not imperative, — indeed, it may be made so formal and ostentatious when compared with the rest of the description as to be ridiculous; yet even in the short description some important detail should close it. In a long description the repetition of the opening statement in a new form sometimes stands at the end. If the description be of movement or change, the end will be the climax of the movement, the result of the change.

The End of a Description.

In the examples already given there are illustrations of the methods of closing. In each case, there is an important detail or an artistic repetition of the general impression. Many examples of short characterization can be found in all narratives. In Irving's description of Ichabod Crane, the next to the last sentence give the significant detail, and the last gives another general impression. It reads: —

"The cognomen of Crane was not inapplicable to his person. He was tall, but exceedingly lank, with narrow shoulders, long arms and legs, hands that dangled a mile out of his sleeves, feet that might have served for shovels, and his whole frame most loosely hung together. His head was small, and flat at top, with huge ears, large green glassy eyes, and a long snipe nose, so that it looked like a weathercock perched upon his spindle neck to tell which way the wind blew."

So far this is but an amplification of his likeness to a crane; certainly " a long snipe nose " " upon his spindle neck" is the most important detail. Next the author gives another general impression : —

"To see him striding along the profile of a hill on a windy day, with his clothes bagging and fluttering about him, one might have mistaken him for the genius of famine descending upon the earth, or some scarecrow eloped from a cornfield."

The following is from "The House of Usher:"—

"Shaking off from my spirit what *must* have been a dream, I scanned more narrowly the real aspect of the building. Its principal feature seemed to be that of an excessive antiquity. The discoloration of ages had been great. Minute fungi overspread the whole exterior, hanging in a fine tangled web-work from the eaves. Yet all this was apart from any extraordinary dilapidation. No portion of the masonry had fallen, and there appeared to be a wild inconsistency between its still perfect adaptation of parts and the crumbling condition of the individual stones. In this there was much that reminded me of the specious totality of old woodwork which has rotted for long years in some neglected vault with no disturbance from the breath of the external air. Beyond this indication of extensive decay, however, the fabric gave little token of instability. Perhaps the eye of a scrutinizing observer might have discovered a barely perceptible fissure, which, extending from the roof of the building in front, made its way down the wall in a zigzag direction, until it became lost in the sullen waters of the tarn."

In this every detail emphasizes the "excessive antiquity" of the house; and on reading the story there is no question of the importance of the "barely perceptible fissure." Thereby hangs the tale.

The two following are descriptions of dawn, of change; they have marked climaxes. The first is by Edward Everett, the second by Stevenson. The similarity in choice of words and in the feelings of the men is remarkable.

"Such was the glorious spectacle as I entered the train. As we proceeded, the timid approach of twilight became more perceptible; the intense blue of the sky began to soften; the smaller stars, like little children, went first to rest; the sister-beams of the Pleiades soon melted together; but the bright constellations of the west and north remained unchanged. Steadily the wondrous transfiguration went on. Hands of angels, hidden from mortal eyes, shifted the scenery of the heavens; the glories of night dissolved into the glories of dawn. The blue sky now turned more softly gray; the great watch-stars shut up their holy eyes; the east began to kindle. Faint streaks of purple soon blushed along the sky; the whole celestial concave was filled with the inflowing tides of the morning light, which came pouring down from above in one great ocean of radiance, till at length, as we reached the Blue Hills, a flash of purple blazed out from above the horizon, and turned the dewy teardrops of flower and leaf into rubies and diamonds. In a few seconds, the everlasting gates of morning were thrown wide open, and the lord of day, arrayed in glories too severe for the gaze of man, began his state."

"At last she began to be aware of a wonderful revolution, compared to which the fire of Mittwalden Palace was but a crack and flash of a percussion cap. The countenance with which the pines regarded her began insensibly to change; the grass, too, short as it was, and the whole winding staircase of the brook's course, began to wear a solemn freshness of appearance. And this slow transfiguration reached her heart, and played upon it, and transpierced it with a serious thrill. She looked all about; the whole face of nature looked back, brimful of meaning, finger on lip, leaking its glad secret. She looked up. Heaven was almost emptied of stars. Such as still lingered shone with a changed and waning brightness, and began to faint in their stations. And the color of the sky itself was most wonderful; for the rich blue of the night had now melted and softened and brightened; and there had succeeded a hue that has no name, and that is never seen but as the herald of the morning. 'Oh!' she cried, joy catching at her voice, 'Oh! it is the dawn!'

"In a breath she passed over the brook, and looped up her skirts and fairly ran in the dim alleys. As she ran, her ears were aware of many pipings, more beautiful than music; in the small, dish-shaped houses in the fork of giant arms, where they had lain all night, lover by lover, warmly pressed, the bright-eyed, big-hearted singers began to awaken for the day. Her heart melted and flowed forth to them in kindness. And they, from their small and high perches in the clerestories of the wood cathedral, peered down sidelong at the ragged Princess as she flitted below them on the carpet of the moss and tassel.

"Soon she had struggled to a certain hilltop, and saw far before her the silent inflooding of the day. Out of the East it welled and whitened; the darkness trembled into light; and the stars were extinguished like the street-lamps of a human city. The whiteness brightened into silver; the silver warmed into gold, and the gold kindled into pure and living fire; and the face of the East was barred with elemental scarlet. The day drew its first long breath, steady and chill; and for leagues around the woods sighed and shivered. And then, at one bound the sun had floated up; and her startled eyes received day's first arrow, and quailed under the buffet. On every side, the shadows leaped from their ambush and fell prone. The day was come, plain and garish; and up the steep and solitary eastern heaven, the sun, victorious over his competitors, continued slowly and royally to mount."

One thing further should be said regarding Mass. Not everything can stand first or last; some important details must be placed in the midst of a description. These particulars will not be of equal importance. The more important details may be given their proportionate emphasis by relatively increasing the length of their treatment. If one detail is more important than another, it requires more to be

Proportion.

said about it; unimportant matters should be passed over with a word. Proportion in the length of treatment is a guide to the relative importance of the matters introduced into a description.

In the description of "The House of Usher," position emphasizes the barely perceptible fissure. Proportion singles out the crumbling condition of the individual stones and makes this detail more emphatic than either the discoloration or the fungi. And in Newman's description, the olive-tree, the brilliant atmosphere, the thyme, the bees, all add to the charms of bright and beautiful Athens; but most of all the Ægean, with its chain of islands, its dark violet billows, its jets of silver, the heaving and panting of its long waves, — the restless living element fascinates and enraptures "yon pilgrim student." Position and proportion are the means of emphasis in a paragraph of description.

Having settled the massing of the description, the next matter for consideration is the arrangement. In order that the parts of a description may be coherent, hold together, they should be arranged in the order in which they would naturally be perceived. What strikes the eye of the beholder as most important, often the general characteristic of the whole, should be mentioned first; and the details should follow as they are seen. In a building, the usual way of observing and describing is from foundation to turret stone. A landscape may be described by beginning with what is near and extending the view; this is common. Sometimes the very opposite plan is pursued; or one may begin on either hand and advance toward the other. Of a person near by, the face is the first thing observed; for it is there that his character can be best discovered. Afterward details

Arrangement must be natural.

of clothing follow as they would naturally be noticed. If a person be at a distance his pose and carriage would be about all that could be seen; as he approaches, the other details would be mentioned as they came into view. To arrange details in the order in which they are naturally observed will result in an association in the description of the details that are contiguous in the objects. Jumping about in a description is a source of confusion. How entirely it may ruin a paragraph can be estimated by the effect upon this single sentence, " He was tall, with feet that might have served for shovels, narrow shoulders, hands that dangled a mile out of his sleeves, long arms and legs, and his whole frame most loosely hung together." This rearrangement makes but a disjointed and feeble impression; and the reason is entirely that an order in which no person ever observed a man has been substituted for the commonest order, — from head to foot. Arrange details so that the parts which are contiguous shall be associated in the description, and proceed in the order in which the details are naturally observed.

The following is by Irving; he is describing the stage-coachman: —

"He has commonly a broad, full face, curiously mottled with red, as if the blood had been forced by hard feeding into every vessel of the skin; he is swelled into jolly dimensions by frequent potations of malt liquors, and his bulk is still further increased by a multiplicity of coats, in which he is buried like a cauliflower, the upper one reaching to his heels. He wears a broad-brimmed, low-crowned hat; a huge roll of colored handkerchief about his neck, knowingly knotted and tucked in at the bosom; and has in summer time a large bouquet of flowers in his buttonhole, the present, most probably, of some enamored country lass. His waistcoat is commonly of some bright color, striped, and his small-clothes extend far below the knees, to meet a pair of jockey boots which reach about half way up his legs."

When the materials have been selected and arranged, the hardest part of the work has been done. It now remains to express in language the picture. A few suggestions regarding the kind of language will be helpful. The writer must always bear in mind the fact that in constructing a mental picture each reader does it from the images he already possesses. "Quaint arabesques" is without meaning to many persons; and until the word has been looked up in the dictionary, and the picture seen there, the beautiful line of "Sir Launfal" suggests no image whatever. So when Stevenson speaks of the birds in the "clerestories of the wood cathedral," the image is not distinct in the mind of a young American. Supposing a pupil in California were asked to describe an orange to an Esquimau. He might say that it is a spheroid about the size of an apple, and the color of one of Lorraine's sunsets. This would be absolutely worthless to a child of the frigid zone. Had he been told that an orange was about the size of a snowball, much the color of the flame of a candle, that the peeling came off like the skin from a seal, and that the inside was good to eat, he would have known more of this fruit. The images which lie in our minds and from which we construct new pictures are much like the blocks that a child-builder rearranges in many different forms; but the blocks do not change. From them he may build a castle or a mill; yet the only difference is a difference in arrangement. So it is with the pictures we build up in imagination: our castle in Spain we have never seen, but the individual elements which we associate to lift up this happy dwelling-place are the things we know and have seen. A reader creates nothing new;

Use Familiar Images.

all he does is to rearrange in his own mind the images already familiar. Only so may he pass from the known to the unknown.

The fact that we construct pictures of what we read from those images already in our minds warns the writer against using materials which those for whom he writes could not understand. It compels him to select definite images, and it urges him to use the common and the concrete. It frequently drives him to use comparisons.

To represent the extremely bare and unornamented appearance of a building, one might write, "It looked like a great barn," or "It was a great barn." In either case the image would be definite, common, and concrete. In both cases there is a comparison. In the first, where the comparison is expressed, there is a *simile;* in the second, where the comparison is only implied, there is a *metaphor.* These two figures of speech are very common in description, and it is because they are of great value. One other is sometimes used, — *personification,* which ascribes to inanimate things the attributes of life which are the property of animate nature. What could be happier than this by Stevenson: "All night long he can hear Nature breathing deeply and freely; even as she takes her rest she turns and smiles"? or this, "A faint sound, more like a moving coolness than a stream of air"? And at the end of the chapter which describes his "night under the pines," he speaks of the "tapestries" and "the inimitable ceiling" and "the view which I command from the windows." In this one chapter are personification, simile, metaphor, — all comparisons, and doing what could hardly be done without them. Common, distinct, concrete images are surest.

To body forth these common, distinct, concrete

images calls for a discriminating choice of words; for in the choice of words lies a large part of the vividness of description. If the thing described be unknown to the reader, it requires the right word to place it before him; if it be common, still must the right word be found to set it apart from the thousand other objects of the same class. The words that may justly be called describing words are adjectives and nouns; and of these the adjective is the first descriptive word. The rule that a writer should never use two adjectives where one will do, and that he should not use one if a noun can be found that completely expresses the thought, is a good one to follow. One certain stroke of the crayon is worth a hundred lines, each approaching the right one. One word, the only one, will tell the truth more vividly than ten that approach its expression. For it must be remembered that a description must be done quickly; every word that is used and does nothing is not only a waste of time, but is actually in the way. In a description every word must count. It may be a comparison, an epithet, personification, or what not, but whatever method is adopted, the right word must do it quickly.

Choice of 8. Adjectives and Nouns.

How much depends on the nice choice of words may be seen by a study of the selections already quoted; and especially by a careful reading of those by Stevenson and Everett. To show the use of adjectives and nouns in description, the following from Kipling is a good illustration. Toomai had just reached the elephants' "ball-room" when he saw —

" white-tusked wild males, with fallen leaves and nuts and twigs lying in the wrinkles of their necks and the folds of their ears; fat, slow-footed she-elephants, with restless pinky-black calves only three or four feet high, running under their stomachs; young elephants with their tusks just beginning to show, and very proud of them; lanky, scraggy, old-maid elephants, with their hollow, anxious faces, and trunks like rough bark; savage old bull-elephants, scarred from shoulder to flank with great weals and cuts of bygone fights, and the caked dirt of their solitary mud bath dropping from their shoulders; and there was one with a broken tusk and the marks of the full-stroke, the terrible drawing scrape of a tiger's claw on his side."

One third of the words in this paragraph are descriptive nouns and adjectives, none of which the reader wishes to change.

Verbs also have a great value in description. In the paragraph picturing the dawn, Stevenson has not neglected the verbs. "Welled," "whitened," "trembled," "brightened," "warmed," "kindled," and so on through the paragraph. Try to change them, and it is apparent that something is lost by any substitution. Kaa, the python, "*pours* himself along the ground." If he is angry, "Baloo and Baghecra could see the big swallowing-muscles on either side of Kaa's throat *ripple* and *bulge*" *Use of Verbs.*

Yet in the choice of words, one may search for the bizarre and unusual rather than for the truly picturesque. Stevenson at times seems to have lapsed. When he says that Modestine would feel a switch "more *tenderly* than my cane;" that he "must *instantly* maltreat this uncomplaining animal," meaning constantly; and at another place that he "had to labor so *consistently* with" his stick that the sweat ran into his eyes, there is a suspicion of a desire for the sensational rather than the direct truth. On the other hand, the beginner finds himself using words that have lost their meaning through indiscriminate usage. "Awful good," "awful pretty," and "awful sweet" mean something less than good, pretty, and sweet. "Lovely," "dear," "splendid," "unique," and a large number of good words have been much dulled by the ignorant use of babblers. Superlatives and all words denoting comparison should be used with stinginess. One cannot afford to part with this kind of coin frequently; the cheaper coins should be used, else he will find an empty purse when need arises. Thackeray has this: "Her voice was the sweetest, low song." How much better this, Her voice was a sweet, low song. All the world is shut out from this, while in the former he challenges the world by the comparison. Shakespeare was wiser when he made Lear say, —

"Her voice was ever soft,
Gentle, and low, — an excellent thing in woman."

Avoid words which have lost their meaning by indiscriminate use; shun the sensational and the bizarre; use superlatives with economy; but in all you do, whether in unadorned or figurative language, choose the word that is quick and sure and vivid — the one word that exactly suggests the picture.

SUGGESTIVE QUESTIONS AND EXERCISES

QUESTIONS.

THE OLD MANSE.

(Riverside Literature Series, No. 69.)

ARE there narrative portions in "The Old Manse"? paragraphs of exposition?

Do you term the whole narration, description, or exposition? Why?

Frame a sentence which you think would be an adequate topic sentence for the whole piece.

What phrase in the first paragraph allows the author to begin the second with the words, "Nor, in truth, had the Old Manse," etc.? Where in the second paragraph is found the words which are the source of "my design," mentioned in the third? How does the author pass from the fourth paragraph to the fifth? In the same way note the connections between the succeeding paragraphs. They are most skillfully dovetailed together. Now make a list of the phrases in the first fifteen pages which introduce paragraphs, telling from what in the preceding paragraph each new paragraph springs. Do you think that such a felicitous result just happened? or did Hawthorne plan it?

Does Hawthorne generally introduce his descriptions by giving the feeling aroused by the object described, a method very common with Poe?

In the paragraph beginning at the bottom of p. 18, what do you think of the selection of material? What have guided in the inclusion and exclusion of details?

Write a paragraph upon this topic: There could not be a more joyous aspect of external nature than as seen from the windows of my study just after the passing of a cooling shower. Be careful to select things that have been made happy, and to use adjectives and nouns that are full of joy.

Make a list of the words used to describe "The Old Apple Dealer."

Has this description Unity?

What relation to the whole has the first sentence of paragraph three? the last?

Do you think there is a grammatical error in the third sentence of this paragraph?

By contrasts to what has Hawthorne brought out better the character of the Apple Dealer? When can contrasts help?

AN INDIAN-SUMMER REVERIE, AND OTHER POEMS.

(Riverside Literature Series, No. 30.)

In this poem what purpose is served by the first two stanzas?

Where in the landscape does the author begin? Which way does he progress?

Quote stanzas in which other senses than sight are called upon.

Make a list of the figures of speech. How many similes? metaphors? examples of personification? Which seems most effective? Which instance of its use do you prefer? Has Lowell used too many figures?

Read "The Oak," "The Dandelion," and "Al Fresco."

Are they description or exposition? Do they bear out Lowell's estimate of himself?

THE SKETCH-BOOK.

(Riverside Literature Series, Nos. 51, 52.)

Why has Irving given four pages to the description of Sleepy Hollow before he introduces Ichabod Crane?

Why, then, seven pages to Ichabod before the story begins?

What gives the peculiar interest to this tale?

In the "Legend of Sleepy Hollow" how many paragraphs of description close with an important detail?

In how many with a general characterization?

In all the descriptions of buildings by Irving that you have read, what are the first things mentioned, — size, shape, color, or what? Make a list, so as to be sure.

Does Irving use many comparisons? Are the likenesses to common things? Select the ten you think best. Are there more in narrative or descriptive passages? What do you gather from this fact?

In "Christmas Day," on p. 51 (R. L. S., No. 52), does Irving proceed from far to near in the landscape? Is this common? Find another example.

How has Irving emphasized the littleness of the minister described on p. 56 (R. L. S., No. 52)?

THE FALL OF THE HOUSE OF USHER.

(Riverside Literature Series, No. 119.)

Is the arrangement of the details in the last two lines of the first paragraph stronger than the arrangement of the same details on p. 63? Why, or why not?

In the description of the hall, pp. 67 and 68, do the details produce the effect upon you which they did upon Poe?

Find a description in this piece which closes with an important detail.

Is Usher described at all when Poe says, "I gazed upon him with a feeling half of pity, half of awe"? Do the details enumerated arouse such feelings in you? Would the feeling have been called forth if it had not been suggested by Poe? Is there, then, any advantage in this method of opening a description?

What good was done by describing Usher as Poe knew him in youth?

Why is the parenthetical clause on p. 72 necessary?

On p. 80, should Poe write "previously to its final interment"?

What do you think of the length of the sentence quoted on p. 85?

Does Poe use description to accent the mood of the narrative, or to make concrete the places and persons?

Why is "The Haunted House" introduced into the story?

Is this story as good as "The Gold-Bug"?

SILAS MARNER.

(Riverside Literature Series, No. 83.)

Why is not the early history of Silas Marner related first in the story?

By what steps has the author approached the definite time?

From the fragments about his appearance, do you get a clear idea of how Marner looks?

Do you approve this method of scattering the description along through the story? Write a description of Marner on the night he was going to the tavern.

Could not the quarrel between Godfrey and Dunsey be omitted?

Describe the interior of Marner's cottage.

Why should Sally Oates and her dropsy be admitted to the story?

Do you know as well how George Eliot's characters look as how they think and feel?

What do you think of the last sentence of Chapter IV.? Why does not Chapter V. go on with Dunsey's story? Why is Chapter VI. introduced at all? What of its close?

What figure in the last sentence of Chapter X.?

Would you prefer to know how tall Eppie was, what kind of clothes she wore, etc., to the knowledge you gain of her on p. 178?

Suppose that Dunsey came home the night he staked Wildfire, recite the conversation between him and Godfrey.

Have Dolly Winthrop, Priscilla Lammeter, and Mr. Macey talk over "The New Minister."

Write on "What I see in George Eliot's Face."

THE DESERTED VILLAGE.

(Riverside Literature Series, No. 68.)

Is this piece description or exposition?

In the first stanza where is the topic sentence?

The author has made two groups of charms. Would it be as well to change them about? Give your reasons.

Where has he used the ear instead of the eye to suggest his picture? Is it clear?

What method is adopted in lines 125-128? See also lines 237-250.

Can you unite the paragraphs on p. 25? Why do you think so?

Could you suggest a new arrangement of details in lines 341-362 that would be as good as the present? What are the last four lines for?

EXERCISES.

Enumerative Description may well employ a few lessons. In it accuracy of detail must be studied, and every detail must be introduced.

1. The Teacher's Desk.

2. Write a letter to a carpenter giving details for the construction of a small bookcase.

3. By telling how you made it, describe a camp, a kite, a dress, or a cake. Narration may be employed for the purpose of description. A good example may be found in "Robinson Crusoe" in the chapter describing his home after the shipwreck.

4. Describe an unfurnished room. Shape, size, position, and number of windows, the fireplace, etc., should be definite. Be sure to give the point of view. To say "On my right hand," "In front of me," or any similar phrases means nothing unless the reader knows where you are.

In these exercises the pupil will doubtless employ the paragraph of particulars. This is the most common in description. Other forms are valuable.

5. Using a paragraph telling what it was not, finish this:

I followed the great singer to her home. Imagine my surprise in finding that the house in which this lady lived was not a home of luxury and splendor, — not even a home of comfort. Go on with the details of a home of luxury which were *not* there. Finish with what you did see. This is really a description of two houses set in artistic contrast to heighten the effect. Remember you are outside.

6. By the use of comparison finish this: The home of my poor little friend was but little better than a barn. Choose only such details as emphasize the barn-like appearance of the home. There is but one room. Remember where you are standing; and keep in mind the effect you wish to produce.

7. Using a moving point of view, describe an interior. Do not have too many rooms.

8. Furnish the room described in number four to suit your taste. Tell how it looks. Remember that a few things give character to a room.

9. Describe your childhood's home as it would look to you after years of absence.

10. Using a paragraph of the obverse, describe the appearance of the house from which you were driven by the cruelty of a drunken father.

11. Describe a single tree standing alone in a field. It will be well for the teacher to read to the class some descriptions of trees, — Lowell's "Birch" and "Oak," "Under the Willows," and some stanzas from "An Indian Summer Reverie." Holmes has some good paragraphs on trees in "The Autocrat." Any good tree descriptions will help pupils to do it better than they can without suggestion. They should describe their own tree, however.

12. Describe some single flower growing wild. Read Lowell's "Dandelion," "Violet, Sweet Violet," Wordsworth's "Daisy," "The Daffodils," "The Small Celandine," and Burns's "Daisy." These do not so much describe as they arouse a feeling of love for the flowers which will show itself in the composition.

13. Describe a view of a lake. If possible, have your

point of view above the lake and use the paragraph of comparison.

14. Describe a landscape from a single point of view. Read Curtis's " My Castles in Spain " from " Prue and I," many descriptions in " An Inland Voyage " by Stevenson, and " Bay Street " by Bliss Carman in " The Atlantic Monthly."

15. Describe your first view of a small cluster of houses or a small town.

16. Approach the town, describing its principal features. Keep the reader informed as to where you are.

17. Describe a dog of your own.

18. Describe a dog of your neighbor's. Before the description is undertaken read " Our Dogs " and " Rab " by Dr. Brown; " A Dog of Flanders " by Ouida. Scott has some noble fellows in his novels.

19. Describe a flock of chickens. There are good descriptions of chickens in " The House of the Seven Gables " and in " Sketches " by Dickens.

20. Describe the burning of your own home. Be careful not to narrate.

21. Describe a stranger you met on the street to-day. It is easier to describe a person if you and the person you describe move toward each other. Remember that you begin the description at a distance. Details should be mentioned as they actually come into view.

22. Describe your father in his favorite corner at home.

23. Describe a person you do not like, by telling what he is not.

24. Describe a person you admire, but are not acquainted with, using the paragraph of comparisons.

25. Describe a picture.

It would be well to have at the end of this year four or five stories written, in which description plays a part. Its principal use is to give the setting to the story, to give concreteness to the characters, and to accent the mood of the story.

Most passages of description are short. Rarely will any

pupil write over three hundred words. One hundred are often better. The short composition gives an opportunity for the study of accuracy of expression. What details to include ; in what order to arrange them that they produce the best effect, both of vividness and naturalness ; and the influence of the point of view and the purpose of the author on the unity of description should be kept constantly present in the exercises. Careful attention should be paid to choice of words, for on right words depends in a large degree the vividness of a description. Right words in well-massed paragraphs of vivid description should be the object this term.

CHAPTER V

EXPOSITION

So far we have studied discourse which deals with things, — things active, doing something, considered under the head of narration; and things at rest, and pictured, considered in description. Now we come to exposition, which deals with ideas either separately or in combinations. Instead of Mr. Smith's horse, exposition treats of the general term, horse. "The Great Stone Face" may have taught a lesson by its story, but the discussion of the value of lofty ideals is a subject for exposition.

That general terms and propositions are harder to get hold of than concrete facts is readily apparent in the first reading of an author like Emerson. To a young person it means little. Yet when he puts in the place of the general terms some specific examples, and so verifies the statements, the general propositions have a mine of meaning, and "the sense of the author is as broad as the world." This stanza from Lowell is but little suggestive to young readers : — *[General Terms Difficult.]*

> "Such earnest natures are the fiery pith,
>   The compact nucleus, round which systems grow!
> Mass after mass becomes inspired therewith,
>   And whirls impregnate with the central glow."

Yet when Columbus and Luther and Garrison are mentioned as illustrations of the meaning, it becomes world-wide in its application. Still in order to get at the thought, there is first the need of the specific and the concrete; afterward we pass to the general and the abstract.

As abstract ideas are harder to get hold of than concrete facts, so exposition has difficulties greater than those found in narration and description. It is not so hard to tell what belongs in a story; the events are all distinct. Nor is it so difficult to know what to include in a description; one can look and see. In exposition this is not so. In most minds ideas do not have distinct limits; the edges rather are indistinct. It is hard to tell where the idea stops. In writing of "The Uses of Coal," it is easy to wander over an indistinct boundary and to take a survey of "The Origin of Coal." Not only may one include what unquestionably should be excluded, but there is no definite guide to the arrangement of the materials, such as was found in narration. There a sequence of time was an almost infallible rule; here the writer must search carefully how to arrange hazy ideas in some effective form. As discourse comes to deal more with general ideas, the difficulties of writing increase; and the difficulties are not due to any new principles of structure which must be introduced. When one says that the material should be selected according to the familiar law of Unity, he has given the guiding principle. Yet the real difficulty is still before an author: it is to decide what stamp to put upon such elusive matter as ideas. They cannot be kept long enough in the twilight of consciousness to analyze them; and often ideas that have been marked "accepted" have, upon reexamination, to be "rejected." To examine ideas — the material used in this form of discourse — so thoroughly that they may be accurately, definitely known in their backward relation and their bearing upon what follows, this is the seat of the difficulty in exposition.

Exposition may conveniently be classified into exposition of a term, or definition; and exposition of a proposition, which is generally suggested by the term exposition.

Definition of a word means giving its limits or boundaries. Of man it might be said that it is a living animal, having a strong bony skele- **Definition.** ton; that this skeleton consists of a trunk from which extend four limbs, called arms and legs, and is surmounted by a bony cavity, called a skull; that the skeleton protects the vital organs, and is itself covered by a muscular tissue which moves the bones and gives a rounded beauty to their ugliness; that man has a highly developed nervous system, the centre of which is the brain placed in the skull. So a person might go on for pages, enumerating the attributes which, taken together, make up the general idea of man.

This sort of exposition is very near description; indeed, were the purpose different, it would be description. The purpose, however, is not to tell how an individual looks, but to place the object in a class. It is therefore not description, but exposition. Moreover, the method is different. In description those characteristics are given that distinguish the object from the rest of the class; while in exposition those qualities are selected which are common to all objects of its class. *Exposition and Description distinguished.*

On account of the length of the definition by an enumeration of all the attributes, it is not frequently used except in long treatises. For it there has been substituted what is called a *logical defini-* **Logical** *tion.* Instead of naming all the characteris- **Definition.** tics of an object, a logical definition groups many attributes under one general term, and then adds a quality which distinguishes the object from the others of the general class. Man has been defined as the "reasoning animal." In this definition a large number of attributes have been gathered together in the general term "animal;" then man is separated from the whole class "animal" by the word "reasoning." A logical definition consists, then, of two parts: the general term naming the genus, and the limiting term naming the distinguishing attribute called the differentia.

Genus and differentia are found in every good definition. The *genus* should be a term more general than the term defined. "Man is a person who reasons" is a poor definition; because "person" is no more general than "man." "A canine is a dog that is wild" is very bad, because "dog," the general term in the definition, is less general than the word defined. However,to say that "a dog is a canine that has been domesticated," is a definition in which the genus is more general than the term defined.

Genus and Differentia.

Next, the genus should be a term well understood. "Man is a mammal who reasons" is all right, in having a genus more general than the term defined, but the definition fails with many because "mammal" is not well understood. "Botany is that branch of biology which treats of plant life" has in it the same error. "Biology" is not so well understood as "botany," though it is a more general term. In cases of this sort, the writer should go farther toward the more general until he finds a term perfectly clear to all. "Man is an animal that reasons," "botany is the branch science that treats of plant life," would both be easily understood. The genus should be a term better understood than the term defined; and it should be a term more general than the term defined.

A definition may be faulty in its *differentia* also. The differentia is that part of a definition which names the difference between the term defined and the general class to which it belongs. "Man is a reasoning animal." "Animal" names the general class, and "reasoning" is the differentia which separates "man" from other "animals." On the selection of this limiting word depends the accuracy of the definition. "Man is an animal that walks," or "that has hands," or "that talks," are all faulty; because bears walk, monkeys have hands, and parrots talk. Supposing the following definitions were given: "A cat is an animal that catches rats and mice;" "A rose is a flower that bears thorns;" "Gold is a metal that is heavy;" all would be faulty because the differentia in each is faulty. Notice, too, the definitions of "dog" and "canine" already given. Even "man is a reasoning animal" may fail; since many men declare that other animals reason. The differentia should include all the members that the term denotes, and it should exclude all that it does not denote.

The requisites of a good definition are: first, that it shall include or denote all the members of the class; second, that it shall exclude everything which does not belong to its class; third, that the words used in the definition shall be better understood than the word defined; fourth, that it shall be brief. *Requisites of a good definition.*

A definition may perfectly expound a term; and because of the very qualities that make it a good definition, accuracy and brevity, it may be almost valueless to the ordinary reader. For instance, this definition, "An acid is a substance, usually sour and sharp to the taste, that changes vegetable blue colors to red, and, combining with an earth, an alkali, or a metallic oxide, forms a salt," would not generally be understood. So it frequently becomes necessary to do more than give a definition in order to explain the meaning of a term. This brings us to the study of exposition, as it is generally understood, in which all the resources of language are called into service to explain a term or a proposition.

What, then, are the methods of explaining a proposition? First, *a proposition may be explained by the repetition of the thought in some other form.* To be effective, repetition must add something to what has been said; the words used may be more specific or they may be more general. For example, " A strong partisan may not be a good citizen. The stanchest Republican may by reason of a blind adherence to party be working an injury to the country he loves. Indeed, one can easily conceive a body of men so devoted to a theory, beautiful though it may be in many respects, that they stand in the way of the world's progress." The second sentence repeats the thought of the first in more specific terms; the third repeats it in more general terms. The specific may be explained by the general; more often the general is cleared up by the specific. In either case, the proposition must be brought one step nearer to the reader by the restatement, or the repetition is not good.

<small>How do Men explain? First, by Repetition.</small>

Speaking of written or printed words, Barrett Wendell writes : —

" In themselves, these black marks are nothing but black marks more or less regular in appearance. Modern English type and script are rather simple to the eye. Old English and German are less so ; less so still, Hebrew and Chinese. But all alphabets present to the eye pretty obvious traces of regularity ; in a written or printed page the same mark will occur over and over again. This is positively all we see, — a number of marks grouped together and occasionally repeated. A glance at a mummy-case, an old-fashioned tea-chest, a Hebrew Bible, will show us all that any eye can ever see in a written or printed document. The outward and visible body of style consists of a limited number of marks which, for all any reader is apt to know, are purely arbitrary."

In this paragraph every sentence is a repetition of some part of the opening or topic sentence, and serves to explain it.

Second, *a proposition may be explained by telling what it is not.* At times this is as valuable as telling what it is. Care should be taken that the thing excluded or denied have some likeness to the proposition or term being explained; that the two be really in some danger of being confused. Unless to a hopelessly ignorant person, it would not explain anything to say "a horse is not a man;" but to assert that "a whale is not a fish, though they have many points in common," would prepare the way for an explanation of what a whale is. The obverse statement is nearly always followed by a repetition of what the thing is.

<small>Second, by telling the</small>

The following from Newman illustrates the method:

" Now what is Theology? First, I will tell you what it is not. And here, in the first place (though of course I speak on the subject as a Catholic), observe that, strictly speaking, I am not assuming that Catholicism is true, while I make myself the champion of Theology. Catholicism has not formally entered into my argument hitherto, nor shall I just now assume any principle peculiar to it, for reasons which will appear in the sequel, though of course I shall use Catholic language. Neither, secondly, will I fall into the fashion of the day, of identifying Natural Theology with Physical

Theology; which said Physical Theology is a most jejune study, considered as a science, and really no science at all, for it is ordinarily no more than a series of pious or polemical remarks upon the physical world viewed religiously, whereas the word 'Natural' comprehends man and society, and all that is involved therein, as the great Protestant writer, Dr. Butler, shows us. Nor, in the third place, do I mean by Theology polemics of any kind; for instance, what are called 'Evidences of Religion,' or 'the Christian Evidences.' . . . Nor, fourthly, do I mean by Theology that vague thing called 'Christianity,' or 'our common Christianity,' or 'Christianity the law of the land,' if there is any man alive who can tell what it is. . . . Lastly, I do not understand by Theology, acquaintance with the Scriptures; for, though no person of religious feeling can read Scripture but he will find those feelings roused, and gain much knowledge of history into the bargain, yet historical reading and religious feeling are not a science. I mean none of these things by Theology. I simply mean the Science of God, or the truths we know about God put into a system; just as we have a science of the stars, and call it astronomy, or of the crust of the earth, and call it geology."

Third, *a common way of explaining a proposition is to go into particulars about it.* Enough particulars should be given to furnish a reasonable explanation of the proposition. Macaulay, writing of the "muster-rolls of names" which Milton uses, goes into details. He says : —

Third, by Details.

"They are charmed names. Every one of them is the first link in a long chain of associated ideas. Like the dwelling place of our infancy revisited in manhood, like the song of our country heard in a strange land, they produce upon us an effect wholly independent of their intrinsic value. One transports us back to a remote period of history. Another places us among the novel scenes and manners of a distant region. A third evokes all the dear classical recollections of childhood, — the schoolroom, the dog-eared Virgil, the holiday, and the prize. A fourth brings before us the splendid phantoms of chivalrous romance, the trophied lists, the embroidered housings, the quaint devices, the haunted forests, the enchanted gardens, the achievements of enamoured knights, and the smiles of rescued princesses."

Fourth, *a proposition may be explained by the use of a single example or illustration.* The value of this method depends on the choice of the example. It must in no essential way differ from the general case it is intended to illustrate. Supposing this proposition were advanced by some woman-hater: "All women are, by nature, liars," and it should be followed by this sentence, "For example, take this lady of fashion." Such an illustration is worthless. The individual chosen does not fairly represent the class. If, on the other hand, a teacher in physics should announce that "all bodies fall at the same rate in a vacuum," and should illustrate by saying, "If I place a bullet and a feather in a tube from which the air has been exhausted, they will be found to fall equally fast," his example would be a fair one, as the two objects differ in no manner essential to the experiment from "all bodies."

Fourth, by Illustration.

Here should be included anecdotes used as illustrations. They are of value if they are of the same type as the general class they are intended to explain. They may be of little value, however. It could safely be said that half the stories told in campaign speeches are not instances in point at all, but are told only to amuse and deceive. Specific instances must be chosen with care if they are to serve a useful purpose in exposition.

This example is from Newman: —

"To know is one thing, to do is another; the two things

are altogether distinct. A man knows that he should get up in the morning, — he lies abed; he knows that he should not lose his temper, yet he cannot keep it. A laboring man knows that he should not go to the ale-house, and his wife knows that she should not filch when she goes out charing, but, nevertheless, in these cases, the consciousness of a duty is not all one with the performance of it. There are, then, large families of instances, to say the least, in which men may become wiser, without becoming better."

Last, *a thing may be explained by telling what it is like, or what it is not like.* This method of comparison is very frequently employed. To liken a thing to something already known is a vivid way of explaining. Moreover in many cases it is easier than the method of repetition or that of details. By this method Macaulay explains his proposition that "it is the character of such revolutions that we always see the worst of them first." He says: —

<small>Fifth, by Compari-</small>

"A newly liberated people may be compared to a northern army encamped on the Rhine or the Xeres. It is said that when soldiers in such a situation first find themselves able to indulge without restraint in such a rare and expensive luxury, nothing is to be seen but intoxication. Soon, however, plenty teaches discretion, and, after wine has been for a few months their daily fare, they become more temperate than they had ever been in their own country. In the same manner, the final and permanent fruits of liberty are wisdom, moderation, and mercy. Its immediate effects are often atrocious crimes, conflicting errors, skepticism on points the most clear, dogmatism on points the most mysterious."

The comparison may be a simile or a metaphor, as when Huxley writes, explaining "the physical basis of life:" —

"Protoplasm, simple or nucleated, is the formal basis of all life. It is the clay of the potter: which, bake it and paint it as he will, remains clay, separated by artifice, and not by nature, from the commonest brick or sun-dried clod."

These, then, are the methods commonly adopted for explaining terms and propositions. First, by the use of definitions; second, by repeating the proposition either directly or obversely, adding something to the thought by each repetition; third, by enumerating particulars which form the ground for the statement; fourth, by selecting an instance which fairly illustrates the proposition; fifth, by the use of comparisons and analogies.

Some general considerations regarding the choice of a subject have been given. A subject should lend itself to the form of discourse employed; next, it should be a subject interesting to the readers; and third, it should be interesting to the writer and suited to his ability. The last condition makes it advisable to limit the subject to a narrow field. Few persons have the ability to view a general subject in all its relations. "Books" everybody knows something of; yet very few are able to treat this general subject in all its ramifications. A person writing of the general topic "books" would not only be compelled to know what a book is, what may truly be called a book, and what is the value of books to readers, and therefore the influence of the different kinds of literature; he would also be driven to study the machinery for making books, the history of printing, illustrating, and binding books, and all the mechanical processes connected with the manufacture of books. The subject might take quite another turn, and be the development of fiction or drama; it might be a discussion of the influences, political or social, that have moulded literature; it might be a study of character as manifested in an author's works. No one is well

The Subject.

fitted to write on the general topic " books." A subject should be limited.

The subject should be concrete.

For young persons *the subject should be so selected and stated that the treatment may be concrete.* As persons advance they make more generalizations; few, however, go so far as to think in general terms. Macaulay says, "Logicians may reason about abstractions, but the great mass of men must have images." That author depended largely for his glittering effects upon the use of common, concrete things which the masses understand. The subject should be such that it can be treated concretely. "Love," as a general proposition, is beautiful; but what more can a young writer say about it? Let him leave the whole horde of abstract subjects found in old rhetorics alone. They are subjects for experience; they cannot be handled by youth.

The Theme.

After the subject has been chosen, the writer next considers how he shall treat it. He selects the attitude he will assume toward the proposition, his point of view; and this position he embodies in a short sentence, called his *theme.* For instance, "patriotism" is the subject; as it stands it is abstract and very general. However, this, " Can a partisan be a patriot?" would be sufficiently concrete to be treated. Even yet there is no indication of the author's point of view. Should he write, "A real partisan is no patriot," his theme is announced, and his point of view known.

A theme, either explicit or implicit, *is essential in exposition.* It is not necessary that it shall be stated to the reader, but it must be clearly stated by the writer for his own guidance. It is, however, usually announced at the opening of the essay. Whether announced or not, it is most essential to the success of the essay. It is the touchstone by which the author tries all the material which he has collected. Not everything on the subject of patriotism should be admitted to an essay that has for its theme, "A real partisan cannot be a true patriot." It would save many a digression if the theme were always written in bold, black letters, and placed before the author as he writes. Every word in a theme should be there for a purpose, expressing some important modification of the thought. For instance, the statement above regarding a partisan may be too sweeping; perhaps the essayist would prefer to discuss the modified statement that "a blind partisan cannot always be a true patriot." The theme should state exactly what will be treated in the essay. The statement of it should employ the hardest kind of thinking; and when the theme is determined definitely and for all, the essay is safe from the intrusion of foreign ideas which disturb the harmony of the whole.

Another advantage in the theme is that, when once chosen, it will go far toward writing the essay. One great trouble with the young writer is that he is not willing to rely on his theme to suggest his composition. Mr. Palmer well says: —

"He examines his pen point, the curtains, his inkstand, to see if perhaps ideas may not be had from these. He wonders what the teacher will wish him to say, and he tries to recall how the passage sounded in the Third Reader. In every direction but one he turns, and that is the direction where lies the prime mover of his toil, his subject. Of that he is afraid. Now, what I want to make evident is that his subject is not in reality the foe, but the friend. It is his only helper. His composition is not to be, as he seems to suppose, a mass of laborious inventions, but it is made up exclusively of what the subject dictates. He has only to attend. At present he stands in his own way, making such a din with his private anxieties that he cannot hear the rich suggestions of his subject. He is bothered with considering how he feels, or what he or somebody else will like to see on his paper. This is debilitating business. He must lean on his subject, if he would have his writing strong, and busy himself with what it says, rather than with what he would say."

Having selected a subject, and with care stated the theme, it yet remains to give the essay a name. There is something in a name, and those authors who make a living by the pen are the shrewdest in displaying their wares under the most attractive titles. *The title should be attractive*, but it should not promise what the essay does not give. Newspaper headlines are usually attractive enough, but shamefully untruthful. Next, the title should *indicate the scope of the essay*. When Mr. Palmer calls his little book " Self-Cultivation in English," it is evident that it is not a text-book, and that it will not treat English as literature or as a science. Then, the title should be *short*. The theme can rarely be used as a title; it is too long. But the paramount idea developed in the essay should be embodied in the title. "Partisanship and Patriotism" would be a good subject to give the essay we have spoken of. The title, then, should be attractive; it should be short; and it should truthfully indicate the contents of the essay.

The Title.

One of the important factors in the construction of an essay is the selection of material. Though theme and title have already been discussed, it was not because they are the things for a writer to consider next after he has chosen his subject, but because they are so intimately bound up in the subject that their consideration at that time was natural. Before a writer can decide upon the position he will

Selection of Material.

assume toward a proposition, he should have looked over the field in a general way; for only with the facts before him is he competent to choose his point of view and to state his theme. The title is not in the least essential to the writing of the essay; it may be deferred until the essay is finished. It is necessary, however, that the writer have much knowledge of his subject, and that from this knowledge he be able to frame an opinion regarding the subject. When this has been done he is ready to begin the work of constructing his essay; and the first question in exposition, as in narration and description, is the selection of material to develop the theme he has chosen.

The selection of material is a more difficult matter in exposition than in narration and description. It requires the shrewdest scrutiny to keep out matter that does not help the thought forward. In narration we decided by the main incident; in description by the purpose and the point of view; in exposition we test all material by its relation to the theme. Does it help to explain the theme? If not, however good material it may be, it has no business in the essay.

Association of ideas is a law by which, when one of two related ideas is mentioned, the other is suggested. To illustrate, when Manila is mentioned, Admiral Dewey appears; when treason is spoken of, Arnold is in the mind. This law is of fundamental importance in arranging an essay; one thing should suggest the next. But valuable as it is, even indispensable, it may become the source of much mischief. For instance, a pupil has this for a topic, " Reading gives pleasure to many." He writes as his second sentence, " By pleasure I mean the opposite of pain," and goes on. "All things are understood by their opposites. If we did not know sickness, we could not enjoy our health. Joy is understood through sorrow. I remember my first sorrow. My father had just given me a new knife, — my first knife," and so on from one thing to another. And not so unnaturally either; each sentence has suggested the next, but not one is on the topic. The most anxious watch must be kept in the selection of material. Some will be admitted without any question; some will be excluded with a brusqueness almost brutal. There is a third class, however, that is allied with the subject, yet it is not so easy to determine whether it should be admitted or rejected. This class requires the closest questioning. It must contribute to the strength of the essay, not to its pages, or it has no place there.

There is another condition which must be considered **Scale of** *in the selection of material, the scale of treat-* **Treatment.** *ment.* If Macaulay had been asked by a daily paper to contribute a paragraph of five hundred words on Milton, he could not have introduced all the numerous topics which have their place in his essay of one hundred pages. He might have mentioned Milton's poetry and his character, the two main divisions of the present essay; but Dante and Æschylus, Puritan and Royalist, would scarcely have received notice. The second consideration in selecting material is the purpose and length of the essay, and the consequent thoroughness with which the subject is to be treated.

The exhaustiveness with which an author treats a subject depends, first, on his knowledge. Any person could write a paragraph on Milton; Macaulay and Lowell wrote delightful essays on the topic; David Masson has written volumes about him. These would have been impossible except to a person who had been a special student of the subject. Second, the thoroughness of the treatment depends *on the knowledge of the readers*. For persons acquainted with the record of the momentous events of Milton's time, it would have been quite unnecessary, it might be considered even an insult to intelligence, to go into such details of history. The shortest statement suffices when the reader is already familiar with the subject and needs only to know the application in this case. Third, the scale of treatment depends *on the purpose for which the essay is written*. If a newspaper paragraph, it is one thing; if for a magazine, it is quite another; if it is to be the final word on the subject, it may reach to volumes.

An apt illustration of proportion in the scale of treatment has been given by Scott and Denny in their "Composition-Rhetoric." They suggest that three maps of the United States, one very large, another half the size of the first, and a third very small, be hung side by side. If a comparison be made, it will be found that, whereas a great number of cities are represented on the largest map, only half as many appear on the middle-sized map. If the smallest map be examined, only the largest cities, the longest rivers, the greatest lakes, and the highest mountains can be found; all others must be omitted. On all three maps the same relation of parts is maintained. In proportion to the whole, New York State will hold the same position in all of them. The Mississippi River will flow from Minnesota to the Gulf of Mexico, and the Gulf will sweep in a curve from Texas to Florida. The scale is different, but the proportion does not change.

This principle applies in the construction of themes. In a paragraph only very important topics will receive any mention. In an essay these important topics retain their proper place and relation, while many other points of subordinate rank will be introduced. If the treatment be lengthened to a book, a host of minor sub-topics will be considered, each adding something to the development of the theme, and each giving to its principal topic the relative importance which belongs to the main divisions of the essay. The scale of treatment will have much to do with the selection of material.

Using Macaulay's "Milton" as an illustration, the analyses below will show how by increasing the size of the essay new subjects come into the field for notice. The first is but a paragraph and has the two main divisions of the essay. The second is an outline for an essay of two thousand words. In the third only one of the sub-topics is analyzed as Macaulay has discussed it. It would take too much space to analyze minutely the whole essay.

MILTON.

A. Milton's poetry has given him his position among great men.
B. His conduct was such as was to be expected from a man of a spirit so high and of an intellect so powerful.

In the following outline the same main headings are retained, and the sub-topics which explain them are introduced. The numbers indicate the paragraphs in Macaulay's essay given to each topic.

INTRODUCTION (1–8).

A. Milton's poetry has given him his position among men. (9–46.)
  I. No poet has ever triumphed over greater difficulties than Milton. (10–19.)
  II. In his lesser works he shows his great power. (20–31.)

III. There is but one modern poem that can be compared with " Paradise Lost;" Dante's " Divine Comedy" has great power, is upon a kindred subject, but in style of treatment widely different. (32-46.)
Transition. (47-49.)
B. His conduct was such as was to be expected from a man of a spirit so high and of an intellect so powerful. (50-90.)
 I. He lived at one of the most memorable eras in the history of mankind, and his conduct must be judged as that of the people is judged. (50-78.)
 II. There were some peculiarities which distinguished him from his contemporaries. (79-90.)
Conclusion. (91-94.)

Again, taking up but one section, B, II., the analysis is as follows: —

II. There were some peculiarities which distinguished him from his contemporaries. (79-90.)
  A. Milton adopted the noblest qualities of every party —
    1. Puritans. (80-84.)
      a. They excited contempt. However
      b. They were no vulgar fanatics; but
      c. They derived their peculiarities from their daily contemplation of superior beings and eternal interests.
      d. Thus the Puritan was made up of two men, — the one all self-abasement, the other all pride.
      e. Résumé of character of Puritans.
    2. Heathens were passionate lovers of freedom. (85.)
    3. Royalists had individual independence, learning, and polite manners of the Court.
  B. But he alone fought the battle for the freedom of the mind. (88.)
    1. This led him to discard parties; and (89)
    2. To dare the boldest literary services. (90.)

The fundamental principle guiding in the selection of material is unity. It decides what may with propriety be admitted to the essay, and it determines in part what must be left out. Another principle, secondary to this, is scale of treatment. If the essay is to be short, only essentials may be used; if long, many related sub-topics must take their subordinate positions in the essay.

Following the selection of material comes its arrangement. Here also there is greater difficulty than was experienced in narration or description. Though the same principles of Coherence and Mass guide, they are more difficult to apply. The seat of the difficulty is in the elusiveness of the material. It is hard to picture distinctly the value and relation of the different topics of an essay. Suppose the subject is "The Evils of War." The first paragraph might contain a general statement announcing the theme. Then these topics are to be discussed: —

Arrangement.

1. The effect on the *morale* of a nation.
2. The suffering of friends and relatives.
3. The destruction of life.
4. The backward step in civilization.
5. The destruction of property.

The order could not be much worse. How shall a better be obtained?

The most helpful suggestion regarding a method of making the material in some degree visible, capable of being grasped, is that each subdivision be placed on a separate card, and that, as the material is gathered, it be put upon the card containing the group to which it belongs. By different arrangements of these cards the writer can find most easily the order that is natural and effective. It is much like anagrams, this ordering of matter in an

Use Cards for Subdivisions.

essay. Take these letters, s-l-y-w-a-r-e, and in your head try to put them together to make a word; you will have some trouble, probably. If, however, these same letters be put upon separate slips of paper, you may with some arrangement get out the rather common word, lawyers. It is much the same with topic cards in exposition; they can be moved and rearranged in all possible ways, and at last an order distinctly better than any other will be found.

Speaking of cards, it might be well to say that the habit of putting down a fact or an idea bearing on a topic just as soon as it occurs to one is invaluable for a writer. All men have good memories; some persons have better ones than others. But there is no one who does not forget; and each catches himself very often saying, "I knew that, but I forgot it." It is a fact, not perhaps complimentary, that paper tablets are surer than the tablets of memory.

In exposition, where the whole attention of the reader should be given to the thought, where more than ever the mind should be freed from *An Outline.* every hindrance, and its whole energy directed to getting the meaning, the greatest care should be given to making a plan. No person who has attained distinction in prose has worked without a plan. Any piece of literature, even the most discursive, has in it something of plan; but in literature of the first rank the plan is easily discovered. How clear it is in Macaulay's essay has been seen. In Burke it is yet more logical and exact. However beautiful a piece may be, however naturally one thought grows out of another, as though it were always so and could be no other way, be sure it is so because of some man's thought, on account of careful planning. And it may be said without a chance of contradiction that when an essay has been well planned it is half done, and that half by far the harder. "We can hardly at the present day understand what Menander meant, when he told a man who inquired as to the progress of his comedy that he had finished it, not having yet written a single line, because he had constructed the action of it in his mind. A modern critic would have assured him that the merit of his piece depended on the brilliant things which arose under his pen as he went along." The brilliant things are but the gargoyles and the scrolls, the ornaments of the structure; and when so brilliant as to attract especial attention, they divert the mind from the total effect much as a series of beautiful marbles set between those perfect columns would have ruined the Parthenon. It was not in any single feature — not in pediment, column, or capital, not in frieze, architrave, or tympanum — that its glorious beauty lay, but in the simple strength and the harmonious symmetry of the whole, in the general plan. Webster planned his orations, Newman planned his essays, Carlyle planned his Frederick the Great. Their works are not a momentary inspiration; they are the result of forethought, long and painstaking. The absolute essential in the structure of an essay, that without which it will fail to arrive anywhere, that compared to which all ornament, all fine writing, is but sounding brass and a tinkling cymbal, that absolute essential is the total effect secured by making a plan.

<small>Mass the End.</small> The principles governing the arrangement of material are Mass and Coherence. Both are equally essential, but in practice some questions regarding Mass are settled first. *The important positions in an essay are the beginning and the end; of these the more important is the end.* In this place, then, there shall be those sentences or those

paragraphs which deserve that distinction. Here frequently stands the theme, the conclusion of the whole matter, that for which the composition was constructed. So that if one wished to know the theme of an essay, he would be justified in looking at its conclusion to find it. In the essay on "Milton," it is evident from the last paragraph that Macaulay never intended it to be only a criticism of his poetry, though he has devoted many pages to this discussion. Here is just the last sentence: "Nor do we envy the man who can study either the life or the writings of the great poet and patriot without aspiring to emulate, not indeed the sublime works with which his genius has enriched our literature, but the zeal with which he labored for the public good, the fortitude with which he endured every private calamity, the lofty disdain with which he looked down on temptations and dangers, the deadly hatred which he bore to bigots and tyrants, and the faith which he so sternly kept with his country and his fame." Notice the last sentence of a delightful essay by George William Curtis; one could easily guess the contents and the title. "Fear of yourself, fear of your own rebuke, fear of betraying your consciousness of your duty and not doing it — that is the fear that Lovelace loved better than Lucasta; that is the fear which Francis, having done his duty, saved, and justly called it honor." Examples of the ending in which the theme of the essay stands in the place of greatest distinction are so plentiful that there needs no collector to establish the assertion.

In a single paragraph of exposition not exceeding two or three hundred words, it is a very safe rule for a beginner always to have the theme in the last sentence; or if he has stated the theme in the opening, to have a restatement of it in different form, fuller and more explicit usually, sometimes a shorter and more epigrammatic form, in the conclusion.

If the pupil should obey this little rule to have at the end something worthy of the position, a vast amount of time would be saved both to teacher and to pupil. It can be safely said that not more than one half the essays end when the thought ends. Instead of quitting when he has finished, the writer dribbles on, repeating in diluted fashion what he has said with some force before, and often introducing matters that are not within hailing distance of his theme. When one has said what he started out to say, it is time to stop. If he stops then, he will have something important in the place of distinction.

The position of second importance is the beginning.

The Beginning. If but a paragraph be written, the topic is usually announced at the opening. In short essays this is the most frequent beginning, and it may safely be used at all times. Exposition is explanation; the natural thing is to let the reader know at once what the writer is attempting to explain. Then the reader knows what the author is talking about and can relate every statement to the general proposition. To delay the topic compels the reader to hold in mind all that has been said up to the time the real theme is uncovered; this frequently results in inattention. In the little book by Mr. Palmer, the first paragraph opens with these two sentences: " English as a study has four aims: the mastery of our language as a science, as a history, as a joy, and as a tool. I am concerned with but one, the mastery of it as a tool." So, too, the essay of which the last sentence has been quoted begins: " These are very precious words of Lovelace: —

'I could not love thee, dear, so much,
Loved I not honor more.'

And Francis First's message to his mother after Pavia, ' All is lost but honor,' is in the same key."

Instead of announcing the theme at the very beginning, in essays of some length there is sometimes an account of the occasion which led to the composition. Macaulay has used this opening in the essay on " Milton." Second, the opening may be the clearing away of matters unrelated in reality, but which people have commonly associated with the topic. And third, the essay may open with definitions of the terms that will be used in the discussion. Of these three, only the first will be much used by young persons. It makes an easy approach to the subject, and avoids the unpleasant jar of an abrupt start. It is common with Macaulay, Lowell, and many essayists that write in an easy, almost conversational style.

There is one case in which the theme should not be announced at the opening. If the proposition were distasteful, if it were generally believed to be false, it would not be policy to announce it at the beginning. However reasonable men may be, it is still true that reason is subject to emotions and beliefs to a greater degree than is praiseworthy. If a man should open an address upon Abraham Lincoln by saying that he was a cringing coward, he would have difficulty to get an audience to hear anything he said after that, no matter how much truth he spoke. The author of such a statement would be so disliked that nothing would win for him favor. When an unwelcome theme is to be discussed, it must be approached carefully by successive steps which prepare the reader for the reception of a truth that before seemed false to him. In this case the theme will be stated at the end, but not at the beginning of the essay.

Get started as soon as you can, and stop when you

have finished; by so doing you will have important matters in those places which will emphasize them. Shun the allurements of high-sounding introductions and conclusions. Professor Marston used to tell his pupils to write the best introduction they could, to fashion their most gorgeous peroration, and to be sure to have the discussion clear, logical, and well expressed. Then he said that when he had cut off both ends, he generally had left a good essay. An essay should be done much as a business man does business. He does not want the gentleman who calls on him during business hours to bow and scatter compliments before he takes up the matter which brought him there; nor does he care to see him swaying on the doorknob after the business is finished. To the business at once, and leave off when you have done. Introductions, exordiums, perorations, and conclusions are worthless unless they be in reality a part of the discussion and necessary to the understanding of the whole.

Everything, however, cannot occupy the first and last places. How can other matters be emphasized? To refer to the parallel of the map, in order to make people see that the Mississippi River is longer than the Hudson, the designer made it longer on the map. That is exactly what is done in an essay. If one matter is of greater importance than another, it should take up a larger part of the essay. When Macaulay passes over Milton's sonnets with a paragraph, while he devotes sixteen paragraphs to "Paradise Lost," he indicates by the greater mass the greater value he ascribes to the epic. So again, a very good proof that he did not intend this essay to be a literary criticism primarily, another evidence beside the closing paragraph, is found in his division of the whole essay. To Milton's poetry he has given forty-one paragraphs, and to his character fifty-two paragraphs. The most common way of emphasizing important divisions of an essay is by increasing the length of treatment.

However, there are times when this cannot be done: a point may be so well known that it needs no amplification. In such a case there may be an emphasis of emotion; that is, the statement may be made with an intensity that counterbalances the weight of the larger treatment. It might be said that the one has great velocity and little mass, while the other has great mass and little velocity. By hurling forth the smaller mass at a higher velocity, the momentum may be as great as when the larger mass moves with little velocity. The dynamic force of burning words may give an emphasis to a paragraph out of all proportion to the length of treatment. In one paragraph Macaulay dashes aside all the defenses of Charles. He writes: —

Emphasis of Emotion.

"The advocates of Charles, like the advocates of other malefactors against whom overwhelming evidence is produced, generally decline all controversy about the facts, and content themselves with calling testimony to character. He had so many private virtues! And had James II. no private virtues? Was Oliver Cromwell, his bitterest enemies themselves being the judges, destitute of private virtues? And what, after all, are the virtues ascribed to Charles? A religious zeal, not more sincere than that of his son, and fully as weak and narrow-minded, and a few of the ordinary household decencies which half the tombstones in England claim for those who lie beneath them. A good father! A good husband! Ample apologies indeed for fifteen years of persecution, tyranny, and falsehood."

Moreover, phrases and sentences may be introduced to show that a writer considers some topics of equal importance to others, or even of greater importance, though they do not demand the same length of treatment. *Of equal importance, not less weighty, beyond question the most pertinent,* illustrate what is meant by phrases which indicate values. These and many of their class which the occasion will call forth are necessary to give certain topics the rank they hold in the writer's conception of the whole subject. In discussing the temper and character of the American people, Burke ascribes it to six powerful causes. The relative value of these is indicated in the last three by phrases. I quote only the opening sentences.

<blockquote>
"First, the people of the colonies are descendants of Englishmen." ... "They were further confirmed in this pleasing error by the form of their provincial legislative assemblies." ... "If anything were wanting to this necessary operation of the form of government, religion would have given it a complete effect." ... "There is a circumstance attending these [southern] colonies which makes the spirit of liberty *still more* high and haughty than in those to the northward." ... "Permit me, Sir, to add another circumstance which contributes *no mean part* towards the growth and effect of this untractable spirit." ... "The last cause of this disobedient spirit in the colonies is *hardly less powerful* than the rest."
</blockquote>

Emphasis is indicated, then, by position; by the length of treatment; by dynamic statement; and by phrases denoting values.

Coherence is the second principle which modifies the internal structure of a composition. That arrangement should be sought for that places in proximity one to another those ideas which are most closely related. More than in composition dealing with things, in those forms of discourse dealing with intangible, invisible ideas, — with thoughts, with speculations, — the greatest care is necessary to make one topic spring of necessity from a preceding topic. And this is not impossible when the material has been carefully selected. The principal divisions of the subject bear a necessary and logical relation to the whole theme, and the subordinate divisions have a similar relation to their main topic. In the essay on "Milton," Macaulay is seeking to commend his hero to the reader for two reasons: first, because his writings " are powerful, not only to delight, but to elevate and purify ; " second, because " the zeal with which he labored for the public good, the fortitude with which he endured every private calamity, the lofty disdain with which he looked down on temptations and dangers, the deadly hatred which he bore to bigots and tyrants, and the faith which he so sternly kept with his country and with his fame " made him a patriot worthy of emulation. We feel instinctively that this arrangement, poetry first and character next, and not the reverse, is the right order. To discuss character first and poetry last would have been ruinous to Macaulay's purpose. Notice next the development of a sub-topic in the same essay. Only one sentence from a paragraph is given. The defenders of Charles do not choose to discuss " the great points of the question," but " content themselves with exposing some of the crimes and follies to which public commotions necessarily give birth." " Be it so." " Many evils were produced by the Civil War." " It is the character of such revolutions that we always see the worst of them first." Yet " there is only one cure for the evils which newly acquired freedom produces, and that cure is freedom." " Therefore it is that we decidedly approve of the conduct of Milton and the other wise and good men who, in spite of much that was ridiculous and hateful in the conduct of their associates, stood firmly by the cause of public liberty." No other arrangement of these paragraphs seems possible. To shift the sequence would break the chain. Each paragraph grows naturally from the paragraph preceding. Closely related topics stand together. There is Coherence.

The logical connection between topics which have
<small>Transition Phrases.</small> been well arranged may be made more evident by the skillful use of words and phrases that indicate the relation of what has been said to what is to be said. These phrases are guideposts pointing the direction the next topic will take. They advise the reader where he is and whither he is going. Cardinal Newman, who had the ability to write not only so that he could be understood, but so that he could not be misunderstood, made frequent use of these guides. The question in one of his essays is "whether knowledge, that is, acquirement, is the real principle of enlargement, or whether that is not rather something beyond it." These fragments of sentences open a series of paragraphs. 1. "For instance, let a person . . . go for the first time where physical nature puts on her wilder and more awful forms," etc. 2. "Again, the view of the heavens which the telescope opens," etc. 3. "And so again, the sight of beasts of prey and other foreign animals," etc. 4. "Hence Physical Science generally," etc. 5. "Again, the study of history," etc. 6. "And in like manner, what is called seeing the world," etc. 7. "And then again, the first time the mind comes across the arguments and speculations of unbelievers," etc. 8. "On the other hand, Religion has its own enlargement," etc. 9. "Now from these instances, . . . it is plain, first, that the communication of knowledge certainly is either a condition or a means of that sense of enlargement, or enlightenment of which at this day

we hear so much in certain quarters: this cannot be denied; but next, it is equally plain, that such communication is not the whole of the process." How extremely valuable such phrases are may be realized from the fact that, though the matter is entirely unknown, any one can know the relation of the parts of this essay, whither it tends, and can almost supply Newman's thoughts.

To secure coherence between the main divisions of an essay, instead of words and phrases, there are employed sentences and paragraphs of summary and transition. *Summary and Transition.* Summaries gather up what has been said on the topic, much like a conclusion to a theme; transitions show the relation between the topic already discussed and the one next to be treated. Summaries at the conclusion of any division of the whole subject are like the seats on a mountain path which are conveniently arranged to give the climber a needed rest, and to spread out at his feet the features of the landscape through which he has made his way. Summaries put the reader in possession of the situation up to that point, and make him ready for the next stage of the advance. At the end of the summary there is frequently a transition, either a few sentences or sometimes a short paragraph. The sentence or paragraph of transition is much more frequent than the paragraph which summarizes.

The examples of these summaries and transitions are so frequent in Macaulay and Burke that one transition is sufficient to indicate their use. Macaulay writes: —

"There are several minor poems of Milton on which we would willingly make a few remarks. . . . Our limits, however, prevent us from discussing the point at length. We hasten on to that extraordinary production which the general suffrage of critics has placed in the highest class of human compositions."

To conclude, exposition embraces definition and explanation. Definition is usually too concise to be clear, and needs an added explanation. In any piece of exposition there must be unity, and this principle will dispense with everything that is not essential to the theme; there must be judicious massing, that those parts of the essay deserving emphasis may receive it; and there must be a coherence between the parts, large and small, so close and intimate that the progress from one topic to another shall be steady and without hindrance. Unity, Mass, and Coherence should be the main considerations in composition the aim of which is to explain a term or a proposition.

SUGGESTIVE QUESTIONS AND EXERCISES.

QUESTIONS.

MACAULAY'S ESSAY ON MILTON.

(Riverside Literature Series, No. 103.)

What makes up the introduction of this essay? Does he use the same method in the Essay on Addison? Take a volume of his essays and see how many begin in similar fashion. At what paragraph of this Essay on Milton does the introduction end? Would it be as well to omit it? Give reasons for your opinion.

Make an analysis of his argument of the proposition, "No poet has ever triumphed over greater difficulties than Milton."

Does Macaulay give a definition of poetry on page 13, or is it an exposition of the term?

What figure of speech do you find in the last sentence of the paragraph on page 43?

When Macaulay begins to discuss "the public conduct of Milton," what method of introduction does he adopt? What value is there in it?

Do the trifles mentioned at the end of the paragraph on page 55 make an anticlimax?

What arrangement of sentences in the paragraph does he use most, individual or serial?

Does he close his paragraphs with a repetition of the topic more frequently than with a single detail emphasizing the topic?

Is his last sentence, in case it is a repetition of the topic, longer or shorter than the topic sentence?

Does Macaulay frequently use epigrams? antitheses?

Find all transition paragraphs.

Find ten full sentence transitions outside of the transition paragraphs.

Where, in such paragraphs, is the topic sentence?

In this essay find examples of the five methods of expounding a proposition.

Which method does Macaulay use oftenest?

Is his treatment of the subject concrete?

What advantage is there in such treatment?

OF KINGS' TREASURIES.

(Riverside Literature Series, No. 142.)

Do you think the title good?

Is Ruskin wise in disclosing his subject at once?

In section 3 what purpose does the first paragraph fulfill? What method of exposition is adopted in the last paragraph? What method in section 4?

For what purpose is the first paragraph of section 5 introduced? Is the last paragraph of this section a digression?

Do you think the last sentence of section 9 upon the topic announced in the first sentence? Where does Ruskin begin to treat the second topic? Should there be two paragraphs?

Find the genus and differentia in the definition of "a good book of the hour."

What is the use of the analogy in section 13?

What figure do you find in section 14?

Do you think a large part of section 30 a digression?

What do you think of the structure of sentences 4 and 8 in section 32? Could you improve it by a change of punctuation?

What is the effect of the supposed case at the end of section 33? Is it a fair deduction? Is it at the right place in the paragraph, and why?

Where would you divide the paragraph in section 37?

Is the example in section 36 a fair one, and does it prove the case?

What is a very common method with Ruskin of connecting paragraphs?

Could you break up the sixth sentence of section 31 so that it would be better?

If his audience had been hostile to him would he have been fortunate in some of his assertions? Make an analysis of the whole essay. Does he seem to you to have digressed from his topic? At what point? Should it be two essays?

What led Ruskin into this long criticism of English character?

Could you include all the main topics that Ruskin has included, and by a change in proportion keep the essay on the subject?

WEBSTER'S BUNKER HILL ORATION.

(Riverside Literature Series, No. 56.)

Number the paragraphs in this oration.

Why is paragraph 3 introduced?

What method of development is used in paragraph 7? In paragraph 8?

In how many paragraphs is the last sentence short?

In how many is the last sentence a repetition of the topic?

What purpose is served in paragraphs 8, 9, and 10?

In paragraph 12 note the use of contrast.

What kind of development in paragraph 27?

Analyze the oration from paragraph 28?

Does he place the topic sentence near the beginning of the paragraphs?

Does he frequently use transition sentences?

Do you think the outline of this as distinct as that of Macaulay's Essay on Milton? Should it be?

What figure of speech in the word "axe" in paragraph 32, and "bayonet" in paragraph 36?

What figure at the end of paragraph 40?

Does he use figures as frequently as Macaulay?

EXERCISES.

This year, taking up the study of exposition, offers especially good opportunities for exercises in paragraph and sentence construction. During the first eight or ten weeks the pupils will write isolated paragraphs. The unity and arrangement of these should be carefully criticised. Also the exercises should be arranged so that the pupils will employ all forms of paragraphs. Before he begins to write a paragraph, the pupil should know what he is to include in it, and in what order; otherwise the paragraph will fail in unity and effective massing. Paragraphs are made by forethought, not by inspiration.

Following the writing of isolated paragraphs is the composition of the long essay. The first thing is a study of outlines. This will take up six or eight weeks. To secure the view of the whole in different arrangements, use the cards.

When the class has gained some grasp of outlines, the writing of essays should be begun. At the option of the pupils, they may write some of the essays already outlined, or study new themes. Two or three paragraphs are all that can be well done for a lesson. Good, not much, should be the ideal. In this way a single essay may occupy a class from three to six weeks.

It should be remembered that these exercises are written consciously for practice. They are exercises — no more. Their purpose is to give skill and judgment in composition. It is because they are exercises that they may be somewhat stereotyped and artificial in form, just as exercises in music may be artificially constructed to meet the difficulties the young musician will have to confront.

During the writing of these essays special attention should be given to sentence construction. The inclusion of just the ideas needed in the sentence and no more; the massing that makes prominent the thought that deserves prominence; and the nice adjustment of one sentence to the next: these objects should be striven for during this semester.

1, 2. Write definitions of such common terms as jingoism, civil service, gold standard, the submerged tenth, sweat shop, internal revenue, cyclonic area, foreign policy, imperialism, free silver, mugwump, political pull, Monroe doctrine, etc. Five or six terms which are not found in a dictionary will make a hard exercise; and two or three lessons in definitions will set the pupils in the direction of accurate and adequate statements.

For isolated paragraphs write upon the following subjects: —

3. Novel reading gives one a knowledge of the world not to be gained in any other way. Particulars.

4. Novel reading unfits people for the actualities of life. Specific instances.

5. Among the numerous uses of biography three stand forth preeminent, — it furnishes the material of history, it lets us into the secrets of the good and great, and it sets before us attainable ideals of noble humanity. Repetition.

6. It is beyond any possibility of successful contradiction that the examination system encourages cheating. Proofs.

7. Electric cars and automobiles are driving horses out of the cities. Instances.

8. Every great development in the culture of a nation has followed a great war. Proofs.

9. From the following general subjects have the pupils state definite themes. Write isolated paragraphs on a few of them.

Political Parties.
War.
Books.
Machines.
Inventions.
Great Men.
Planets.
Civil Service.
Coeducation.
Roads.
Tramps.
Boycotts.

10. Place another similar list on the board and have the pupils vote on what three they prefer. Use these in making outlines. Then select more.

Supposing they had settled upon this theme: The tramp

is the logical result of our economic system; have it outlined. The result might be as follows: —
- A. What is a tramp?
  1. Who become tramps?
  2. Their number.
  3. Where are they?
- B. Why is he a tramp?
  1. Inventions have increased the power of production more rapidly than the demand for products has grown.
     - a. On the farm.
     - b. Transportation.
     - c. Factories.
     - d. Piecework.
  2. Women now do much work formerly done by men.
     - a. As clerks.
     - b. As typewriters, stenographers, and bookkeepers.
     - c. In the professions.
  3. The result of these causes is that many men willing to work are out of employment.
- C. What must be done?

11. Fill out the following outline.
    Subject: The Thermometer.
    - A. Its Invention.
    - B. Its Construction.
    - C. Its Value and Uses.

12. Outline six more themes.

13. Beginning the writing of long essays, write essays in sections. Using "Tramps" for an illustration, as it is outlined it contains about twelve paragraphs. All of section "A" may be included in one paragraph. "B, 1" may be a paragraph of repetition; "a," "b," "c," "d," may each make a paragraph of particulars. By stating "B, 2" in the following way, it may be a paragraph of "what not:" It was once considered unladylike for women to engage in any occupation outside of the home. Men said that they could not retain, etc.— Go on with the things woman could not do, closing with a statement of what she does do.

"B, 2, a." On account of their fidelity, honesty, and courtesy, women succeed as clerks. Repetition.
    b. The quickness of their intelligence and the accuracy of their work have made women more desirable for routine work in an office than men. Comparison and Contrast.
    c. There are certain feminine qualities which especially fit women for the practice of teaching and medicine. Details.

"B, 3." By Combination of Forms.

"C." By Details.

It would be a pleasure to go on with this list of exercises, but it is unnecessary and it is unwise. These indicate the objects to be sought for in the exercises. They are not a specific course, though they might suit a certain environment. Each teacher knows her own pupils, — their attainments and their interests. The subjects should be chosen to suit their special cases. Only make them interesting; put them into such form that there is something to get hold of; and adapt them so that all the topics to be studied will be illustrated in the work. The pupils should be able to write any form of paragraph, to arrange it so that any idea is made prominent, and to make easy transitions. Arrange the exercises to accomplish definite results.

During the third year, attention should be given to words and to the refinements of elegant composition. These the pupils will best learn by careful watch of the literature. The teacher should be quick to feel the strength and beauty of any passage and able to point out the means adopted to obtain the delightful effect. Clearness first is the thing to be desired; if to this can be added force and a degree of elegance during the last two years, the work of the instructor has been well done.

CHAPTER VI

ARGUMENT

ARGUMENT has been defined as that form of discourse the purpose of which is to convince the reader of the truth or falsity of a proposition. It is closely allied with exposition. To convince a person, it is first necessary that the proposition be explained to him. This is all that is necessary in many cases. Did men decide all matters without prejudice, and were they willing to accept the truth at any cost, even to discard the beliefs that have been to them the source of greatest happiness, the simple explanation would be sufficient. However, as men are not all-wise, and as they are not always " reasonable," they are found to hold different opinions regarding the same subject; and one person often wishes to convince another of the error of his beliefs. Men continually use the words *because* and *therefore;* indeed, a great deal of writing has in it an element of argument.

From the fact that argument and exposition are so nearly alike, it follows that they will be governed by much the same principles. As argument, in addition to explaining, seeks to convince, it is necessary, in addition to knowing how to explain, to know what is considered convincing, — what are proofs; and secondly, what is the best order in which to arrange proofs.

Arguments have been classified as inductive and deductive.[1] Induction includes arguments that proceed

[1] A text-book on Logic, such as Jevons's, should be used to illustrate the kinds of argument more fully.

from individual cases to establish a general truth. Deduction comprises arguments that proceed from a general truth to establish the proposition in specific instances, or groups of instances. *Induction and Deduction.*

If one should say "Socrates is mortal because he is a man," or "Socrates will die because all men are mortal," or "Socrates is a man, therefore he will die," by any of these he has expressed a truth which all men accept. In any of these expressions are bound up two propositions, called premises, from which a third proposition, called a conclusion, is derived. If expanded, the three propositions assume this form: All men are mortal. Socrates is a man. Therefore Socrates is mortal. This is termed a syllogism. A syllogism consists of a major premise, a predication about all the members of a general class of objects; a minor premise, a predication that includes an individual or a group of individuals in the general class named by the major premise; and a conclusion, the proposition which is derived from the relation existing between the other two propositions. The propositions above would be classified as follows:— *Syllogism. Premises.*

Major premise: All men are mortal, a predication about *all* men.
Minor premise: Socrates is a man, including an individual in the general class.
Conclusion: Socrates is mortal.

In every syllogism there are three terms,— major, minor, and middle. The middle term is found in both the premises, but not in the conclusion. It is the link connecting the major and minor terms. The major term is usually the predicate of the major premise and the predicate of the conclusion. The minor term is the subject of the minor pre- *Terms.*

mise and the subject of the conclusion. "Men" is the middle term, "are mortal" the major term, and "Socrates," the minor term.

It is rarely the case in literature that the syllogism is fully stated: generally one of the premises is omitted. Such a form of statement is termed an enthymeme. "Socrates will die because all men are mortal" is an enthymeme. The minor premise has been omitted. "Socrates is mortal because he is a man" is also an enthymeme, because the major premise which states that "all men are mortal" has been omitted.

<small>Enthymeme.</small>

The conclusions arrived at by means of syllogisms are irresistible, provided the form be correct and the premises be true. It is impossible here to discuss the forms of syllogisms; they are too many. It will be of value, however, to call attention to a few of the commonest errors in syllogisms.

The first error arises from a misunderstanding of terms. It is often said that George Eliot is a poet; there are some who disagree. Certain it is that she wrote in verse form; and it is true that she has embodied noble thoughts in verse; but it is quite as true that she lacks "the bird-note." If this were reduced to a syllogism, it would not be a discussion of whether George Eliot be a poet, but rather a discussion of what is a poet. Stated, it reads: All persons who embody noble thoughts in verse form are poets. George Eliot is a person who has embodied noble thoughts in verse form. Therefore George Eliot is a poet. If the major premise of this syllogism be granted, the conclusion is unquestionable. The terms should be defined at the beginning; then this error, springing from a misunderstanding of terms, perhaps the most common, would be avoided.

<small>Definition of Terms.</small>

The second error arises from the fact that the middle term is not "distributed;" that is, the major premise makes no statement about all the members of a class. The premises in the following are true, but the conclusion is nonsense.

Undistributed Middle.

A horse is an animal.
Man is an animal.
Therefore, man is a horse.

The middle term, in this case "animal," must be "distributed;" some statement must be made of *all* animals. The following would be true: All animals have life; therefore man has life. The major premise predicates life of all animals.

A third error in a syllogism is in the premises themselves. If either premise be false, the conclusion is not necessarily true. A parent might say to his son, "You are doing wrong, and you will pay the penalty for it soon." Generally he would be right. However, if this were put into a syllogism, it would read as follows: All persons who do wrong pay the penalty soon. You are such a person. Therefore, etc. Admitting the son is breaking the law, the fact is that the major premise is not always true, and the conclusion holds the weakness of the weak premise. Again, supposing everybody accepted the general truth, "All unrepentant sinners will be punished." The minister might then say to a young man, "You will certainly be punished, because all unrepentant sinners will be punished." The young man might deny the suppressed minor premise, which is, "You are an unrepentant sinner." Both premises must be true if they prove anything. The conclusion contains the weakness of either premise. In both of these examples note that the mistake is in the premise which does not appear. In an enthymeme, great care

False Premises.

should be taken with the suppressed premise. Be sure it is true when you use this form of argument, and be sure to look for it and state it in full when examining another's argument. It is a common way of hiding a weak point to cover it in the suppressed premise of an enthymeme.

Induction, which proceeds directly opposite to the method of deduction, is the method by which all our ultimate knowledge has been obtained. By observing individual instances man has gathered a great store of general truths. There was a time when the first man would not have been justified in saying, "The sun will rise in the east to-morrow." The general law had not been established. To-day it is practically certain that the sun will rise in the east to-morrow morning, because it has done so for thousands of years; the large number of instances establishes the general truth. Yet there may come a day when it will rise in the south, or not rise at all. Until every case has been tried and found to conform to the law, theoretically man cannot be absolutely certain of any general truth. There may come an exception to the general rule that all men must die. So far, however, there is no experience to justify any man in hoping to escape death. "As sure as death" means in practice absolutely sure, though this is not what is called a perfect induction; that is, an induction in which every possible case has been included. "All the other States are smaller than Texas" is a perfect induction, but it forms no basis for argument. All the cases must be known for a perfect induction; there is no unknown to argue to. This, then, is only a short statement of many individual truths, and has but little of value. Induction that is imperfect is more valuable; for with many cases the probability becomes so strong that it is a practical certainty. It is the method of science.

More valuable for literature is another division of arguments into arguments from cause, arguments from sign, and arguments from example.

Arguments from cause include those propositions which, if they were granted, would account for the fact or proposition maintained. The decisive test is to suppose the proposition to be true; then, if it will account for the condition, it is an argument from cause. A child holds its finger in a flame; therefore its finger is burned. If the first proposition be supposed to be true, it will account for a burned finger. It is an argument from cause, and it is conclusive. Again, if a man severs his carotid artery, he will die. If the first proposition be supposed to be true, it will account for the man's subsequent death. Now, supposing a man takes strychnine, he will die. This is not quite so sure. If a stomach-pump were used or an antidote given, he might not die. The cause has been hindered in its action, or another cause has intervened to counterbalance the first. If, then, a cause be adequate to produce the effect, and if it act unhindered or unmodified, the effect will certainly follow the active cause. An argument that uses as a premise such a cause may predicate its effect as a conclusion with absolute certainty. Such an argument is conclusive.

The argument from cause is used more frequently to establish a probability than to prove a fact or proposition. However strong the proofs of a statement may be, men hesitate to accept either the statement or the proofs if the proposition is not plausible, or, as people say, if "they do not understand it," or if "it is not reasonable." If a murder be done and circumstances all point to your friend, you do not believe your friend to be the criminal until some fact is pro-

[margin: Arguments from cause.]

duced sufficient to cause your friend to commit the crime, — until some motive is established. If it be shown that the friend hated the murdered man and would be benefited by his death, a motive is established, — the proposition is made plausible. A man could "understand how he came to do it." The hatred and the benefit being granted, they would account for his deed. It is an argument from cause, used not as a proof, but to establish a probability. It makes the proposition ready for proof.

The second class of arguments, arguments from sign, is most often used for proof. If two facts or conditions always occur together, the presence of one is a sign of the presence of the other. Cause and effect are so related that if either be observed, it is an indication of the other. No cause acts without a consequent effect; an effect is a sure sign of a preceding cause. Supposing one should say, "Because the flowers are dead, there was a frost," or "If ice has formed on the river, it must have been cold," in both instances the argument would be an argument from sign. Both also proceed from the effect to the cause. Only a low temperature forms ice on the river; the argument from effect to cause is conclusive. In the first case, the argument is not conclusive, because flowers may die from other causes. In a case like this, it is necessary to find all possible causes, and then by testing each in succession to determine which could not have acted and leave the one that is the only actual cause. A man is found dead; death has resulted from natural causes, from murder, or from suicide. Each possible cause would be tested; and by elimination of the other possible causes the one right cause would be left. This method of elimination is frequently employed in arguments from effect to cause.

When this method is used the alternatives should be few, else it gives rise to confusion and to lack of attention caused by the tediousness of the discussion. And an enumeration of all possible causes must be made; for if one be omitted it may be the one that is in fact the right one.

The relation between cause and effect is so intimate that the occurrence of one may be regarded as a sure sign of the presence of the other. If an effect is produced by only one cause, the presence of the effect is a certain indication of the cause. If several causes produce the same effect, some other methods must be used to determine the cause operating in this special case.

In reasoning from effect to cause, one must be sure that he is dealing with a cause. As effect Sequence follows cause, there is danger that anything and Cause. that follows another may be considered as caused by it. Because a man died just after eating, it would not be quite reasonable to connect eating and death as cause and effect. The fact is that death is surer to follow starvation. The glow at evening is generally followed by fair weather the next day; but the fair weather is not an effect of a clear sunset. Common sense must be used to determine whether the relation is one of cause and effect; something more than a simple sequence is necessary.

Another argument from sign associates conditions that frequently occur together, though one is not the cause of the other. "James is near, because there is his blind father," means that James always accompanies his father; where the father is, the son is too. If one had noticed that potatoes planted at the full of the moon grew well, and potatoes planted at other times did not thrive, he might say as a result of years of observation that a certain crop would be a failure because it was not planted at the right time. This argument might have weight with ignorant people, but intelligent persons do not consider it a sure sign. All signs belong to this class of arguments; they are of value or worthless as they come true more or less frequently. Every time there is an exception the argument is weakened; another case of its working strengthens it. Where there is no sure relation like cause and effect, the strength of the argument depends on the frequency of the recurrence of the associated conditions.

A third argument from sign associates two effects of the same cause. A lad on waking exclaims, "The window is covered with frost; I can go skating to-day." The frost on the window is not the cause of the ice on the river. Rather, both phenomena are results of the same cause. This kind of argument is not necessarily conclusive; yet with others it always strengthens a case.

Testimony is usually called an argument from sign. The assertion by some one that a thing occurred is not sure proof; it is only a sign that it occurred. People have said that they have seen witches, ghosts, and sea serpents, and unquestionably believed it; men generally do not accept their testimony. In a criminal case, it would be difficult to accept the testimony of both sides. Though testimony seems a strong argument, it is or it is not, according to the conditions under which it is given. One would care little for the testimony of an ignorant man in a matter that called for wisdom; he would hesitate to accept the testimony of a man who claimed he saw, but upon cross-examination could not report what he saw; and he would not think it fair to be condemned upon the testimony of his enemies. Books have been written upon evidence, but three principles are all that are needed in ordinary arguments. First, the person giving testimony must be capable of observation; second, he must be able to report accurately what he has observed; third, he must have a desire to tell the exact truth.

The third large division comprises arguments from example. That is, if a truth be asserted of an individual, it can therefore be predicated of the class to which the individual belongs. For instance, if the first time a person saw a giraffe, he observed that it was eating grass, he would be justified in saying that giraffes are herbivorous. All gold is yellow, heavy, and not corroded by acid, though no one has tested it all. However, every giraffe does not have one ear brown and the other gray because the first one seen happened to be so marked; neither is all gold in the shape of ten-dollar gold pieces. Only common sense will serve to pick out essential qualities; but if essential and invariable qualities be selected, the argument from the example of an individual to all members of its class is very powerful.

Analogies resemble examples. In exposition they are used for illustration; in argument they are employed as proofs. Though two things belong to different classes of objects, they may have some qualities that are similar, and so an argument may be made from one to another. "Natural Law in the Spiritual World" is a book written to show how the physical laws hold true in the region of spirit. It is not because an enemy sowed tares in a neighbor's field that there are wicked men in the world; nor is it because a lover of jewels will sell everything that he has to buy the pearl of greatest price that men devote everything they have to the kingdom of heaven. Analogies prove nothing. They clear up relations and often help the reader to appreciate other arguments. They are valuable when the likeness is broad and easily traced. They should never be used alone.

These, then, are the principal forms of argument: deduction and induction; arguments from cause, from sign, and from example. Upon these men depend when they wish to convince of truth or error.

In argument the material is selected with reference to its value as proof. Every particle of matter must be carefully tested. While a piece of material that could be omitted without loss to the explanation may sometimes find a place in exposition, such a thing must not occur in argument. As soon as a reader discovers that the writer is off the track, either he loses respect for the author's words, or he suspects him of trying to hide the weakness of his position in a cloud of worthless and irrelevant matters. Every bit of material should advance the argument one step; it should fill its niche in the well-planned structure; it should contribute its part to the strength of the whole.

When the material has been selected, it must be arranged. An argument is a demonstration. Each of its parts is the natural result of what has preceded, and, up to the last step, each part is the basis for the next step. As in geometry a demonstration that omits one step in its development, or, which comes to the same thing, puts the point out of its logical order, is worthless as a demonstration, so in argument not one essential step can be omitted, nor can it be misplaced. The plan in an argument may be more evident than in exposition. We are a little offended if the framework shows too plainly in exposition; but there is no offense in a well-articulated skeleton in an argument. It is quite the rule that the general plan and the main divisions of the argument are announced at the very beginning. Any device that will make the relation of the parts clearer should be used. Over and over again the writer should arrange the cards with the topics until he is certain that no other order is so good. The writing is a mere trifle compared with the outline, called in argument the brief.

Though the brief is so essential, it is unfortunately a thing about which but few suggestions can be given. The circumstances under which arguments are written — especially whether written to defend a position or to attack it — are so various that rules cannot be given. Still a few general principles may be of value.

Proofs should be arranged in a climax. This does not mean that the weakest argument should come first, and the next stronger should follow, and so on until the last and strongest is reached. **Climax.** It is necessary to begin with something that will catch the attention; and in argument it is frequently a proof strong enough to convince the reader that the writer knows what he is contending for, and that he can strike a hard blow. Then again, it is evident that in all arguments there are main points in the discussion that must be established by points of minor importance. The main points should be arranged in a logical climax, and the sub-topics which go to support one of the main divisions should have their climax. At the end of the whole should be the strongest and the most comprehensive argument. It should be a general advance of the whole line of argument, including all the propositions that have previously been called into action, sweeping everything before it.

To gain this climax what kind of arguments should precede? Of inductive and deductive, the inductive proofs generally go first. The advance from particular instances to general truths is the best suited to catch the attention, for men think with individual examples, and general truths make little appeal to them. Moreover, if one is addressing people of opposing views, — and in most cases he is, else why is he arguing? — it is unwise to begin with bald statements of unwelcome truths. They will be rejected without consideration. They can with advantage be delayed until they are reached in the regular development, and the reader has been prepared for their reception. General truths and their application by deductive arguments usually stand late in the brief.

Inductive precedes Deductive.

Of arguments from cause, sign, or example, it is ordinarily wise to place arguments from cause first. A person does not listen to any explanation of an unknown truth until he knows that the explanation is plausible; that the cause assigned is adequate to produce the result. After one knows that the cause is sufficient and may have brought about the result, he is in a position to learn that it is the very cause that produced the effect. Arguments from cause are very rarely conclusive proofs of fact. They only establish a probability. And it would be unwise to prove that a thing might be a possibility after one had attempted to prove that it is a fact. It would be a long step backward, a retreat. Therefore arguments from cause, unless absolutely conclusive proof of fact, should not come last; but by other arguments, — by testimony, by example, by analogy, — the possibility, which has been reached by the argument from cause, may be established as a fact.

Cause precedes Sign.

Of the two, sign and example, example generally follows sign. In arguments about human affairs, examples seldom prove anything; for under similar conditions one person may not act like another. Though this be true, the argument from example is one of the most effective — it is not at all conclusive — in that class of cases where oratory is combined with argument to convince and persuade. This is because men learn most readily from examples. To reason about matters of conduct on abstract principles of morality convinces but few; to point to a Lincoln or a Franklin has persuaded thousands. Examples are of most use in enforcing and illustrating and strengthening a point already established, and they generally follow arguments from sign.

Example follows sign.

One other class of arguments finds a place in debate: namely, indirect arguments. It is often as much an advantage to a debater to dispose of objections as it is to establish his own case. This is because a question usually has two alternatives. If one can refute the arguments in favor of the opponent's position, he has by that very process established his own. If the points of the refutation are of minor importance and are related to any division of his own direct argument, the refutation of such points should be taken up in connection with the related parts of the direct argument. If, however, it is an argument of some weight and should be considered separate and apart from the direct argument, it is generally wisest to proceed to its demolition at the end of the direct argument and before the conclusion of the whole. For then the whole weight of the direct argument will be thrown into the refutation and will render every word so much the more destructive. Again, if the opposing argument be very strong and have taken complete possession of the audience, it must be attacked and disposed of at the very beginning. Otherwise it is impossible for the direct argument to make any advance.

Refutation.

From these suggestions one derives the general principle that each case must be considered by itself. There will be cases of conflict among the rules, and there must be a careful weighing of methods. Common sense and patient labor are the most valuable assistants in arranging a powerful argument.

It hardly needs to be said that the suggestions made in the chapter on Exposition regarding Mass and Coherence should be observed here. In argument as in exposition, topics are emphasized by position, and by proportion in the scale of treatment. Here as there, matters that are closely related in thought should be connected in the discourse, and matters that are not related in thought should not be associated in the essay.

It will be an advantage now to look through "Conciliation with the Colonies" and note its general plan of structure. Only the main divisions of this powerful oration can be given, as to make a full brief would deprive this piece of literature of half its value for study.

Analysis of Burke's Oration. Mr. Burke begins by saying that it is "an awful subject or there is none this side of the grave." He states that he has studied the question for years, and while Parliament has pursued a vacillating policy and one aggravating to the colonies, he has a fixed policy and one sure to restore "the former unsuspecting confidence in the Mother Country." His policy is simple peace. This by way of introduction. He then divides the argument into two large divisions and proceeds.

I. OUGHT YOU TO CONCEDE?

   A. What are "the true nature and the peculiar circumstances of the object which we have before us?"

      1. America has a rapidly growing population.

II. It has a rapidly increasing commercial value, shown by
1. Its demand for our goods.
2. The value of its agricultural products.
3. The value of the products of its fisheries.
III. There is in the people a "fierce spirit of liberty." This is the result of
1. Their descent from Englishmen.
2. Their popular form of government.
3. Religion in the North.
4. The haughty spirit of the South.
5. Their education.
6. Their remoteness from the governing body.

B. "You have before you the object." "What . . . shall we do with it?" "There are but three ways of proceeding relative to this stubborn spirit in the colonies."
I. To change it by removing the causes. This is impracticable.
II. To prosecute it as criminal. This is inexpedient.
III. *To comply with it as necessary.* This is the answer to the first question.

II. OF WHAT NATURE OUGHT THE CONCESSION TO BE?
A. A concession that grants to any colony the satisfaction of the grievances it complains of brings about conciliation and peace. This general proposition is established by the following examples. It has done so in
1. Ireland,
2. Wales,
3. Durham, and
4. Chester.
B. The grievances complained of in America are unjust taxation and no representation.
C. Therefore these resolutions rehearsing facts and calculated to satisfy their grievances will bring about conciliation and peace.

    I. They are unrepresented.
    II. They are taxed.
    III. No method has been devised for procuring a representation in Parliament for the said Colonies.
    IV. Each colony has within itself a body with powers to raise, levy, and assess taxes.
    V. These assemblies have at sundry times granted large subsidies and aids to his Majesty's service.
    VI. Experience teaches that it is expedient to follow their method rather than force payment.
D. As a result of the adoption of these resolutions, "everything which has been made to enforce a contrary system must, I take it for granted, fall along with it. On that ground, I have drawn the following resolutions."
    I. It is proper to repeal certain legislation regarding taxes, imports, and administration of justice.
    II. To secure a fair and unbiased judiciary.
    III. To provide better for the Courts of Admiralty.
E. He next considers objections.
Conclusion.

Notice first the introduction. It goes straight to the question. To tell a large opposition that it has vacillated on a great question is not calculated to win a kind hearing; yet this point, necessary to Burke's argument, is so delicately handled that no one could be seriously offended, nor could any one charge him with weakness. The introduction serves its purpose; it gains the attention of the audience and it exactly states the proposition.

He then divides the whole argument into two parts. The framework is visible, and with intent. These great divisions he takes up separately. First, that there may be a perfect understanding of the question, he explains "the true nature and the peculiar circumstances of the object which we have before us." This illustrates the use of exposition in argument. The descent and education did not prove that the Americans had a fiery spirit; that was acknowledged and needed no proof. It simply sets forth the facts, — facts which he afterward uses as powerful instruments of conviction. As long as a man can use exposition, he can carry his readers with him; it is when he begins to argue, to force matters, that he raises opposition. So this use of exposition was fortunate. America was an English colony. Her strength and riches were England's strength and wealth. It would be pleasing to all Englishmen to hear the recital of America's prosperity. Up to the time he asks, "What, in the name of God, shall we do with it," the oration is not essentially argument; it does nothing more than place "before you the object."

In the section marked "I. B," Burke begins the real argument by the method of elimination. He asserts that there are only three ways of dealing with this fierce spirit of liberty. Then he conclusively proves the first impracticable and the second inexpedient. There is left but the one course, concession. This method of proof is absolutely conclusive if every possible contingency is stated and provided for. Notice that in this section "B" everything that was mentioned in the first section "A" is used, and the whole is one solid mass moving forward irresistibly to the conclusion of the first and the most important part of this argument.

The second main division is devoted to the conclusion of the first. If you must concede, — the conclusion of the first half, — what will be the nature of your concession? A concession, to be a concession, must grant what the colonists wish, not what the ministry thinks would be good for them. Then by the history of England's dealings with Ireland, Wales, Chester, and Durham, he proves that such a concession has been followed by peace. This makes the major premise of his syllogism, stated in " II. A." The minor premise is a statement of the grievances of the colonies. The conclusion is in the resolutions for the redress of th grievances of the colonies. The second part is th one great syllogism, the premises of which are established by ample proof, the conclusion of which cannot well be disputed.

"And here I should close," says the orator; the direct argument is finished. There are some objections which demand dignified consideration. At this point, however, it is easy to refute any objections, for behind each word there is now the crushing weight of the whole argument.

The conclusion recites the advantages of Burke's plan over all others, and reasserts its value, now proven at every point. It is a powerful summary, and a skillful plea for the adoption of a policy of conciliation with the colonies of America.

Every kind of argument is used in this oration. One would look long for a treasury better supplied with illustrations. The great conclusions are reached by the certain methods of elimination and deduction. In establishing the minor points Burke has used arguments from sign, cause, example, and induction. He calls in testimony; he quotes authority; he illustrates. Not any device of sound argument that a man honest in his search for truth may use has been omitted. It is worthy of patient study.

In conclusion, the student of argument should learn well the value of different kinds of argument; he should exercise the most careful scrutiny in selecting his material, without any hesitation rejecting irrelevant matter; he should state the proposition so that it cannot be misunderstood; he must consider his readers, guiding his course wisely with regard for all the conditions under which he produces his argument; he should remember that the law in argument is climax, and that coherence should be sought with infinite pains. Above all, the man who takes up a debate must be fair and honest; only so will he win favor from his readers, and gain what is worth more than victory, — the distinction of being a servant of truth.

SUGGESTIVE QUESTIONS.

QUESTIONS.

MACAULAY'S ESSAY ON MILTON.

(Riverside Literature Series, No. 103.)

Put into a syllogism, Macaulay's opponents said, "An educated man living in an enlightened age has better facilities for writing poetry than an uneducated man at the dawn of civilization. Macaulay was an educated man, living in an enlightened age; therefore Macaulay had better facilities," etc.

Which premise does Macaulay attack? Does he demolish it?

What value is there in an analogy between experimental sciences and imitative arts? Between poetry and a magic-lantern? Is either an argument that is convincing? Are both effective in the essay?

What do you think of Macaulay's estimate of Wordsworth? Granting that this estimate is true, what kind of a proof is it of the proposition that "his very talents will be a hindrance to him"?

Is it a uniform phenomenon that as civilization advances, poetry declines? Name some instances that prove it.

Name some instances that disprove it. What method of proof have you used in both?

Is an uncivilized state of society the cause of good poetry, or only an attendant circumstance?

What method of proof is adopted on pages 34 and 35?

Granting that you cannot conceive "a good man and an unnatural father," does that prove anything about the first sentence at the bottom of page 55?

Does the example of the prisoner on page 60 prove anything?

Burke's Speech on Conciliation with the Colonies.

(Riverside Literature Series, No. 100.)

What argument does Burke use to prove that hedging in the population is not practicable?

When he says that they will occupy territory because they have done so, is that an inductive or deductive argument, or is it an argument from sign?

If it is deductive, what is the suppressed premise?

Are the arguments from 48 to 64 more in the nature of direct or indirect proofs?

What value is there in an indirect argument?

"Americans speak the English language, therefore they are English." Is the argument good? Where is the fault? Look for the suppressed premise.

Is paragraph 55 direct or indirect argument?

Does he prove that criminal procedure against the colonies would fail, by sign or by deduction?

Do the four precedents which he cites of Ireland, Wales, Durham, and Chester prove that his plan will work in America?

Upon what general principle do all arguments from example depend?

Is paragraph 79 in itself exposition or argument?

What method is adopted in paragraph 88 to prove that the principle of concession is applicable to America?

How does he prove that Americans were grieved by taxes?

How does he establish the competence of the colony assemblies?

How could the arguments have made "the conclusion irresistible"? (Paragraph 112.)

What principle of argument is stated in paragraph 114?

In paragraph 127 is the one example cited enough to prove the rule?

Find an example of argument from sign. Is it a relation of cause and effect? Is it conclusive?

In paragraph 129 what does Burke mention as arguments of value?

What kind of arguments in paragraphs 128 to 136? What is the conclusion?

Whenever Burke states a general truth it forms a part of what? Supply the other premise in five cases, and derive a conclusion.

Does he ever use an argument from cause to establish a probability? To establish a fact?

Does he use deduction more frequently than sign?

Does he seek for a climax in the arrangement of the parts of his brief?

CHAPTER VII

PARAGRAPHS

So far we have been dealing with whole compositions; we now take up the study of paragraphs, sentences, and words. A paragraph in many respects resembles a whole composition. It may be narrative, descriptive, expositive, or argumentative. It must have a beginning, a middle, and an end. It is constructed with regard to Unity, Mass, and Coherence. And as a whole composition treats a single theme, so a paragraph treats one division of a theme. It has been defined as a composition in miniature. A paragraph is a sentence or a group of sentences serving a single purpose in the development of a theme. The purpose may be simply to announce the theme-subject, to make a conclusion, to indicate a transition; but in the great majority of cases its purpose is to treat a single topic. So true is this that many authors, with good reason, define a paragraph as a group of sentences treating a single topic. *[Definition.]*

Nobody would have trouble in telling where on a page a paragraph began and where it ended. The indention at the beginning, and usually the incomplete line at the end, mark its visible limits. Unfortunately there is no specified length after which the writer is to make a break in the lines and begin a new paragraph. The length of a paragraph depends on something deeper than appearances; as the topic requires a lengthy or but a short treatment, as *[Long and Short Paragrap]* the paragraph may be a long summary or a short transition, the length of a paragraph varies. Yet there is one circumstance which should counsel an author to keep his paragraphs within certain bounds: he should always have regard for his readers. Readers shirk heavy labor. If a book or an article looks hard, it is passed by; if it looks easy, it is read. If the paragraphs be long and the page solid, the composition looks difficult; if the paragraphs be short and the page broken, the piece looks easy. This fact should advise a writer to make the page attractive by using short paragraphs; provided, and the provision is important, he can so make real paragraphs, divisions of composition that fully treat one topic. These divisions may in reality be but one sentence, and they may just as unquestionably be two pages of hard reading.

Successive paragraphs, each more than a page of ordinary print in length, repel as too hard; and a series of paragraphs of less than a quarter of a page impresses a reader as scrappy, and the work seems to lack the authority of complete treatment. An author will serve his readers and himself best by so subdividing his subject that the paragraphs are within these limits.

The following paragraph is much too long and can with no difficulty be subdivided. The paragraphs in the next group are too short, and they are incomplete.

"Keating rode up now, and the transaction became more complicated. It ended in the purchase of the horse by Bryce for a hundred and twenty, to be paid on the delivery of Wildfire, safe and sound, at the Batherley stables. It did occur to Dunsey that it might be wise for him to give up the day's hunting, proceed at once to Batherley, and, having waited for Bryce's return, hire a horse to carry him home with the money in his pocket. But the inclination for a run, encouraged by confidence in his luck, and by a draught of brandy from his pocket-pistol at the conclusion of the bargain, was not easy to overcome, especially with a horse under him that would take the fences to the admiration of the field. Dunstan, however, took one fence too many, and got his horse pierced with a hedge-stake. His own ill-favored person, which was quite unmarketable, escaped without injury; but poor Wildfire, unconscious of his price, turned on his flank, and painfully panted his last. It happened that Dunstan, a short time before, having had to get down to arrange his stirrup, had muttered a good many curses at this interruption, which had thrown him in the rear of the hunt near the moment of glory, and under this exasperation had taken the fences more blindly. He would soon have been up with the hounds again, when the fatal accident happened; and hence he was between eager riders in advance, not troubling themselves about what happened behind them, and far-off stragglers, who were as likely as not to pass quite aloof from the line of road in which Wildfire had fallen. Dunstan, whose nature it was to care more for immediate annoyances than for remote consequences, no sooner recovered his legs, and saw that it was all over with Wildfire, than he felt a satisfaction at the absence of witnesses to a position which no swaggering could make enviable. Reinforcing himself, after his shake, with a little brandy and much swearing, he walked as fast as he could to a coppice on his right hand, through which it occurred to him that he could make his way to Batherley without danger of encountering any member of the hunt. His first intention was to hire a horse there and ride home forthwith, for to walk many miles without a gun in his hand, and along an ordinary road, was as much out of the question to him as to other spirited young men of his kind. He did not much mind about taking the bad news to Godfrey, for he had to offer him at the same time the resource of Marner's money; and if Godfrey kicked, as he always did, at the notion of making a fresh debt, from which he himself got the smallest share of advantage, why, he would n't kick long: Dunstan felt sure he could worry Godfrey into anything. The idea of Marner's money kept growing in vividness, now the want of it had become immediate; the prospect of having to make his appearance with the muddy boots of a pedestrian at Batherley, and to encounter the grinning queries of stablemen, stood unpleasantly in the way of his impatience to be back at Raveloe and carry out his felicitous plan; and a casual visitation of his waistcoat-pocket, as he was ruminating, awakened his memory to the fact that the two or three small coins his fore-finger encountered there were of too pale a color to cover that small debt, without payment of which the stable-keeper had declared he would never do any more business with Dunsey Cass. After all, according to the direction in which the run had brought him, he was not so very much farther from home than he was from Batherley; but Dunsey, not being remarkable for clearness of head, was only led to this conclusion by the gradual perception that there were other reasons for choosing the unprecedented course of walking home. It was now nearly four o'clock, and a mist was gathering: the sooner he got into the road the better. He remembered having crossed the road and seen the finger-post only a little while before Wildfire broke down; so, buttoning his coat, twisting the lash of his hunting-whip compactly round the handle, and rapping the tops of his boots with a self-possessed air, as if to assure himself that he was not at all taken by surprise, he set off with the sense that he was undertaking a remarkable feat of bodily exertion, which somehow, and at some time, he should be able to dress up and magnify to the admiration of a select circle at the Rainbow. When a young gentleman like Dunsey is reduced to so exceptional a mode of locomotion as walking, a whip in his hand is a desirable corrective to a too bewildering dreamy sense of unwontedness in his position; and Dunstan, as he went along through the gathering mist, was always rapping his whip somewhere. It was Godfrey's whip, which he had chosen to take without leave because it had a gold handle; of course no one could see, when Dunstan held it, that the name *Godfrey Cass* was cut in deep letters on that gold handle — they could only see that it was a very handsome whip. Dunsey was not without fear that he might meet some acquaintance in whose eyes he would cut a pitiable figure, for mist is no screen when people get close to each other; but when he at last found himself in the well-known Raveloe lanes without having met a soul, he silently remarked that that was part of his usual good luck. But now the mist, helped by the evening darkness, was more of a screen than he desired, for it hid the ruts into which his feet were liable to slip — hid everything, so that he had to guide his steps by dragging his whip along the low bushes in advance of the hedgerow. He must soon, he thought, be getting near the opening at the Stone-pits: he should find it out by the break in the hedgerow. He found it out, however, by another circumstance which he had not expected — namely, by certain gleams of light, which he presently guessed to proceed from Silas Marner's cottage. That cottage and the money hidden within it had been in his mind continually during his walk, and he had been imagining ways of cajoling and tempting the weaver to part with the immediate possession of his money for the sake of receiving interest. Dunstan felt as if there must be a little frightening added to the cajolery, for his own arithmetical convictions were not clear enough to afford him any forcible demonstration as to the advantages of interest; and as for security, he regarded it vaguely as a means of cheating a man by making him believe that he would be paid. Altogether, the operation on the miser's mind was a task that Godfrey would be sure to hand over to his more daring and cunning brother: Dunstan had made up his mind to that; and by the time he saw the light gleaming through the chinks of Marner's shutters, the idea of a dialogue with the weaver had become so familiar to him, that it occurred to him as quite a natural thing to make the acquaintance forthwith. There might be several conveniences attending this course: the weaver had possibly got a lantern, and Dunstan was tired of feeling his way. He was still nearly three quarters of a mile from home, and the lane was becoming unpleasantly slippery, for the mist was passing into rain. He turned up the bank, not without some fear lest he might miss the right way, since he was not certain whether the light were in front or on the side of the cottage. But he felt the ground before him cautiously with his whip-handle, and at last arrived safely at the door. He knocked loudly, rather enjoying the idea that the old fellow would be frightened at the sudden noise. He heard no movement in reply: all was silence in the cottage. Was the weaver gone to bed, then? If so, why had he left a light? That was a strange forgetfulness in a miser. Dunstan knocked still more loudly, and, without pausing for a reply, pushed his fingers through the latch-hole, intending to shake the door and pull the latch-string up and down, not doubting that the door was fastened. But, to his surprise, at this double motion the door opened, and he found himself in front of a bright fire, which lit up every corner of the cottage — the bed, the loom, the three chairs, and the table — and showed him that Marner was not there."

"The country, all white, lit up by the fire, shone like a cloth of silver tinted with red.

"A bell, far off, began to toll.

"The old 'Sauvage' remained standing before her ruined dwelling, armed with her gun, her son's gun, for fear lest one of those men might escape.

"When she saw that it was ended, she threw her weapon into the brasier. A loud report rang back.

"People were coming, the peasants, the Prussians.

"They found the woman seated on the trunk of a tree, calm and satisfied.

"A German officer, who spoke French like a son of France, demanded of her: —

"'Where are your soldiers?'

"She extended her thin arm towards the red heap of fire which was gradually going out, and she answered with a strong voice: —

"'There!'

"They crowded round her. The Prussian asked: —

"'How did it take fire?'

"She said: —

"'It was I who set it on fire.'"

Paragraphs are developments of a definite topic; and this topic is generally announced at the beginning of the paragraph. In isolated paragraphs, paragraphs that are indeed compositions in miniature, the topic-sentence is the first sentence. The reader is then advised of the subject of the discussion; and as sentence after sentence passes him, he can relate it to the topic, and the thought is a cumulative whole. If the subject be not announced, the individual sentences must be held in mind until the reader catches the drift of the discussion, or the author at last presents the topic. _{Topic Sentence.}

Below are four paragraphs, one from each form of discourse, all having the topic-sentence at the beginning.

"*But success or defeat was a minor matter to them, who had only thought for the safety of those they loved.* Amelia, at the news of the victory, became still more agitated even than before. She was for going that moment to the army. She besought her brother with tears to conduct her thither. Her doubts and terrors reached their paroxysm; and the poor girl, who for many hours had been plunged into stupor, raved and ran hither and thither in hysteric insanity, — a piteous sight. No man writhing in pain in the hard-fought field fifteen miles off, where lay, after their struggles, so many of the brave — no man suffered more keenly than this poor harmless victim of the war. Jos could not bear the sight of her pain. He left his sister in the charge of her stouter female companion and descended once more to the threshold of the hotel, where everybody still lingered, and talked, and waited for more news." (Thackeray.)

"*Yet the fact remains that the honey-bee is essentially a wild creature, and never has been and cannot be thoroughly domesticated.* Its proper home is the woods, and thither every new swarm counts on going; and thither many do go in spite of the care and watchfulness of the bee-keeper. If the woods in any given locality are deficient in trees with suitable cavities, the bees resort to all kinds of makeshifts; they go into chimneys, into barns and outhouses, under stones, into rocks, and so forth. Several chimneys in my locality with disused flues are taken possession of by colonies of bees nearly every season. One day, while bee-hunting, I developed a line that went toward a farmhouse where I had reason to believe no bees were kept. I followed it up and questioned the farmer about his bees. He said he kept no bees, but that a swarm had taken possession of his chimney, and another had gone under the clapboards in the gable end of his house. He had taken a large lot of honey out of both places the year before. Another farmer told me that one day his family had seen a number of bees examining a knot-hole in the side of his house; the next day as they were sitting down to dinner their attention was attracted by a loud humming noise, when they discovered a swarm of bees settling upon the side of the house and pouring into the knothole. In subsequent years other swarms came to the same place." (Burroughs.)

"*It is important, therefore, to hold fast to this: that poetry is at bottom a criticism of life;* that the greatness of a poet lies in his powerful and beautiful application of ideas to life, — to the question: How to live. Morals are often treated in a narrow and false fashion; they are bound up with systems of thought and belief which have had their day; they have fallen into the hands of pedants and professional dealers; they grow tiresome to some of us. We find attraction, at times, even in a poetry of revolt against them; in a poetry which might take for its motto Omar Khayyam's words: 'Let us make up in the tavern for the time which we have wasted in the mosque.' Or we find attractions in a poetry indifferent to them ; in a poetry where the contents may be what they will, but where the form is studied and exquisite. We delude ourselves in either case ; and the best cure for our delusion is to let our minds rest upon that great and inexhaustible word *life*, until we learn to enter into its meaning. A poetry of revolt against moral ideas is a poetry of revolt against *life* ; a poetry of indifference toward moral ideas is a poetry of indifference toward *life*." (Arnold.)

" *The advantages arising from a system of copyright are obvious.* It is desirable that we should have a supply of good books : we cannot have such a supply unless men of letters are liberally remunerated ; and the least objectionable way of remunerating them is by means of copyright. You cannot depend for literary instruction and amusement on the leisure of men occupied in the pursuits of active life. Such men may occasionally produce compositions of great merit. But you must not look to such men for works which require deep meditation and long research. Works of that kind you can expect only from persons who make literature the business of their lives. Of these persons few will be found among the rich and the noble. The rich and the noble are not impelled to intellectual exertion by necessity. They may be impelled to intellectual exertion by the desire of distinguishing themselves, or by the desire of benefiting the community. But it is generally within these walls that they seek to signalize themselves and to serve their fellow-creatures. Both their ambition and their public spirit, in a country like this, naturally take a political turn. It is then on men whose profession is literature, and whose private means are not ample, that you must rely for a supply of valuable books. Such men must be remunerated for their literary labor. And there are only two ways in which they can be remunerated. One of those ways is patronage ; the other is copyright." (Macaulay.)

Frequently the topic-sentence is delayed until after the connection between what was said in the preceding paragraph and what will be said has been made. To establish this relation requires sometimes but a word or a short phrase, and sometimes sentences. In these cases the topic-sentence follows the transition, and it may come as late as the middle of the paragraph.

"The crows we have always with us, but it is not every day or every season that one sees an eagle. *Hence I must preserve the memory of one I saw the last day I went bee-hunting.* As I was laboring up the side of a mountain at the head of a valley, the noble bird sprang from the top of a dry tree above me and came sailing directly over my head. I saw him bend his eye down upon me, and I could hear the low hum of his plumage, as if the web of every quill in his great wings vibrated in his strong, level flight. I watched him as long as my eye could hold him. When he was fairly clear of the mountain he began that sweeping spiral movement in which he climbs the sky. Up and up he went without once breaking his majestic poise till he appeared to sight some far-off alien geography, when he bent his course thitherward, and gradually vanished in the blue depths. The eagle is a bird of large ideas, he embraces long distances; the continent is his home. I never look upon one without emotion; I follow him with my eye as long as I can. I think of Canada, of the Great Lakes, of the Rocky Mountains, of the wild and sounding sea-coast. The waters are his, and the woods and the inaccessible cliffs. He pierces behind the veil of the storm, and his joy is height and depth and vast spaces." (Burroughs.)

"Now these insinuations and questions shall be answered in their proper places; here I will but say that I scorn and detest lying, and quibbling, and double-tongued practice, and slyness, and cunning, and smoothness, and cant, and pretence, quite as much as any Protestants hate them; and I pray to be kept from the snare of them. But all this is just now by the bye; *my present subject is my Accuser;* what I insist upon here is this unmanly attempt of his, in his concluding pages, to cut the ground from under my feet; — to poison by anticipation the public mind against me, John Henry Newman, and to infuse into the imaginations of my readers suspicion and mistrust of everything that I may say in reply to him. This I call poisoning the wells." (Newman.)

In exposition and argument, and sometimes in the other forms of discourse, the topic-sentence may be at the end of the paragraph. This is for emphasis in narration and description. In exposition and argument it is better to lead up to an unwelcome truth than to announce it at once.

"Thus the matter of life, so far as we know it (and we have no right to speculate on any other), breaks up, in consequence of that continual death which is the condition of its manifesting vitality, into carbonic acid, water, and nitrogenous compounds which certainly possess no properties but those of ordinary matter. And out of these same forms of ordinary matter, and from none which are simpler, the vegetable world builds up all the protoplasm which keeps the animal world a-going. *Plants are the accumulators of the power which animals distribute and disperse.*" (Huxley.)

Sometimes no topic-sentence appears in the paragraph. In such a case it is easily discovered; No Topic-or at times it is too fragile to be compressed Sentence. into any definite shape — a feeling, or a sentiment too delicate, too volatile for expression. A paragraph with no topic-sentence is most common in narration and description.

"The tide of color has ebbed from the upper sky. In the west the sea of sunken fire draws back; and the stars leap forth, and tremble, and retire before the advancing moon, who slips the silver train of cloud from her shoulders, and, with her foot upon the pine-tops, surveys heaven." (Meredith.)

The Plan. Whether the topic form a part of the paragraph or not, it should be distinctly before the writer, and he should write upon the topic. Nothing contributes so much to the success of paragraphs as a definite treatment of one single topic. The paragraph is the development, the growth of this topic, as the plant is the development of its seed. Moreover, the development is according to a definite plan. The different steps are not usually laid out, as was done in the outline of a theme. Genung, in the "Practical Elements of Rhetoric," presents what he calls a typical form for a paragraph. It shows that a paragraph which is fully developed is in reality a miniature theme. It is as follows: —

   The Subject proposed.
 I. Whatever is needed to explain the subject.
   Repetition.
   Obverse.
   Definition.
 II. Whatever is needed to establish the subject.
   Exemplification or detail.
   Illustration.
   Proof.
 III. Whatever is needed to apply the subject.
   Result or consequence.
   Enforcement.
   Summary or recapitulation.

This typical form of a paragraph embodies all that paragraphs may do, and it is the logical arrangement. However, it is rare, perhaps it never occurs, that a paragraph is found having all these elements developed. The purpose determines which part of a paragraph should receive the amplification. If it be narrative or descriptive, there is no definition or proof; but the development by details will predominate. In an argument, definition and proof will form the large part of the paragraphs. Again, the position in the theme determines what kind of a paragraph should be used. In exposition the first paragraphs would be devoted to stating the proposition, and would therefore be largely given up to definition and repetition; the body would be especially paragraphs of detail and illustration; while the closing paragraph would be taken up with results and a summary. As one of the elements of a paragraph has been especially developed, paragraphs have been named paragraphs of repetition,[1] of the obverse, of details, of instances or examples, and of comparisons. Such a division is somewhat mechanical; but for purposes of study and for conscious practice in construction it has value.

Kind of Paragraphs.

The paragraph of details is by far the most common. It is found in all kinds of discourse. It originates from the fact that persons generally give the general truth first and follow this statement with the details or particulars. Whether the storyteller begins by saying, "Now I'll tell you just how they happened to be there;" or the traveler writes, "From the Place de la Concorde one has about him magnificent views," or "There were many unfortunate circumstances about the Dreyfus affair;" in each case he will follow the general statement of the opening sentence with sentences going into particulars or details.

Details.

" *All was now bustle and hubbub in the late quiet school-*

[1] See Scott and Denney's *Composition-Rhetoric*.

room. The scholars were hurried through their lessons without stopping at trifles; those who were nimble skipped over half with impunity, and those who were tardy had a smart application now and then in the rear, to quicken their speed or help them over a tall word. Books were flung aside without being put away on the shelves, inkstands were overturned, benches thrown down, and the whole school was turned loose an hour before the usual time, bursting forth like a legion of young imps, yelping and racketing about the green in joy at their early emancipation." (Irving.)

" It was toward evening that Ichabod arrived at the castle of the Heer Van Tassel, *which he found thronged with the pride and flower of the adjacent country*. Old farmers, a spare leathern-faced race, in homespun coats and breeches, blue stocking, huge shoes, and magnificent pewter buckles. Their brisk, withered little dames, in close crimped caps, long-waisted short-gowns, homespun petticoats, with scissors and pincushions, and gay calico pockets hanging on the outside. Buxom lasses, almost as antiquated as their mothers, excepting where a straw hat, a fine ribbon, or perhaps a white frock gave symptoms of city innovation. The sons, in short square-skirted coats, with rows of stupendous brass buttons, and their hair generally queued in the fashion of the times, especially if they could procure an eelskin for the purpose, it being esteemed throughout the country as a potent nourisher and strengthener of the hair." (Irving.)

" The enemies of the Parliament, indeed, rarely choose to take issue in the great points of the question. They content themselves with exposing some of *the crimes and follies* to which public commotions necessarily give birth. They bewail the unmerited fate of Strafford. They execrate the lawless violence of the army. They laugh at the scriptural names of the preachers. Major-generals fleecing their districts; soldiers reveling on the spoils of a ruined peasantry; upstarts, enriched by the public plunder, taking possession of the hospitable firesides and hereditary trees of the old gentry; boys smashing the beautiful windows of cathedrals; Quakers riding naked through the market-place; Fifth-monarchy men shouting for King Jesus; agitators lecturing from the tops of tubs on the fate of Agog, — all these, they tell us, were the offspring of the great Rebellion." (Macaulay.)

In narration and in a short paragraph of description this paragraph of details is frequently without a topic-sentence. The circumstances that make up a transaction are grouped, but there is no need of writing, "I will now detail this." In the following, since the paragraph is plainly about the preparation for the fight, it is unnecessary to say so. Such a patent statement would hinder the movement of the story.

"Alan drew a dirk, which he held in his left hand in case they should run in under his sword. I, on my part, clambered up into the berth with an armful of pistols and something of a heavy heart, and set open the window where I was to watch. It was a small part of the deck that I could overlook, but enough for our purpose. The sea had gone down, and the wind was steady and kept the sails quiet; so that there was a great stillness on the ship, in which I made sure I heard the sound of muttering voices. A little after, and there came a clash of steel upon the deck, by which I knew they were dealing out the cutlasses, and one had been let fall; and after that silence again." (Stevenson.)

The paragraph of comparisons tells what a thing is like and what a thing is not like. It is much used in description and exposition. It is often the clearest way to describe an object or to explain a proposition. One thing may be likened to a number of things, drawing from each a quality that more definitely pictures it; or it may be compared with but one, and the likeness may be followed out to the limit of its value. In the same manner it is often of value

<small>Comparisons.</small>

to tell what a thing or a proposition does not resemble, to contrast it with one or more ideas, and by this means exclude what might otherwise be confusing. Note that after the negative comparison the paragraph closes with what it is like, or what it is.

From Macaulay's long comparison of the writings of Milton and Dante, one paragraph is enough to illustrate the use of contrast.

"Now let us *compare* with the exact details of Dante the dim intimations of Milton. We will cite a few examples. The English poet has never thought of taking the measure of Satan. He gives us merely a vague idea of vast bulk. In one passage the fiend lies stretched out, huge in length, floating many a rood, equal in size to the earth-born enemies of Jove, or to the sea-monster which the mariner mistakes for an island. When he addresses himself to battle against the guardian angels, he stands like Teneriffe or Atlas; his stature reaches the sky. Contrast with these descriptions the lines in which Dante has described the gigantic spectre of Nimrod: 'His face seemed to me as long and as broad as the ball of St. Peter's at Rome, and his other limbs were in proportion; so that the bank, which concealed him from the waist downwards, nevertheless showed so much of him that three tall Germans would in vain have attempted to reach to his hair.'"

The following indicates the use of similarity.

"It is the character of such revolutions that we always see the worst of them at first. Till men have been some time free, they know not how to use their freedom. The natives of wine countries are generally sober. In climates where wine is a rarity intemperance abounds. A newly liberated people may be *compared to* a northern army encamped on the Rhine or the Xeres. It is said that, when soldiers in such a situation first find themselves able to indulge without restraint in such a rare and expensive luxury, nothing is to be seen but intoxication. Soon, however, plenty teaches discretion, and, after wine has been for a few months their daily fare, they become more temperate than they had ever been in their own country. In the same manner, the final and permanent fruits of liberty are wisdom, moderation, and mercy. Its immediate effects are often atrocious crimes, conflicting errors, skepticism on points the most clear, dogmatism on points the most mysterious. It is just at this crisis that its enemies love to exhibit it. They pull down the scaffolding from the half-finished edifice; they point to the flying dust, the falling bricks, the comfortless rooms, the frightful irregularity of the whole appearance, and then ask in scorn where the promised splendor and comfort is to be found. If such miserable sophisms were to prevail, there would never be a good house or a good government in the world." (Macaulay.)

A third method of developing a paragraph from a topic-sentence is by repetition. Simply to repeat in other words would be useless redundancy; but so to repeat that with each repetition the thought broadens or deepens is valuable in proposing a subject or explaining it. No person has attained greater skill in repetition than Matthew Arnold, and much of his clearness comes from his repetition, often of the very same phrases. Repetition.

" Wordsworth has been in his grave for some thirty years, and certainly his lovers and admirers cannot flatter themselves that this great and steady light of glory as yet shines over him. He is not fully recognized at home; he is not recognized at all abroad. Yet I firmly believe that the poetical performance of Wordsworth is, after that of Shakespeare and Milton, of which all the world now recognizes the worth, undoubtedly the most considerable in our language from the Elizabethan age to the present time. Chaucer is anterior; and on other grounds, too, he cannot well be brought into the comparison. But taking the roll of our chief poetical names, besides Shakespeare and Milton, from the age of Elizabeth downwards, and going through it, — Spenser, Dryden, Pope, Gray, Goldsmith, Cowper, Burns, Coleridge, Scott, Campbell, Moore, Byron, Shelley, Keats (I mention those only who are dead), — I think it certain that Wordsworth's name deserves to stand, and will finally stand, above them all. Several of the poets named have gifts and excellencies which Wordsworth has not. But taking the performance of each as a whole, I say that Wordsworth seems to me to have left a body of poetical work superior in power, in interest, in the qualities which give enduring freshness, to that which any one of the others has left." (Arnold.)

"Perhaps no person can be a poet, or can even enjoy poetry, without a certain unsoundness of mind, if anything which gives so much pleasure ought to be called unsoundness. By poetry we mean not all writing in verse, nor even all good writing in verse. Our definition excludes many metrical compositions which, on other grounds, deserve the highest praise. By poetry, we mean the art of employing words in such a manner as to produce an illusion on the imagination, the art of doing by means of words what the painter does by means of colors. Thus the greatest of the poets has described it, in lines universally admired for the vigor and felicity of their diction, and still more valuable on account of the just notion which they convey of the art in which he excelled : —

'As imagination bodies forth
The forms of things unknown, the poet's pen
Turns them to shapes, and gives to airy nothing
A local habitation and a name.'

These are the fruits of the 'fine frenzy' which he ascribes to the poet, — a fine frenzy, doubtless, but still a frenzy. Truth, indeed, is essential to poetry, but it is the truth of madness. The reasonings are just, but the premises are false. After the first suppositions have been made, everything ought to be consistent; but those first suppositions require a degree of credulity which almost amounts to a partial and temporary derangement of the intellect. Hence, of all people, children are the most imaginative. They abandon themselves without reserve to every illusion. Every image which is strongly presented to their mental eye produces in them the effect of reality. No man, whatever his sensibility may be, is ever affected by Hamlet or Lear as a little girl is affected by the story of poor Red Riding Hood. She knows it is all false, that wolves cannot speak, that there are no wolves in England. Yet in spite of her knowledge she believes; she weeps; she trembles; she dares not go into a dark room lest she should feel the teeth of the monster at her throat. Such is the despotism of the imagination over uncultivated minds." (Macaulay.)

A fourth method of building up a paragraph from a topic-sentence consists in telling what it is not; that is, giving the obverse. This is very effective in argument, and is employed in exposition and description. The obverse usually follows a positive statement, and again is followed by the affirmative; that is, first what it is, then what it is not, and last, what it is again. In the following description by Ruskin, the method appears and reappears. Notice the "nots" and "buts," indicating the change from the negative to the positive statement. It would be a sacrilege to omit the last paragraph, though it does not illustrate this manner of development.

Obverse.

"For all other rivers there is a surface, and an underneath, and a vaguely displeasing idea of the bottom. But the Rhone flows like one lambent jewel; its surface is nowhere, its ethereal self is everywhere, the iridescent rush and translucent strength of it blue to the shore, and radiant to the depth.

"Fifteen feet thick, not of flowing, but flying water; not water, neither — melted glacier, rather, one should call it; the force of the ice is with it, and the wreathing of the clouds, the gladness of the sky, and the continuance of Time.

"Waves of clear sea are, indeed, lovely to watch, but they are always coming or gone, never in any taken shape to be seen for a second. But here was one mighty wave that was always itself, and every fluted swirl of it, constant as the wreathing of a shell. No wasting away of the fallen foam, no pause for gathering of power, no helpless ebb of discouraged recoil; but alike through bright day and lulling night, the never-pausing plunge, and never-fading flash, and never-hushing whisper, and, while the sun was up, the ever-answering glow of unearthly aquamarine, ultramarine, violet-blue, gentian-blue, peacock-blue, river-of-paradise blue, glass of a painted window melted in the sun, and the witch of the Alps flinging the spun tresses of it forever from her snow.

"The innocent way, too, in which the river used to stop to look into every little corner. Great torrents always seem angry, and great rivers are often too sullen; but there is no anger, no disdain in the Rhone. It seemed as if the mountain stream was in mere bliss at recovering itself again out of the lake-sleep, and raced because it rejoiced in racing, fain yet to return and stay. There were pieces of wave that danced all day, as if Perdita were looking on to learn; there were little streams that skipped like lambs and leaped like chamois; there were pools that shook the sunshine all through them, and were rippled in layers of overlaid ripples, like crystal sand; there were currents that twisted the light into golden braids, and inlaid the threads with turquoise enamel; there were strips of stream that had certainly above the lake been mill-stream, and were looking busily for mills to turn again; and there were shoots of stream that had once shot fearfully into the air, and now sprang up again, laughing, that they had only fallen a foot or two; — and in the midst of all the gay glittering and eddied lingering, the noble bearing by of the midmost depth, so mighty, yet so terrorless and harmless, with its swallows skimming in spite of petrels, and the dear old decrepit town as safe in the embracing sweep of it as if it were set in a brooch of sapphires."

This extract from Burke's speech is a good example of the same method.

"I put this consideration of the present and the growing numbers in the front of our deliberation, because, Sir, this consideration will make it evident to a blunter discernment than yours, that *no* partial, narrow, contracted, pinched, occasional system will be at all suitable to such an object. It will show you that it is *not* to be considered as one of those *minima* which are out of the eye and consideration of the law; *not* a paltry excrescence of the state; *not* a mean dependent, who may be neglected with little damage and provoked with little danger. It will prove that some degree of care and caution is required in the handling such an object; it will show that you ought not, in reason, to trifle with so large a mass of the interests and feelings of the human race. You could at no time do so without guilt; and be assured you will not be able to do it long with impunity."

A fifth method of expanding a topic is by means of illustrations and examples. It is used largely in establishing or enforcing a proposition. **Examples.**
The author selects one example, or perhaps more than one, to illustrate his proposition. Note the words that may introduce specific instances: *for example, for instance, to illustrate, a case in point*, and so forth.

In the first of the following quotations, Cardinal Newman is showing that simply to acquire is not true mental enlargement. The paragraph is made up of a series of instances. The second paragraph is by **Macaulay.**

"The *case is the same still more strikingly when* the persons in question are beyond dispute men of inferior powers and deficient education. Perhaps they have been much in foreign countries, and they receive, in a passive, otiose, unfruitful way, the various facts which are forced upon them there. Seafaring men, *for example*, range from one end of the earth to the other; but the multiplicity of external objects which they have encountered forms no symmetrical and consistent picture upon their imagination; they see the tapestry of human life, as it were, on the wrong side, and it tells no story. They sleep, and they rise up, and they find themselves, now in Europe, now in Asia; they see visions of great cities and wild regions; they are in the marts of commerce, or amid the islands of the South; they gaze on Pompey's Pillar, or on the Andes; and nothing which meets them carries them forward or backward, to any idea beyond itself. Nothing has a drift or relation; nothing has a history or a promise. Everything stands by itself and comes and goes in its turn, like the shifting scenes of a show, which leave the spectator where he was. Perhaps you are near such a man on a particular occasion, and expect him to be shocked or perplexed at something which occurs; but one thing is much the same to him as another; or, if he is perplexed, it is as not knowing what to say, whether it is right to admire, or to ridicule, or to disapprove, while conscious that some expression of opinion is expected from him; for in fact he has no standard of judgment at all, and no landmarks to guide him to a conclusion. Such is mere acquisition, and, I repeat, no one would dream of calling it philosophy."

"I will give *another instance*. One of the most instructive, interesting, and delightful books in our language is Boswell's 'Life of Johnson.' Now it is well known that Boswell's eldest son considered this book, considered the whole relation of Boswell to Johnson, as a blot in the escutcheon of the family. He thought, not perhaps altogether without reason, that his father had exhibited himself in a ludicrous and degrading light. And thus he became so sore and irritable that at last he could not bear to hear the 'Life of Johnson' mentioned. Suppose that the law had been what my honorable and learned friend wishes to make it. Suppose that the copyright of Boswell's 'Life of Johnson' had belonged, as it well might, during sixty years, to Boswell's eldest son. What would have been the consequence?

An unadulterated copy of the finest biographical work in the world would have been as scarce as the first edition of Camden's 'Britannia.'"

As was said at the beginning, a paragraph is seldom made exclusively of one form. One part of the typical paragraph is usually developed more than any other and gives to the paragraph its character and its name. By far the most common variety of paragraph is that which combines two or more of the other forms. It is not necessary to cite examples; they are everywhere. Though combination is the commonest method of development, it should be guarded. It is a poor paragraph that combines the forms indiscriminately. It should follow some plan; and the best plan is the one already given in the typical paragraph. *Combines Two or More Forms.*

All paragraphs, whatever be the special method of development, are governed by the three principles which have guided in the structure of whole compositions. Whether the purpose be to prove or to narrate, to enforce a conclusion or to illustrate, if a paragraph is to produce its greatest effect, it should have unity, it should be well massed, and it should be coherent.

It is not necessary now to define unity in a paragraph; the need is rather to notice the offenses against it that frequently occur. They are manifestly two: too much may be included, and not all may be included. The accompanying circumstance of the one, not necessarily the cause, however, is often a very long paragraph, and of the other a short paragraph.

Violations of the unity of a paragraph most frequently result from including more than belongs there. The theme has been selected; it is narrow and concise. When one begins to write, many *Unity.*

things crowd in pell-mell. Impressions, which come and go, we hardly know how or why, are the only products of most minds. Impressions, not shaped and logical thoughts, make up the mixed confusion frequently called a theme. The writer puts down enough of these impressions to make a paragraph, and then goes on to do it again, fancying that so he is really paragraphing. Even should he keep within the limits of his theme, he cannot in this way paragraph. As everything upon a subject does not belong in a theme, so everything in a theme may not be introduced indiscriminately into any paragraph.

The other danger lies in the short paragraph. It does not allow a writer room to say all he has to say upon the topic, so it runs over into the next paragraph. All of the thought-paragraph should appear in one division on the page. This error is not so common as the former. Examples of each are to be found on pages 152–157.

Need of Outline. The remedy for this confusion clearly is hard thinking; and a great assistance is the outline. Before a word is written, think through the theme; get clearly the purpose of each paragraph in the development of the whole. Then write just what the paragraph was intended to include, and no more. More will be suggested because the parts of a whole theme are all closely related, but that more belongs somewhere else. Make a sharp outline, and follow it.

Mass. A paragraph should be so arranged that the parts which arrest the eye will be important.[1] When a person glances down a page, his eye rests upon the beginning and the end of each paragraph. A reader going rapidly through an article to get what he wants of it does not read religiously every

---

[1] Barrett Wendell's *English Composition.*

word; he knows that he will be directed to the contents of each paragraph by the first and last sentences. If a writer considers his readers, if he desires to arrange his paragraph so that it will be most effective, he will have at these points such sentences as will accurately indicate its contents and the trend of the discussion; and he will form these sentences so well that they will deserve the attention which is given them by reason of their position in the paragraph.

What are the words that deserve the distinction of opening and closing a paragraph? As in the theme, so in a paragraph, the first thing is to announce the subject of discussion. When the subject is simply announced without giving any indication as to the drift of the discussion, the conclusion of the discussion is generally stated in the last sentence. Burke says, "The first thing we have to consider with regard to the nature of the object is the number of people in the colonies." He concludes the paragraph with, "Whilst we are discussing any given magnitude, they are grown to it. Whilst we spend our time in deliberating on the mode of governing two millions, we shall find we have millions more to manage. Your children do not grow faster from infancy to manhood than they spread from families to communities, and from villages to nations." In other cases the opening sentence states the conclusion at which the paragraph will arrive. Then the closing sentence may be a repetition of the opening or topic sentence; or it may be one of the points used to exemplify or establish the proposition which opens the paragraph. Again, in a short paragraph the topic need not be announced at the beginning; in this case it should be given in the concluding sentence. Or, should the topic be given in the opening sentence of a short paragraph,

<small>What begins and ends a Paragraph?</small>

it is unnecessary to repeat it at the end. In any case, whether the paragraph opens with a simple announcement of the topic to be discussed, or with the conclusion which the paragraph aims to explain, establish, or illustrate, or whether it closes with the conclusion of the whole matter, or with one of the main points in the development, the sentences at the beginning and the end of a paragraph should be strong sentences worthy of their distinguished position.

In the first paragraph below, there is a proposition in the first sentence and its repetition in the last. In the two following, though they close with no general statement, the specific assertions used to substantiate and illustrate the first sentences are strong and carry in themselves the truth of the topic-sentence.

"The eloquence of Mr. Adams resembled his general character, and formed, indeed, a part of it. It was bold, manly, and energetic; and such the crisis required. When public bodies are to be addressed on momentous occasions, when great interests are at stake, and strong passions excited, nothing is valuable in speech farther than as it is connected with high intellectual and moral endowments. Clearness, force, and earnestness are the qualities which produce conviction. True eloquence, indeed, does not consist in speech. It cannot be brought from far. Labor and learning may toil for it, but they will toil in vain. Words and phrases may be marshaled in every way, but they cannot compass it. It must exist in the man, in the subject, and in the occasion. Affected passion, intense expression, the pomp of declamation, all may aspire to it; they cannot reach it. It comes, if it come at all, like the outbreaking of a fountain from the earth, or the bursting forth of volcanic fires, with spontaneous, original, native force. The graces taught in the schools, the costly ornaments and studied contrivances of speech, shock and disgust men when their own lives and the fate of their wives, their children, and their country hang on the decision of the hour. Then words have lost their power, rhetoric is vain, and all elaborate oratory contemptible. Even genius itself then feels rebuked and subdued, as in the presence of higher qualities. Then patriotism is eloquent; then self-devotion is eloquent. The clear conception, outrunning the deductions of logic, the high purpose, the firm resolve, the dauntless spirit, speaking on the tongue, beaming from the eye, informing every feature, and urging the whole man onward, right onward to his object — this, this is eloquence: or rather it is something greater and higher than all eloquence; it is action, noble, sublime, godlike action." (Webster.)

"The prejudiced man travels, and then everything he sees in Catholic countries only serves to make him more thankful that his notions are so true; and the more he sees of Popery, the more abominable he feels it to be. If there is any sin, any evil in a foreign population, though it be found among Protestants also, still Popery is clearly the cause of it. If great cities are the schools of vice, it is owing to Popery. If Sunday is profaned, if there is a carnival, it is the fault of the Catholic Church. Then, there are no private houses, as in England; families live in staircases; see what it is to belong to a Popish country. Why do the Roman laborers wheel their barrows so slow in the Forum? why do the Lazzaroni of Naples lie so listlessly on the beach? why, but because they are under the *malaria* of a false religion. Rage, as is well known, is in the Roman like a falling sickness, almost as if his will had no part in it and he had no responsibility; see what it is to be a Papist. Bloodletting is as frequent and as much a matter of course in the South as hair-cutting in England; it is a trick borrowed from the convents, when they wish to tame down refractory spirits." (Newman.)

"Excuse me, Sir, if turning from such thoughts I resume this comparative view once more. You have seen it on a large scale; look at it on a small one. I will point out to your attention a particular instance of it in the single province of Pennsylvania. In the year 1704 that province called for £11,459 in value of your commodities, native and foreign. This was the whole. What did it demand in 1772? Why, nearly fifty times as much; for in that year the export to Pennsylvania was £507,909, nearly equal to the export to all the colonies together in the first period." (Burke.)

The following illustrates the weakness of closing with a specific instance when it does not rise to the level of the remainder of a paragraph. The last sentence would better be omitted.

"We often hear of the magical influence of poetry. The expression in general means nothing; but, applied to the writings of Milton, it is most appropriate. His poetry acts like an incantation. Its merit lies less in its obvious meaning than in its occult power. There would seem, at first sight, to be no more in his words than in other words. But they are words of enchantment. No sooner are they pronounced than the past is present and the distant near. New forms of beauty start at once into existence, and all the burial-places of memory give up their dead. Change the structure of the sentence, substitute one synonym for another, and the whole effect is destroyed. The spell loses its power; and he who should then hope to conjure with it would find himself as much mistaken as Cassim in the Arabian tale, when he stood crying, 'Open Wheat,' 'Open Barley,' to the door which obeyed no sound but 'Open Sesame.' In the miserable failure of Dryden in his attempt to translate into his own diction some parts of the 'Paradise Lost' is a remarkable instance of this." (Macaulay.)

By examination, one finds that the first sentence of a paragraph of exposition and of argument is usually a terse statement of the proposition; and that after the proposition has been established there follows a longer sentence gathering up all the points of the discussion into a full, rounded period which forms a suitable climax and conclusion of the

Length of un, and closing Sentences.

paragraph. Of Macaulay's "Milton" one is quite inside the truth when he says that of those paragraphs containing an opening topic-sentence and its restatement as a conclusion, the closing sentence is the longer in the ratio of two to one. In Burke's "Conciliation," the ratio rises as high as four to one. There are, however, exceptions to the rule. Paragraphs sometimes close with a shorter statement of the proposition, a sort of aphorism or epigram. As this kind of sentence is fascinating, some books have said that paragraphs should close so; that it is like cracking a whip, and gives a snap to the paragraph not gained in any other way. Even if readers enjoyed having paragraphs close in this cracking manner, it must be borne in mind that not all conclusions are capable of such a statement, and, what is worse, that the tendency to seek for epigrams leads to untruth and a degenerated form of witticism. Such forced sentences are only half truths, or they are a bit of cheap repartee. Such a close is effective, if the whole truth can be so expressed; but to seek for such sentences is dangerous. The best rule is the one already stated; it applies to the long sentence and the short sentence alike. It is that a paragraph should close with words that deserve distinction.

The body of a paragraph should have the matter so proportioned that the more important points shall receive the longer treatment. In a paragraph of proof, details, or comparison, that point in the proof, that particular, that part of the comparison, which for the specific purpose has most significance, should have proportionately fuller treatment. It is the same principle already noticed in exposition. Indicate the relative importance of topics in a paragraph by the relative number of words used in their treatment.

For mass in a paragraph, then, keep in mind that

the last sentence should contain matter and form worthy of the position it occupies; that the position of next importance is at the beginning; and that the relative importance of the matters in the body of a paragraph is pretty correctly indicated by the relative length of treatment.

<small>Coherence and Clear-</small> Coherence, the third principle of structure, is the most important; and it is the most difficult to apply. For one can make a beginning and an end, he can select his materials so that there is unity, but to make all the parts stick together, to arrange the sentences so that one grows naturally from the preceding and leads into the next, requires nice adjustment of parts, and rewriting many times. How essential coherence in a paragraph is, simply to make the thought easy to grasp, may be seen by taking a paragraph to pieces and mixing up its sentences, and at the same time removing all words that bind its parts together. The following can hardly be understood at all, but in its original condition it is so clear that it cannot be misunderstood. If the sentences be arranged in the following order, the original paragraph will appear: 1, 5, 3, 9, 8, 6, 2, 4, 7, 10.

1. "The first question which obviously suggests itself is how these wonderful moral effects are to be wrought under the instrumentality of the physical sciences. 2. To know is one thing, to do is another; the two things are altogether distinct. 3. Does Sir Robert Peel mean to say, that whatever be the occult reasons for the result, so it is; you have but to drench the popular mind with physics, and moral and religious advancement follows on the whole, in spite of individual failures? 4. A man knows he should get up in the morning, — he lies abed; he knows he should not lose his temper, yet he cannot keep it. 5. Can the process be analyzed and drawn out, or does it act like a dose or a charm which comes

into general use empirically? 6. It is natural and becoming to seek for some clear idea of the meaning of so dark an oracle. 7. A laboring man knows he should not go to the ale-house, and his wife knows she should not filch when she goes out charing, but, nevertheless, in these cases, the consciousness of a duty is not all one with the performance of it. 8. Or rather, does he mean, that, from the nature of the case, he who is imbued with science and literature, unless adverse influences interfere, cannot but be a better man? 9. Yet when has the experiment been tried on so large a scale as to justify such anticipations? 10. There are, then, large families of instances, to say the least, in which men may become wiser, without becoming better; what, then, is the meaning of this great maxim in the mouth of its promulgators?"

Coherence, so necessary to the easy understanding of a paragraph, is gained in three ways: by the order in which the sentences are arranged; by the use of parallel constructions for parallel ideas; and by the use of connectives.

Material which has been selected with regard to the principle of unity is all informed with one idea. Yet though one thought runs through it all and unites it, the parts do not stand in an equally close relation to the conclusion, nor is each part equally related to every other part. Had they been, the last paragraph quoted would have been as well in one order as another. Rather the sentences seem to fall into groups of more closely related matters; or at times one sentence seems to follow as the direct consequence of the preceding sentence. With respect to the way in which the sentences contribute to the topic of the paragraph, whether the topic be announced first or last, sentences may be said to contribute directly to the proposition or indirectly. If

<small>Two Arrangements of Sentences graph.</small>

directly, the paragraph is a collection of sentences, each having a common purpose, each having a similar relation to the topic, arranged, as it were, side by side, and advancing as one body to the conclusion. This may be termed an individual arrangement of sentences, since as individuals they each contribute to the topic. The conclusion derives its force from the combined mass of all. If indirectly, the paragraph is a series of sentences, each growing out of the one preceding it, each receiving a push from the sentence before, and the last having the combined force of all. This may be styled a serial arrangement of sentences, since in such a case each contributes to the topic only as one in a chain. The former overcomes by its mass; the latter strikes by reason of its velocity. The one advances in rank; the other advances in single file.

An illustration of each will help to an understanding of this. In the following paragraph from Macaulay's essay on Milton, each of the details mentioned points directly to "those days" when the race became a "byword and a shaking of the head to the nations." Their aggregate mass enforces the topic of the paragraph. They are all one body equally informed with the common principle which is the topic. Notice that one sentence is not the source of the next, but that all the sentences stand in a similar relation to the conclusion. This arrangement is common in description. In the second paragraph, from Irving's "Legend of Sleepy Hollow," each detail contributes to the appearance of Ichabod, not through some other sentence, but directly.

"Then came those days, never to be recalled without a blush, the days of servitude without loyalty and sensuality without love; of dwarfish talents and gigantic vices; the paradise of cold hearts and narrow minds; the golden age of the coward, the bigot, and the slave. The king cringed to his rival that he might trample on his people; sank into a viceroy of France, and pocketed with complacent infamy her degrading insults and her more degrading gold. The caresses of harlots and the jests of buffoons regulated the policy of the state. The government had just ability enough to deceive, and just religion enough to persecute. The principles of liberty were the scoff of every grinning courtier, and the Anathema Maranatha of every fawning dean. In every high place, worship was paid to Charles and James, Belial and Moloch; and England propitiated those obscene and cruel idols with the blood of her best and bravest children. Crime succeeded to crime, and disgrace to disgrace, till the race, accursed of God and man, was a second time driven forth to wander on the face of the earth, and to be a byword and a shaking of the head to the nations."

"Ichabod was a suitable figure for such a steed. He rode with short stirrups, which brought his knees nearly up to the pommel of the saddle; his sharp elbows stuck out like grasshoppers'; he carried his whip perpendicularly in his hand, like a sceptre, and as his horse jogged on, the motion of his arms was not unlike the flapping of a pair of wings. A small wool hat rested on the top of his nose, for so his scanty strip of forehead might be called, and the skirts of his black coat fluttered out almost to the horse's tail. Such was the appearance of Ichabod and his steed as they shambled out of the gate of Hans Van Ripper, and it was altogether such an apparition as is seldom to be met with in broad daylight."

The following paragraph in the essay on Milton contains an example of the second method of arrangement. Each sentence is the result of the one before it. The sentences advance in single file. Notice that each sentence does not contribute directly to the conclusion, but that it acts through the succeeding sentence. The phrases from which a succeeding sentence springs are in small capitals; and the phrases which refer back are in italics.

"Most of the remarks which we have hitherto made on the public character of Milton apply to him only as one of A LARGE BODY. WE SHALL PROCEED to notice some of the peculiarities which distinguished him *from his contemporaries*. *And for that purpose* it is necessary to take a short survey of THE PARTIES into which the political world was at that time divided. We must premise that our observations are intended to apply only to THOSE WHO ADHERED, from a sincere preference, to one or to the other side. In days of public commotion, *every faction*, like an Oriental army, is attended by a crowd of camp-followers, a useless and heartless RABBLE, who prowl round its line of march in the hope of picking up something under its protection, but desert it in the day of battle, and often join to exterminate it after defeat. England, at the time of which we are treating, abounded with fickle and *selfish politicians*, who transferred their support to every government as it rose; who kissed the hand of the king in 1640, and spat in his face in 1649; who shouted with equal glee when Cromwell was inaugurated in Westminster Hall, and when he was dug up to be hanged at Tyburn; who dined on calves' heads or broiled rumps, and cut down oak branches or stuck them up, as circumstances altered, without the slightest shame or repugnance. *These* we leave out of account. We take our estimate of parties from *those who* really deserve to be called partisans."

(For other examples of the same arrangement see the next quotation, and also a paragraph quoted on page 222.)

Paragraphs are most frequently found to combine the two methods. In the following, notice that the second sentence grows out of the first, the third from the second, and so the serial arrangement is maintained until the eighth is reached. Sentences nine, ten, eleven, and twelve give body to sentence eight.

Then begins again the regular succession. Sentences sixteen to twenty are the outgrowth of the phrase "on his account."

"1. The Puritans were men whose minds had derived a peculiar character from the daily contemplation of superior beings and eternal interests. 2. Not content with acknowledging in general terms an overruling Providence, they habitually ascribed every event to the will of the Great Being, for whose power nothing was too vast, for whose inspection nothing was too minute. 3. To know Him, to serve Him, to enjoy Him, was with them the great end of existence. 4. They rejected with contempt the ceremonious homage which other sects substituted for the pure worship of the soul. 5. Instead of catching occasional glimpses of the Deity through an obscuring veil, they aspired to gaze full on the intolerable brightness, and to commune with Him face to face. 6. Hence originated their contempt for terrestrial distinctions. 7. The difference between the greatest and the meanest of mankind seemed to vanish when compared with the boundless interval which separated the whole race from Him on whom their own eyes were constantly fixed. 8. They recognized no title to superiority but His favor; and, confident of that favor, they despised all the accomplishments and all the dignities of the world. 9. If they were unacquainted with the works of philosophers and poets, they were deeply read in the oracles of God. 10. If their names were not found in the registers of heralds, they were recorded in the Book of Life. 11. If their steps were not accompanied by a splendid train of menials, legions of ministering angels had charge over them. 12. Their palaces were houses not made with hands; their diadems, crowns of glory which should never fade away. 13. On the rich and the eloquent, on nobles and priests, they looked down with contempt; for they esteemed themselves rich in a more precious treasure, and eloquent in a more sublime language, nobles by the right of an earlier creation, and priests by the imposition of a mightier hand. 14. The very meanest of them was a being to whose fate a mysterious and terrible importance belonged, on whose slightest action the spirits of light and darkne looked with anxious interest; who had been destined, befor heaven and earth were created, to enjoy a felicity which should continue when heaven and earth should have passed away. 15. Events which short-sighted politicians ascribed to earthly causes had been ordained on his account. 16. For his sake empires had risen, and flourished, and decayed. 17. For his sake the Almighty had proclaimed His will by the pen of the Evangelist and the harp of the prophet. 18. He had been wrested by no common deliverer from the grasp of no common foe. 19. He had been ransomed by the sweat of no vulgar agony, by the blood of no earthly sacrifice. 20. It was for him that the sun had been darkened, that the rocks had been rent, that the dead had risen, that all nature had shuddered at the sufferings of her expiring God."

This division has been made because by its aid an approach can be made toward rules for arrangement. In the paragraph quoted on page 183, the different sentences are equally related to the topic. Is there, then, no reason why one should be first rather than another? Notice the topics of the sentences and the order becomes a necessity. King, state policy, government, liberty, religion, — it is an ascending scale. On page 96 is a paragraph on the charmed names used by Milton. "One," "another," "a third," "a fourth," — for all one can see as to the relation of each to the topic, "a fourth" might as well have been "one" as fourth. But upon reading the paragraph it is evident that Macaulay thought the last more important than the first. So in the paragraph just quoted about the Puritans, when the arrangement of the first eight sentences changes in sentences nine through eleven, and again in sentences sixteen to twenty, the order is a climax. Moreover, those topics are associated which are more closely related in thought. King is more closely related to government than to religion, and religion is more intimately associated with the idea of liberty than with king. The order, then, is the natural order of association. From these examples we derive the first principle of arrangement. In a paragraph where several sentences contribute individually to the topic, they must be arranged in the order in which the thoughts are associated and follow each other; and, when possible, they should take the order of a climax.

In the paragraph made up of sentences in a series, each linked to the sentence before and after, the difficulty is in transmitting the force of one sentence to the next one undiminished. This is done by binding the sentences so closely together that one cannot slip on the other. In the paragraph about the Puritans, of the second sentence the "Great Being" goes back to "superior beings" of the first; and "Him" in the next springs from "Great Being." "To know Him, to serve Him, to enjoy Him," — what is it but the "pure worship" of the fourth? while "ceremonious homage" of the fourth is the "occasional glimpses of the Deity through an obscuring veil" of the fifth. One sentence grows out of some phrase of the preceding sentence; the sentences are firmly locked together by the repetition, a little modified, of the thought of a preceding phrase. There is no slipping. To get this result there must be no question of the thought-sequence in the sentences. Each sentence must be a consequence of a preceding sentence. And there must be attention to the choice and position of the words from which the following sentence is to spring. Such words cannot be indefinite, mushy words; they must be definite, firm words. Moreover, they must not be buried out of sight by a mass of unimportant matters; they must be so placed that they are unhindered, free to push forward the thought toward its ultimate conclusion. This often requires inversion in the sentence. That phrase which is the source of the next sentence must be thrown up into a prominent position; and it is usually pressed toward the end of the sentence, nearer to the sentence which is its consequence. In a paragraph quoted on page 222, where this same subject is taken up in connection with sentences, there is an excellent illustration of this. " Slow and obscure," " inadequate ideas," " small circle," and the numerous phrases which repeat the thought, though not the words, are firm words binding the sentences together indissolubly.

Use of Pronouns. Not all sentences permit such clear reference as this. Still it must be said that where the thought is logical and clear, the reference is never missed: the binding words are important words and they occupy prominent positions. There is, however, a whole group of words whose function is to make the references sure. They are pronouns. Pronouns refer back, and they point forward. Their careful use is the commonest method of making sure of references, and so of binding sentences together. The ones in common use are *this, that, the former, the latter;* the relatives *who, which,* and *that;* and the personal pronouns *he, she, it.* To these may be added some adverbs: *here, there, hence, whence, now, then, when,* and *while.* The binding force of these words is manifest in every paragraph of composition.

The following paragraph, from Burke's speech on "Conciliation with the Colonies," illustrates the use of pronouns as words referring back, and binding the whole into one inseparable unit.

" As to the wealth which the colonies have drawn from the

sea by their fisheries, you had all that matter fully opened at your bar. You surely thought *those* acquisitions of value, for *they* seemed even to excite your envy; and yet the spirit by which *that* enterprising employment has been exercised ought rather, in my opinion, to have raised your esteem and admiration. And pray, Sir, what in the world is equal to *it*? Pass by the other parts, and look at the manner in which the people of New England have of late carried on the whale fishery. Whilst we follow *them* among the tumbling mountains of ice, and behold *them* penetrating into the deepest frozen recesses of Hudson's Bay and Davis's Straits, whilst we are looking for *them* beneath the arctic circle, we hear that *they* have pierced into the opposite region of polar cold, that *they* are at the antipodes, and engaged under the frozen Serpent of the south. Falkland Island, which seemed too remote and romantic an object for the grasp of national ambition, is but a stage and resting-place in the progress of *their* victorious industry. Nor is the equinoctial heat more discouraging to *them* than the accumulated winter of both the poles. We know that whilst *some* of *them* draw the line and strike the harpoon on the coast of Africa, *others* run the longitude and pursue *their* gigantic game along the coast of Brazil. No sea but what is vexed by *their* fisheries; no climate that is not witness to *their* toils. Neither the perseverance of Holland, nor the activity of France, nor the dexterous and firm sagacity of English enterprise ever carried *this* most perilous mode of hardy industry to the extent to which *it* has been pushed by *this* recent people; a people who are still, as it were, but in the gristle, and not yet hardened into the bone of manhood. When I contemplate *these* things; when I know that the colonies in general owe little or nothing to any care of ours, and that they are not squeezed into this happy form by the constraints of watchful and suspicious government, but that, through a wise and salutary neglect, a generous nature has been suffered to take her own way to perfection; when I reflect upon *these* effects, when I see how profitable *they* have been to us, I feel all the pride of power sink, and all presumption in the wisdom of human contrivances melt and die away within me. My rigor relents. I pardon something to the spirit of liberty."

Of Conjunctions.
Another group of words which give coherence to a paragraph is conjunctions. They indicate the relations between sentences, and they point the direction of the new sentence. The common relations between sentences indicated by conjunctions are coördinative, subordinative, adversative, concessive, and illative. Each young writer has usually but one word, at the most two words, in his vocabulary to express each of these relations. He knows *and*, *but*, *if*, *although*, and *therefore*. Each person should learn from a grammar the whole list, for no class of words indicates clear thinking so unmistakably as conjunctions.

Two words of advice should be given regarding the use of conjunctions. If the thought all bends one way, if this direction is perfectly clear, there is no need of conjunctions. It is when the course of the discussion is tortuous, when the road is not direct, when the reader may lose the way without these guides, that conjunctions should be used. On the other hand, conjunctions are an annoyance when not needed. Just as guideposts along a road where there is no chance to leave the direct path are useless, and their recurrence is a cause of aggravation, so it is with unnecessary conjunctions. They attract attention to themselves, and so draw it from the thought. The first caution is, Do not use conjunctions unless needed.

In the following, the repetition of *and* is unnecessary and annoying.

"Six shillings a week does not keep body and soul together very unitedly. They want to get away from each other when there is only such a very slight bond as that between them; and one day, I suppose, the pain and the dull monotony of it all had stood before her eyes plainer than usual, and the mocking spectre had frightened her. She had made one last appeal to friends, but, against the chill wall of their respectability, the voice of the erring outcast fell unheeded; *and* then she had gone to see her child — had held it in her arms and kissed it, in a weary, dull sort of way, *and* without betraying any particular emotion of any kind, *and* had left it, after putting into its hand a penny box of chocolate she had bought it, *and* afterwards, with her last few shillings, had taken a ticket *and* come down to Goring.

"It seemed that the bitterest thoughts of her life must have centred about the wooded reaches and the bright green meadows around Goring; but women strangely hug the knife that stabs them, and, perhaps, amidst the gall, there may have mingled also sunny memories of sweetest hours, spent upon those shadowed deeps over which the great trees bend their branches down so low.

"She had wandered about the woods by the river's brink all day, *and* then, when evening fell *and* the gray twilight spread its dusky robe upon the waters, she stretched out her arms to the silent river that had known her sorrow and her joy. *And* the old river had taken her into its gentle arms, *and* had laid her weary head upon its bosom, *and* had hushed away the pain."

The other word is: When possible put the conjunction that connects two sentences into the body of the sentence, rather than at its beginning. In this way its binding power is increased. This principle should limit the use of *and* and *but* at the beginning of a sentence. Rarely is *and* needed in such a place. If the thought goes straight forward — and it must do so if *and* correctly expresses the relation — there is usually no gain in its use. At times when the reader might be led to expect some change of direction from some phrase in the preceding sentence, then it would be wise to set him right by the use of *and*. Moreover, there are times when coordinate thoughts are so important, and the expression of the coordination is so important, that a sentence beginning with *and* is the only adequate means of expressing it. However, be very sure that there is need for every *and* that you use. The same caution may be given about *but*. *But* indicates an abrupt turn in the thought. Is such a contrast in the thought? If so, is there no other word to express the thought? Some persons go so far as to say that these words should never begin a sentence. This is too pedantic and not true. When coordinative and adversative relations are to be expressed, however, it is certainly more elegant if some variety can be obtained, and the union is closer if the conjunction be placed in the body of the sentence. This requires the use of other words besides *and* and *but*. *Also, in like manner, besides, too, nevertheless, however, after all, for all that*, should be as familiar as the two overworked words *and* and *but*. Look for ways to bind sentences in the middle rather than at the end. It is more elegant and it is much safer.

Parallel Constructions. A third principle of arrangement is the use of parallel constructions for parallel thoughts. By parallel structure is meant that the principal elements of the sentences shall be arranged in the same order. If subordinate clauses precede principal clauses in one sentence, they shall in the other; if they follow in one, they shall follow in the other. If an active voice be used in one, it shall be used in the other; if the predicate go before the subject in one, it shall in the other. The use of parallel structure frequently demands repetition of forms and even of identical words and phrases. It is very effective in giving clearness to a paragraph and in securing coherence of its parts.

In the first of the two illustrations below, read one sentence this way and observe the ruin that is wrought. "The North American colonies made such a struggle against the mother country." In the second paragraph, change two of the sentences to the passive voice. The effect is evident loss in clearness and strength.

"All history is full of revolutions, produced by causes similar to those which are now operating in England. A portion of the community which had been of no account, expands and becomes strong. It demands a place in the system, suited, not to its former weakness, but to its present power. If this is granted, all is well. If this is refused, then comes the struggle between the young energy of one class and the ancient privileges of another. Such was the struggle between the Plebeians and Patricians of Rome. Such was the struggle of the Italian allies for admission to the full rights of Roman citizens. Such was the struggle of our North American colonies against the mother country. Such was the struggle which the Third Estate of France maintained against the aristocracy of birth. Such was the struggle which the Roman Catholics of Ireland maintained against the aristocracy of creed. Such is the struggle which the free people of color in Jamaica are now maintaining against the aristocracy of skin. Such, finally, is the struggle which the middle classes in England are maintaining against an aristocracy of mere locality, against an aristocracy, the principle of which is to invest a hundred drunken pot-wallopers in one place, or the owner of a ruined hovel in another, with powers which are withheld from cities renowned to the furthest ends of the earth for the marvels of their wealth and of their industry." (Macaulay.)

"Man is a being of genius, passion, intellect, conscience, power. He exercises these various gifts in various ways, in deeds, in great thoughts, in heroic acts, in hateful crimes. He founds states, he fights battles, he builds cities, he ploughs the forest, he subdues the elements, he rules his kind. He creates vast ideas, and influences many generations. He takes a thousand shapes, and undergoes a thousand fortunes. Literature records them all to the life. . . . He pours out his fervid soul in poetry; he sways to and fro, he soars, he dives, in his restless speculations; his lips drop eloquence; he touches the canvas, and it glows with beauty; he sweeps the strings, and they thrill with an ecstatic meaning. He looks back into himself, and he reads his own thoughts, and notes them down; he looks out into the universe, and tells over and celebrates the elements and principles of which it is the product." (Newman.)

(The principles of Mass and Coherence in paragraphs are closely allied with these same principles regarding sentences. Some further discussion of these important matters, as well as more illustrations, will be found in the next chapter.)

Good sense must be exercised in the use of parallel constructions. Although a short series of sentences containing parallel thoughts is common and demands this treatment, it is not at all frequent that one has such a long series as these paragraphs contain. In these paragraphs the parallel is in the thought; it has not been searched out. Because one is pleased with these effects of parallel construction, he should not be led to seek for opportunities where he can force sentences into similar shapes. The thoughts must be parallel. If the thought is actually parallel, a parallel treatment may be adopted with great advantage to clearness and force; if it is not parallel, any attempt to treat it as such is detected as a shallow trick. To search for thoughts to trail along in a series results in thinnest bombast. As everywhere else in composition, so here a writer must rely on his good taste and good sense.

Whatever may be the special mode of development, of whatever form of discourse it is to be a part, the three fundamental principles which guide in making a paragraph are Unity, Mass, and Coherence. The unity of the paragraph is secured by referring all of the material to the topic, including what contributes to the main thought and excluding what has no value. Paragraphs excessively long or very short may lead to offenses against unity. Mass in a paragraph is gained by placing worthy words in the positions of distinction; by treating the more important matters at greater length; and, when possible without disturbing coherence, by arranging the material in a climax. Coherence is secured by keeping together matters related in thought; by a wise choice and placing of all words which bind sentences together; and by the use of parallel constructions for parallel ideas. Carefully chosen material, arranged so that worthy words occupy the positions of distinction, and all so skillfully knit together that every sentence, every phrase, every word, takes the reader one step toward the conclusion, — this constitutes a good paragraph.

Summary.

SUGGESTIVE QUESTIONS

THE OLD MANSE.
(Riverside Literature Series, No. 69.)

In the paragraph beginning at the bottom of page 19, what do you think of the selection of material? Does the last detail give the finishing touch to the paragraph? Is it a real climax?

On page 25 a paragraph begins, "Lightly as," etc. In the second sentence "bound volume" goes back to what words in the first sentence? "he," of the third, to what of the second? "thus it was" to what before?

Now take the paragraph on pages 34 and 35 and trace the connection of the sentences, drawing two lines under the phrase from which a succeeding sentence springs, and one line under words that refer back to a preceding phrase; also trace out the dovetailing in the sentences on pages 6 and 7. In the paragraph on pages 18 and 19 the development is not so. Each sentence emphasizes "the sombre aspect of external nature." What is the law of their arrangement? (See text-book, pages 181-187.)

Find other paragraphs arranged in this way. (See pages 35, 36.)

What is the topic of the second paragraph?

Can you divide the paragraph filling the middle of page 8? Where?

What is the relation between the first sentence and the last in the paragraph at the bottom of page 11? Give the words that join the sentences of the paragraph together.

In the paragraph beginning on page 13, what is the purpose of the first two sentences?

On page 14, does it seem to you that Hawthorne had forgotten the Old Manse enough so that it could be called a digression? or do you think that the delightful, rambling character of the essay permits it? Can you divide this paragraph on pages 14 and 15? Where?

What figure at the bottom of page 15? Is it the custom to use a capital letter in such a case? Has the paragraph in which the figure occurs unity? Where could you divide it? Give the topic of both new paragraphs.

Of the paragraph on pages 16 and 17, what is the relation of the last three sentences to the topic?

What comment would you make upon the last sentence of the paragraph ending at the top of page 25?

At the opening of the paragraph beginning on page 29, do you like the figure? Trace the relation between the first and second sentences; between the second and the third. Could this paragraph be divided?

RIP VAN WINKLE AND THE LEGEND OF SLEEPY HOLLOW.

(Riverside Literature Series, No. 51.)

In the paragraph on page 11, what is the relation between the first and last sentences? Why is the middle of the paragraph introduced? Is it effective?

What method of development is adopted in the next paragraph?

Trace out the connection of the paragraphs in the first five pages of this essay. What words at the beginning of each paragraph are especially helpful in joining the parts?

On page 13 Irving writes, " Times grew worse and worse for Rip Van Winkle," etc. How many paragraphs are given to this topic? Could all of them be put into one? Should they? What is the last part of the first sentence of this paragraph?

Why are there so few topic sentences in this essay? How did Irving know where to paragraph? Give topics of the paragraphs on pages 16, 17, 18. In the paragraph beginning at the bottom of p. 17, why are the clothes of the man mentioned first?

What method of paragraph development is adopted in the

paragraph beginning in the middle of page 23? Is the last detail important?

From the use on pages 24 and 25, what do you gather as to the rule for paragraphing where dialogue is reported?

In the paragraph on page 40, what reason has Irving for saying "therefore"? From what sentence does the last of this paragraph arise? Do you think the specific closing of the paragraph worthy of the position?

When Irving says on page 41 that he was "an odd mixture of small shrewdness and simple credulity," did he mean that he was shrewd, or that he was not shrewd? Can you find anything in the paragraphs to develop the thought that he was shrewd? How many paragraphs are given to his simple credulity? Why so many?

In the paragraph beginning at the bottom of page 42, what advantage is there in the exclamatory sentences?

Would it be as well to divide the next paragraph into three sentences? Give your reasons. As the paragraph stands, is the sentence loose or periodic?

In the paragraph beginning at the bottom of page 45, what is the method of development? Why is the chanticleer mentioned last?

Are Irving's sentences long? Do they seem long? Why, or why not?

What is the relation of the first sentence of the first paragraph on page 55 to the last?

What is the topic of the next paragraph? Do you think it would be just as well to put the second sentence of this paragraph last?

In the paragraph beginning at the bottom of page 55, what method of development has been used? Why is the "blue jay" mentioned last?

THE FALL OF THE HOUSE OF USHER.

(Riverside Literature Series, No. 119.)

Do you think the first paragraph too long? Where can you divide it? What is the test of the length of a paragraph?

At the bottom of page 67, do you think the first sentence of the paragraph the topic? or is it the last sentence? Give reasons.

Is the detail at the end of the paragraph beginning on the middle of page 71 upon the topic of the paragraph? Is it good there? How do you know that Usher did not say "him"?

Of the paragraph on page 73, what sentence is the topic?

What proportion of the paragraphs have topic sentences? Have the others topics? Give them for the paragraphs on the first five pages.

What method of paragraph development has Poe adopted in the paragraph beginning in the middle of page 81? What is the relation between the opening and the close of the paragraph? Why is the middle needed?

Do you like the second sentence of the next paragraph? What is there disagreeable in it?

As you read along do the paragraphs run into one another? Is such a condition good?

SILAS MARNER.

(Riverside Literature Series, No. 83.)

Divide paragraphs on pages 10 and 11. What is the topic of each of the new paragraphs?

In the first paragraph of chapter two each sentence grows out of the one preceding. Put two lines under the words in each sentence which are the source of the next sentence. Draw one line under the words in each sentence which refer back to the preceding sentence.

In the paragraph beginning at the bottom of page 94, what is the topic sentence? What relation has the last sentence to the first? What method of development in the paragraph?

Can the paragraphs of exposition usually be divided? Do they violate unity? If not, upon what principle can you divide them?

What is the tendency in regard to the length of paragraphs in recent literature?

CHAPTER VIII

SENTENCES

A SENTENCE is a group of words expressing a complete thought. Sentences have been classified
as simple, complex, and compound. In reality
there are but two classes of sentences, — simple and compound. It is not material to the
construction of a sentence whether a modifier be a
word, a phrase, or a clause; it still remains an adjective,
adverb, or noun modifier, and the method in which the
subject and predicate are developed is the same. By
means of modifiers, a subject and predicate of but two
words may grow to the size of a paragraph, and yet
be a group of words expressing one complete thought.

Definition and Classification. Simple Sentences.

In the sentence below, the subject and predicate are
"we are free." This does not, however, express
Burke's complete thought. It is not what he meant.
Free to do what? How free? When may it be done?
Why now? What bill? — All these introduce modifications to the simple assertion, "we are free," modifications which are essential to the completeness of the
thought.

"By the return of this bill, which seemed to have taken
its flight forever, we are at this very instant nearly as free
to choose a plan for our American government as we were
on the first day of the session."

On the other hand, the compound sentence is usually
said to consist of at least two independent
clauses; and the very fact of their independence, which is only a grammatical independence, to be

Compound Sentences.

sure, makes the clauses very nearly independent sentences. So near to sentences may the clauses be in their independence that some writers would make them so. The following group of sentences Kipling certainly could have handled in another way. "The reason for her wandering was simple enough. Coppy, in a tone of too hastily assumed authority, had told her over night that she must not ride out by the river. And she had gone to prove her own spirit and teach Coppy a lesson." Certainly the last two sentences could be united into a compound sentence, nor would it be straining the structure to put all three sentences into one. This example is not exceptional. Many similar cases may be found in all prose writers; and in Macaulay's writings there are certainly occasions when it would be better to unite independent sentences. If the fundamental ideas of the two clauses bear certain definite and evident relations to each other, they should stand in one compound sentence. These evident relations are: first, an assertion and its repetition in some other form; second, an assertion and its contrast; third, an assertion and its consequence; and fourth, an assertion and an example. If the clauses do not bear one of these evident relations to each other, they should receive special attention; for they may be two separate, independent thoughts requiring for their expression two sentences. The following sentences illustrate the common relations that may exist between the clauses of a compound sentence.

Repetition. "Nothing has a drift or relation; nothing has a promise or history."

"But the religion most prevalent in our northern colonies is a refinement on the principle of resistance; it is the dissidence of dissent, and the protestantism of the Protestant religion."

Contrast. "If the people approve the way in which these authorities are interpreting and using the Constitution, they go on; if the people disapprove, they pause, or at least slacken their pace."

"Every court is equally bound to pronounce, and competent to pronounce, on such questions, a State court no less than a Federal court; but as all the more important questions are carried by appeal to the supreme Federal court, it is practically that court whose opinion determines them."

Consequence. "The British and American line had run near it during the war; it had, *therefore*, been the scene of marauding, and infested with refugees, cow-boys, and all kinds of border chivalry."

Example. "He found favor in the eyes of the mothers by petting the children, particularly the youngest; and like the lion bold, which whilom so magnanimously the lamb did hold, he would sit with a child on one knee, and rock a cradle with his foot for whole hours together."

There is another condition which masses many details into one compound sentence. If in narration a writer wishes to give the impression that many things are done in a moment of time, and together form one incident, he may group many circumstances, nearly independent except for the matter of time, into one compound sentence. In description he may present groups of details hastily in one sentence, and so give the impression of unity. The same thing may be done in exposition. Many independent ideas may bear a common relation to another idea, either expressed or understood; and in order to get them before the reader as one whole, the author may group them in a single sentence. The examples below illustrate this method of sentence development.

Narration. "For a moment the terror of Hans Van Ripper's wrath passed across his mind, — for it was his Sunday saddle; but this was no time for petty fears; the goblin was hard on his haunches; and (unskillful rider that he was!) he had much ado to maintain his seat; sometimes slipping on one side, sometimes on another, and sometimes jolted on the high ridge of his horse's backbone, with a violence that he verily feared would cleave him asunder." (Irving.)

Description. "In one corner stood a huge bag of wool, ready to be spun; in another, a quantity of linsey-woolsey just from the loom; ears of Indian corn, and strings of dried apples and peaches, hung in gay festoons along the walls, mingled with the gaud of red peppers; and a door left ajar gave him a peep into the best parlor, where the claw-footed chairs and dark mahogany tables shone like mirrors; andirons, with their accompanying shovel and tongs, glistened from their covert of asparagus tops; mock oranges and conch shells decorated the mantelpiece; strings of various-colored birds' eggs were suspended above it; a great ostrich egg was hung from the centre of the room, and a corner cupboard, knowingly left open, displayed immense treasures of old silver and well-mended china." (Irving.)

Exposition. "That perfection of the Intellect, which is the result of Education, and its *beau idéal*, to be imparted to individuals in their respective measures, is the clear, calm, accurate vision and comprehension of all things, as far as the finite mind can embrace them, each in its place, and with its own characteristics upon it. It is almost prophetic from its knowledge of history; it is almost heart-searching from its knowledge of human nature; it has almost supernatural charity from its freedom from littleness and prejudice; it has almost the repose of faith, because nothing can startle it; it has almost the beauty and harmony of heavenly contemplation, so intimate is it with the eternal order of things and the music of the spheres." (Newman.)

(Notice the use of the semicolon in the last two groups of sentences. The parts of compound sentences such as these should be designated by the use of semi-**colons.**)

Having determined approximately what relations

may be grouped in a single sentence, the first question for consideration is whether sentences should be long or short. This cannot be definitely answered. Since they should be concise, the short sentence is well suited for definitions. Since a proposition should be announced in as few words as can be used, without sacrificing brevity to clearness, short sentences serve best for this purpose. As changes in the direction of the development of a thought should be quickly indicated, a short sentence is generally used for transition. And as at times when the mind is under a stress of strong feeling, or the action of a story is rapid, all explanatory matters are cut away, the barest statements in shortest sentences serve best to express strong emotion and rapid action.

Short Sentences.

Long sentences have the very opposite uses. To amplify a topic, to develop a proposition by repetition, by details, by proofs, or by example, long sentences are serviceable; by them the finer modifications of a thought can be expressed. So, too, a summary of a paragraph or a chapter frequently employs long sentences to express the whole thought with precision and with proper subordination of parts. Again, as short sentences best express haste and intensity, so long sentences give the feeling of quiet deliberation and dignified calm.

Long Sentences.

Illustrations of definitions, propositions, transitions, and exemplifications are to be found everywhere. Slow movement expressed by long sentences is well illustrated in Irving and Hawthorne. One selection from George Meredith, to show the peculiar adaptation of the short sentence to express intensity of feeling, is given. Richard Feverel has just learned that the wife whom he had deserted has borne him a son. Description and narration are mingled. The short, nervous sentences express both the vividness of his impressions and the intensity of his emotions.

"A pale gray light on the skirts of the flying tempest displayed the dawn. Richard was walking hurriedly. The green drenched woods lay all about his path, bent thick, and the forest drooped glimmeringly. Impelled as a man who feels a revelation mounting obscurely to his brain, Richard was passing one of those little forest-chapels, hung with votive wreaths, where the peasants halt to kneel and pray. Cold, still, in the twilight it stood, rain-drops pattering round it. He looked within, and saw the Virgin holding her Child. He moved not by. But not many steps had he gone before the strength went out of him, and he shuddered. What was it? He asked not. He was in other hands. Vivid as lightning the Spirit of Life illumined him. He felt in his heart the cry of his child, his darling's touch. With shut eyes he saw them both. They drew him from the depths; they led him a blind and tottering man. And as they led him he had a sense of purification so sweet he shuddered again and again."

In a sentence, as in a theme or a paragraph, the first question regarding its structure is what to put into it. The germ of a paragraph is usually *Unity.* a sentence; of the sentence it is one word or but very few words. This kernel of a sentence may be developed through the many modifications of the thought; but always the additions must be distinctly related to the germ words. If this relation of parts to the kernel of the sentence be unmistakable, the sentence has unity; if there are parts whose connection with the germ of the sentence cannot be easily traced, they should be rejected as belonging to another sentence. The pith of the whole sentence can be stated in a few words, if the sentence has unity.

Long sentences should be watched. One thing easily suggests another, interesting too, it may be; and when an essay is to be written, anything, — especially if it have so worthy a quality as interest to recommend it, — anything is allowed to go in. Such a sentence as the following can be explained on no other principle: "Just then James came rushing downstairs like mad to find the fellow who had punched a hole in the tire of his bicycle, which was a Columbia which he got two years before at a second-hand store, paying for it in work at fifteen cents an hour." Plainly everything after "bicycle" is nothing to the present purpose and should be excluded. The following from a description of Cologne Cathedral is as bad, in some respects, worse; for there is one point where the break is so abrupt that a child would detect it. "The superintendence was intrusted to Mr. Ahlert, whose ideas were not well adapted to inspire him for his grand task, under his direction much of the former beauty and artistical skill was lost sight of, but at all events it was a great satisfaction to see the work go on and to have the expenses defrayed by the State." In this case the writer, beyond doubt, thinks long sentences the correct thing. Long sentences are necessary at times; but the desire simply to write long sentences or to fill up space should never lead one to forget that a sentence is the expression of one — not more — of one complete thought.

On the other hand, sentences should contain the whole of one thought; none of it should run over into another sentence. Strange as it may seem, sentences are sometimes found like the following: "James was on the whole a bad boy. But he had some redeeming qualities." "The first day at school was all new to me. While it was interesting as well." "He said that he was going. And that I might go with him." There is no ground for an explanation of such errors as these except laziness and grossest illiteracy. It is by no device so simple as the insertion of a period that man can separate what has been joined in thought. *And* and *but* rarely begin sentences; in nearly all cases it will be found that the sentences they purport to connect are but the independent clauses of one compound sentence. *While* or any other subordinating conjunction introduces a dependent clause; a dependent clause is not a sentence; it can never stand alone.

The offenses against the unity of a sentence are including too much and including too little. Both are the result of carelessness or inability to think. The purpose, the kernel, the germ of the sentence, should be so clearly in mind that every necessary modification of the thought shall be included and every unnecessary phrase be excluded. Some further suggestions concerning unity are found in the paragraphs treating primarily of mass and coherence.

As advance is made in the ability to grasp quickly the thought of a book, it becomes more and more evident that the eye must be taken into account when arranging the parts of a composition. **Mass.** The eye sees the headings of the chapters; it catches the last words of one paragraph and the first words of the next; it lights upon the words near the periods; so the parts of a composition should be arranged so that these points shall contain worthy words. Moreover, within the sentence the colon marks the greatest independence of the parts; the semicolon comes next; and the comma marks the smallest division of thought. Following the guidance of the eye, then, the words before a period should be the most important; those near a colon, a semicolon, and a comma will have a descending scale of value. A speaker has no difficulty with punctuation; unconsciously he pauses with the thought. So true is this, that one is inclined to say that if the writer will read aloud his own composition, and punctuate where he pauses in the reading, always remembering the rank of the marks of punctuation, he will not be far from right. It will be noticed that he has paused in the reading after important words, as if the thought stayed a moment there for the help of the reader. Naturally we pause after important words; and conversely, the places of importance in a sentence are near the marks of punctuation, increasing from the comma to the period.

End of a Sentence. The end of a sentence is more important than the beginning; and the difference in value is greater than in a paragraph. In a paragraph the opening is very important, generally containing the topic. In a sentence, however, the beginning more often has some phrase of transition, or some modifier; while it is the end that contains the gist of the sentence. This fact makes it imperative that no unworthy matter stand at the end. How important a position it is, and how much is expected of the final words of a sentence, is evident from the effect of failure produced by a sentence that closes with weak words. In the following sentences, phrases have been moved from their places; the weakness is apparent.

Abstract liberty is not to be found; and this is true of other mere abstractions.

This is a persuasion built upon liberty, and not only favorable to it.

I pass, therefore, to their agriculture, another point of view.

Of course Burke never wrote such sentences as these. However, sentences like them can be found in school compositions.

"Lincoln's character is worthy to be any young man's ideal; having in it much to admire."

"Euclid Avenue, with its broad lawns, and with Wade Park as the fitting climax of its spacious beauty, is the most attractive driveway in the United States, which is saying a good deal."

"Minnesota has many beautiful lakes; Mille Lacs, fringed with dark pines; Osakis, with its beach of glistening sand; Minnetonka, skirted by a lovely boulevard bordered by cool lawns and cosy cottages; and many others not so big."

Such sentences as these are not uncommon. Their ruin is wrought by the closing words. Watch for trailing relatives, dangling participles, and straggling generalities at the end of sentences. The end of a sentence is a position of distinction; it should be held by words of distinction.

So influential is position in a sentence that by virtue of it a word or a clause of equal rank with others can be made to take on a certain added authority. By observing the end of a sentence, a reader can determine what was uppermost in the mind of an author careful of these things. In the following sentence as it was written by Burke the emphasis is on the duration of the time; but by a change of position it is put upon the fact. "Refined policy ever has been the parent of confusion; and ever will be so, as long as the world endures." Changing the last clause it reads, "and, as long as the world endures, ever will be so." This is not weak; but the stress is not where Burke placed it. The position of the words gives them an importance that does not inhere in the words themselves.

Still, as the tenure of a place of distinction cannot save a fool from the reputation of folly, position in a sentence cannot redeem empty words from their truly insipid character. Indeed, as the imbecility of a shallow pate is made all the more apparent by a position of distinction, so is the utter unfitness of certain words for their position painfully manifest. This is the secret of anti-climax. By reason of its very position in a sentence, the last phrase should be distinguished; instead the position is held by a silly nothing. Disappointing anti-climaxes, like those already cited, are frequently made by young writers; and they are sometimes met with in the works of the best authors. The following sentence is from Newman: from the point of view of an ardent churchman, it may be a climax; but from the point of view of the general reader who considers the whole greater than any of its parts, in spite of all the sense preceding the final phrase, that is absurd and disappointing nonsense.

Effect of Anti-climax.

"I protest to you, gentlemen, that if I had to choose between a so-called university, which dispensed with residence and tutorial superintendence, and gave its degrees to any person who passed an examination in a wide range of subjects, and a university which had no professors and examinations at all, but merely brought a number of young men together for three or four years, and then sent them away as the University of Oxford is said to have done some sixty years since, if I were asked which of these methods was the better discipline of the intellect, — mind, I do not say whic is *morally* the better, for it is plain that compulsory study must be a good and idleness an intolerable mischief, — but if I must determine which of the two courses was the more successful in training, moulding, and enlarging the mind, which sent out men the more fitted for their secular duties, which produced better public men, men of the world, men whose names would descend to posterity, I have no hesitation in giving the preference to that university which did nothing, over that which exacted an acquaintance with every science under the sun. And, paradox as this may seem, still if results be the test of systems, the influence of the public schools and colleges of England, in the course of the last century, at least will bear out one side of the contrast as I have drawn it. What could come, on the other hand, of the ideal systems of education which have fascinated the imagination of this age, could they ever take effect, and whether they would not produce a generation frivolous, narrow-minded, and resourceless, intellectually considered, is a fair subject for debate ; but so far is certain, that the universities and scholastic establishments, to which I refer, and which did little more than bring together first boys and then youths in large numbers, these institutions, with miserable deformities on the side of morals, with a hollow profession of Christianity, and a heathen code of ethics, — I say, at least, they can boast of a succession of heroes and statesmen, of literary men and philosophers, of men conspicuous for great natural virtues, for habits of business, for knowledge of life, for practical judgment, for cultivated tastes, for accomplishments, who have made England what it is, — able to subdue the earth, *able to domineer over Catholics* "

From what has been said, it is evident that the parts of a sentence, as far as may be, should be arranged in a climax. The climax should be in the thought, with a corresponding increase in the weight of the phrases. If the thoughts increase in importance, the words that express them should increase in number. The number of words in the treatment bears a pretty constant ratio to the importance of the subject treated. The paragraph quoted from Newman is an excellent illustration of the use of climax, — until it comes to that last phrase. Note in the first sentence the repetition of the condition, three times repeated. Change the second to the third and see how different it is. Then he has " public men, men of the world, men whose names would descend to posterity," — a steady increase in the thought, and a corresponding increase in the length of phrases. The last sentence

Use of Climax.

contains a fine example of climax. " Of heroes and statesmen, of literary men and philosophers, of men conspicuous for great natural virtues, for habits of business, for knowledge of life, for practical judgment, for cultivated tastes, for accomplishments, who have made England what it is, — able to subdue the earth." Climax is the arrangement that produces the effect of vigorous strength. In arranging a succession of modifiers, so far as possible without breaking some other more important principle, a writer will gain in force if he seeks for climax.

Sentences are divided into two classes: loose and periodic. A loose sentence may be broken at some point before the end, and up to that point be grammatically a complete sentence. An arrangement of the parts of a sentence that suspends the meaning until the close is called periodic. The periodic sentence is generally so massed that the end contains words of distinction, and the sentence forms a climax. Not all climaxes are periods; but nearly all periods are climaxes.

Loose and Periodic.

The philosophy of the periodic sentence has been best stated by Herbert Spencer. He starts with the axiom that the whole amount of attention a reader can give at any moment is limited and fixed. A reader must give a part of it to merely acquiring the meaning; the remainder of his attention he can give to the thought itself. In reading Cicero the pupil has to put a large part of his attention upon the vocabulary, upon the order and construction of the words; the barest fragment of attention he can bestow upon the thought of the great orator. So when the reader attacks one of Browning's most involved and obscure passages, he is kept from the thought by the difficulties in the language. As it is the purpose of language

The Period.

to convey thought, and as it is usually the wish of an author to be understood, he should use up as little as possible of the reader's limited attention for the mere acquisition of the thought, and leave the reader as much as he can to put upon the meaning. In applying this to sentences, the question is, which form of sentence demands least effort to get at its meaning: the periodic sentence, which suspends the meaning to the end; or the loose sentence, which may be broken at several points and gives its meaning in installments? The old example is as good as any: shall we say as the French do, a horse black; or shall we say as the English do, a black horse? for in the arrangement of these three words there lies the difference between a loose and a periodic sentence. Consider the French order first. When a person hears the words "a horse," he at once thinks of the horse he knows best; that is, generally, a bay horse. When the word "black" follows, the whole image has to be changed from the bay horse he knows to the black horse he has occasionally seen. There has been a waste of attention. On the other hand, when the words "a black" are heard, the mind constructs no image; it waits until the noun modified is spoken. Then the whole image springs up at once; it is correct and it needs no remodeling. The following sentence illustrates the point. "I am wasting time" is the beginning. It would be difficult to enumerate the many thoughts suggested by these words; each person has his own idea of wasting time. When the rest of the sentence is added, "trying to learn my geometry lesson," the whole has to be reconstructed. On the other hand the periodic statement suspends the meaning to the end. There is no place where, without additions to the words used, the mind can rest. "Trying to learn a geometry lesson is for me a waste of time." Theoretically the periodic sentence is better than the loose sentence; for it economizes attention.

There is another side to the question, however. If the details be many, and if each be long, they would be more than the mind could carry without great effort; and instead of economy of attention, there is improvident waste. The mind will carry a long, carefully arranged period at intervals; but a succession of periods is sure to result in its absolute refusal to do so any longer. There is a limit to the length of a period that economizes attention; and there is a limit to the number of successive periods which a reader can endure.

There is another form of sentence, which combines the loose and the periodic. It generally begins with the periodic form and sustains this until it is better to relieve the mind of the stress, when the period ends or the loose structure begins; and the sentence may as a whole be periodic while containing parts that are loose. This kind of sentence is a common form for long sentences. It gives to prose much of the dignity of the period, together with the familiarity of the loose sentence.

Periodic and Loose

The sentence below may be changed, by putting the last clause first, to a loose sentence; and by placing it after the word "subject" it becomes mixed.

"By all persons who have written of the subject, for the grandeur of its mountains and the deep quiet of its green valleys, for the leaping torrents of its foaming rivers and blue calm of its crag-walled lakes, Switzerland has been named 'the Paradise of Europe.'"

The following paragraph from Burke contains examples of loose, periodic, and mixed sentences: —

"To restore order and repose to an empire so great and so distracted as ours, is, merely in the attempt, an undertaking that would ennoble the flights of the highest genius, and obtain pardon for the efforts of the meanest understanding. Struggling a good while with these thoughts, by degrees I felt myself more firm. I derived, at length, some confidence from what in other circumstances usually produces timidity. I grew less anxious, even from the idea of my own insignificance. For, judging of what you are by what you ought to be, I persuaded myself that you would not reject a reasonable proposition because it had nothing but its reason to recommend it. On the other hand, being totally destitute of all shadow of influence, natural or adventitious, I was very sure that, if my proposition were futile or dangerous — if it were weakly conceived, or improperly timed, — there was nothing exterior to it of power to awe, dazzle, or delude you. You will see it just as it is; and you will treat it just as it deserves."

Which shall be used, loose sentences or periodic? In literature the loose more frequently occur. They are informal and conversational, and are especially suited to letter-writing, story-telling, and the light essay. The period is formal; it has the air of preparation. The oration, the formal essay, well-wrought argument, — forms of literature where preparation is expected, — may use the period with good effect. It has a finish, a scholarly refinement, not found in the loose sentence; and yet a series of periods would be as much out of place in a letter as a court regalia at a downtown restaurant. The loose sentence is easy, informal, and familiar; the periodic is stiff, artificial, and aristocratic. To use none but loose sentences gives a composition an air of familiarity even to the verge of vulgarity; to employ only periodic sentences induces a feeling of stiff artificiality bordering on bombast. The fitness of each for its purpose is the guide for its use.

There is, however, a reason why young persons should be encouraged to use periodic sentences. Usually they compose short sentences, so there is little danger of overburdening the reader's attention. With this danger removed, the result of the generous use of periodic sentences will be nothing worse than a too obvious preparation. The sentences will all be finished to a degree, and unquestionably will give a feeling artificiality. However, the attention to sentence-structure necessary in order to make it periodic is a thing devoutly to be wished at this stage of growth. No other fault is so common in sentence-construction as carelessness. A theme will be logically outlined, a paragraph carefully planned, but a sentence, — anybody standing on one foot can make a sentence. A well-turned sentence is a work of art, and it is never made in moments when the writer "did n't think." The end must be seen at the beginning : else it does not end ; it plays out. There is no other remedy for careless, slipshod sentence-making so effective as the construction of many periodic sentences.

Not only will there be care in the arrangement the material, but when all details must be introduced before the principal thought, there will be little chance of any phrase slipping into the sentence that does not in truth belong there. Dangling participles, trailing relatives, and straggling generalities can find no chance to hang on to a periodic sentence. Every detail must be a real and necessary modification of the general thought of the sentence, else it can hardly be forced in. Periodic sentences, then, besides insuring a careful finish to the work, are also a safeguard against the introduction of irrelevant material, — the commonest offense against sentence-unity.

Closely connected with the emphasis gained by the

periodic arrangement of the parts of a sentence is the emphasis gained by forcing words out of their natural order. In a sentence the points which arrest the eye and the attention are the beginning and the end. However, if the subject stands first and the words of the predicate in their natural order, there is no more emphasis upon them than these important elements of a sentence ordinarily deserve. To emphasize either it is necessary to force it out of its natural position. "George next went to Boston," is the natural order of this sentence. Supposing, however, that a writer wished to emphasize the fact that it was George who went next, not James or Fred, he could do it by forcing the word "George" from its present natural position to a position unnatural. He could write, "It was George who next went to Boston," or, "The next to go to Boston was George." Forcing the subject toward the position usually occupied by the predicate emphasizes the subject. This is similar to the emphasis given by the period. "It was George" is so far periodic, followed by the loose structure; and the last arrangement is quite periodic. Every device for throwing the subject back into the sentence makes the sentence up to the point where the subject is introduced periodic; this arrangement throws the emphasis forward to the word that closes the period.

Other parts of a sentence may be emphasized by being placed out of their natural order. In the natural order, adjectives and adverbs precede the words they modify; conditional and concessive clauses precede the clauses they modify; an object follows a verb; and prepositional phrases and adjective clauses follow the words they modify. These rules are general. Moving a part of a sentence from this general order

Emphasis by Change of Order.

usually emphasizes it. "George went to Boston next" emphasizes a little the time; but "Next George went to Boston" places great emphasis on the time. So "It was to Boston that George went next" emphasizes the place. "Went" cannot be so dealt with. It seems irrevocably fixed that in a prose declarative sentence the verb shall never stand first. It is not allowed by good use.

The rearrangement of the following sentence illustrates the emphasis given by putting words out of their natural order : —

The strong and swarthy sailors of the Patria slowly rowed the party to the shore.

The sailors of the Patria, strong and swarthy, slowly rowed the party to the shore.

Slowly the strong and swarthy sailors of the Patria rowed the party to the shore.

Of the steamer Patria, the sailors, strong and swarthy, rowed the party to the shore.

To show the arrangement of clauses the following will be sufficient : —

He cannot make advancement, even if he studies hard.
Even if he studies hard, he cannot make advancement.
" Your Irish pensioners would starve, if they had no other fund to live on than the taxes granted by English authority.'
If they had no other fund to live on than the taxes granted by English authority, your Irish pensioners would starve.

The latter arrangement emphasizes the conclusion much more than the former; at the same time it subordinates the condition. Burke wished the emphasis to be upon the condition; he placed it after the conclusion.

Emphasis is gained by placing words in important positions in a sentence; by arranging the parts to form a climax; by the use of the period; by forcing words out of their natural order. It is also gained by the subdual of parts not important. This emphasis is a matter of relative intensity. The beauty and strength of any artistic product depend as much upon the subdual of the accessories as upon the intensifying of the necessaries. In order to get the emphasis upon certain phrases, it is necessary to subordinate other phrases. In the talk of a child every thought phrases itself as a simple sentence. Not until it grows to youth does the child recognize that there is a difference in values, and adopt means for expressing it. To grasp firmly the principal idea and then subdue all other ideas is an elegant way of emphasizing.

The subdual of parts is accomplished by reducing to subordinate clauses, to phrases, to words, some of the ideas which in a child's talk would be expressed in sentences. A thought of barely enough importance to be mentioned should be squeezed into a word. If it deserves more notice, perhaps a prepositional phrase will express it. A participial phrase will often serve for a clause or a sentence. A subordinate clause may be needed if the thought is of great importance. And last, if it deserves such a distinction, the thought may demand an independent clause or a sentence for itself. If the following sentence be broken into bits as a child would tell it, the nice effects of emphasis which Irving has given it are ruined : —

"When the dance was at an end, Ichabod was attracted to a knot of the sager folks, who, with old Van Tassel, sat smoking at one end of the piazza, gossiping over former times, and drawing out long stories about the war."

Put into simple sentences, it would be like this : The

dance was at an end. Ichabod was attracted to a knot of folks. The folks were older. They sat at the end of the piazza. Old Van Tassel was with them. They were smoking, etc.

In such sentences, nothing is emphatic; it is all alike. In Irving's sentences, where ideas are reduced to clause, phrase, even a word, there is no question about what is important and what is unimportant. He has secured an exquisite emphasis by a discriminating subdual of subordinate ideas.

This brings up the sentences by Kipling already quoted on page 201. The author has used three independent sentences. They can be written as one, thus: The reason of her wandering was simple enough; for Coppy, in a tone of too-hastily-assumed authority, had told her over night that she must not ride out by the river, and she had gone to prove her own spirit and teach Coppy a lesson.

There is a reason, however, why Kipling wished that last sentence to stand alone. Subordinated as it is here rewritten, it does not half express the spiteful independence she assumed to teach Coppy a lesson. It needs the independent construction. Just as surely as Kipling is right in putting the reasons into two sharp, independent sentences, is Irving right when he puts the reason in the following sentence into a subordinate clause. It is not important enough to deserve a sentence all by itself.

"He was, moreover, esteemed by the women as a man of great erudition, for he had read several books quite through, and was a perfect master of Cotton Mather's 'History of New England Witchcraft,' in which, by the way, he most firmly and potently believed."

In the following sentence, the effect of subordination is unmistakable: —

"He had a name in the village for brutally misusing the ass ; yet it is certain that he shed a tear *which* made a clean mark down one cheek."

Now read it again: —

"He had a name in the village for brutally misusing the ass ; yet it is certain that he shed a tear, *and the tear* made a clean mark down one cheek."

The last clause has burst away from its former submission, and in its independence has made the most important announcement of the sentence, — the witty climax. Emphasis is, to a large degree, a matter of position, but position cannot emancipate any clause from the thralldom of subordination. To emphasize one idea, subordinate ancillary ideas; make them take their proper rank in the sentence. Reduce them to a clause or to a phrase ; and if a word justly expresses the relative importance of the thought, reduce its expression to a single word.

In the chapter on paragraphs it was said that one sentence is often the source of the succeeding sentence ; that such a sentence seemed to be charged like a Leyden jar, and to discharge its whole power through a single word or phrase; and further, that this word or phrase should be left free to act, — it should be uncovered. How a sentence can be arranged so that this word or phrase shall have the prominence it deserves, and can unhindered transmit the undiminished force of one sentence to the next, has now been explained. First, such words can be made dynamic by placing them at the beginning or the end of a sentence ; second, by placing them near the major marks of punctuation ; third, by forcing them from their natural order ; and fourth, by the subdual of the other parts of the sentence. The greatest care in

The Dynamic Point of a Sentence.

massing sentences so that none of their power be lost in transmission is one of the secrets of the literature that carries the reader irresistibly forward. Sometimes he may be annoyed by the repetition of phrases; but he cannot get away; he must go forward. In the paragraph below, quoted from Matthew Arnold, every phrase that is the point from which the next sentence springs is in a position where it can act untrammeled. Through it the whole force of the sentence passes: —

" It will be said that it is a very subtle and indirect action which I am thus prescribing for criticism, and that, by embracing in this manner the Indian virtue of detachment and abandoning the sphere of practical life, it condemns itself as a slow and obscure work. Slow and obscure it may be, but it is the only proper work of criticism. The mass of mankind will never have any ardent zeal for seeing things as they are; very inadequate ideas will satisfy them. On these inadequate ideas reposes, and must repose, the general practice of the world. That is as much as saying that whoever sets himself to see things as they are will find himself one of a very small circle; but it is only by this small circle resolutely doing its own work that adequate ideas will ever get current at all. The rush and uproar of practical life will always have a dizzying and attracting effect upon the most collected spectator, and tend to draw him into its vortex; most of all will this be the case where that life is so powerful as it is in England. But it is only by remaining collected, and refusing to lend himself to the point of view of the practical man, that the critic can do the practical man any service; and it is only by the greatest sincerity in pursuing his own course, and by at last convincing even the practical man of his sincerity, that he can escape misunderstandings which perpetually threaten him."

Good use has been mentioned. In massing the parts of a sentence for the purpose of emphasizing some idea, a writer has not entire freedom. Good use, which is the use of acknowledged masters, decides what may be done. There are certain arrangements of words to which we are accustomed; and the disregard of them leads to obscurity or downright contrariety in the thought. "Brutus stabbed Cæsar" is the common order; "Brutus Cæsar stabbed," or "Stabbed Brutus Cæsar," is obscure; while "Cæsar stabbed Brutus" is the very opposite of the truth. Those who have studied Latin know that as far as understanding the sentence is concerned, it would make no difference in which order the three Latin words should be arranged; though it would make a mighty difference in the emphasis. In Latin the case endings determine the construction of the words. In an inflected language the words may be massed almost to suit the writer; in an uninflected language, within certain limits the order determines the relation between groups of words. Though for emphasis it might be advisable to have the object first, for the sake of clearness in a short sentence the object cannot stand first. The primary consideration in making any piece of literature is that it may be understood. To be understood, the sentence must be arranged in the order to which we are accustomed. The order to which we are accustomed has been determined by good use.

Good Use.

The variety in the arrangement of the parts of a sentence that has been sanctioned by good usage is great, yet there are limits. Grammar is based upon the usage of the best writers. Any offense against the grammar of our language is a sin against good use. Browning may use constructions so erratic that the ordinary reader does not know what he is reading about; Carlyle may forge a new word rather than take the trouble to find one that other people have used. But the young writer, at least, is far safer while keeping within the limits of good use.

Coherence in a sentence is that principle of structure by which its parts are best arranged to stick together. The parts of a sentence containing related ideas should be so associated that there can be no mistake regarding the reference or the modification. Such a sentence as the following cannot be understood; the reference is obscure. "James told him that he did not see what he was to do in the matter." If the reader were sure of the first "he," he could not come nearer than a guess at the reference of the second "he." The third personal pronoun — he, she, it — in all its cases is especially uncertain in its references.

[margin: Clearness gained by coherence.]

The first sentence below is from an English grammar. The second is from a recently published biography. Both are obscure in the reference of the pronouns.

"When 'self' is added to a pronoun of the First and Second person, it is preceded by the Possessive case. But when it is added to a pronoun of the Third person, it is preceded by a pronoun in the Objective case."

"I am reminded of Swinburne's view of Providence when he said that he never saw an old gentleman give a sixpence to a beggar, but he was straightway run over by a 'bus."

The relative pronoun is also uncertain in its references.

Some Southerners were among the ship's passengers, of whom a few had served in the Rebellion. (Obscure reference.)

Red lights were displayed in a peculiar succession, which warned of impending storm. (No antecedent.)

To make the reference of pronouns, personal and relative, distinct, the antecedent must be made prominent; sometimes the only way out of the difficulty is a repetition of the antecedent. And the pronoun should stand near the word to which it refers. Keep associated ideas together.

Like pronouns in the uncertainty of their reference are participles. Either the subject is not expressed, or it is uncertain.

Hastening up the steps, the door opened. (None.)
Coming from the spring, with a pail of water in either hand, he saw her for the first time. (Uncertain.)

Adverbs are sometimes placed so that they make a sentence ridiculous; and frequently their meaning is lost by being separated from the words they modify. "Only" is a word to be watched. Like adverbs are correlative conjunctions. They are frequently so placed that they do not join the elements they were intended to unite.

He seized the young girl as she rose from the water almost roughly.
I think I hardly shall.
I only went as far as the gate.
"Who shall say, of us who know only of rest and peace by toil and strife?"
He not only learned algebra readily but also Latin.

Phrases and clauses may lose their reference by being removed from the words they modify.

Toiling up the hill, he arrived at Hotel Bellevue through a drizzling rain.
Addison rose to a post which dukes, the heads of the great houses of Talbot, Russell, and Bentinck, have thought it an honor to fill without high birth, and with little property.
"Fred was liked well; but he had the habit of that class that cannot get the English Language in the right order when a little excited."

All the classes of errors which have been exemplified here are due to the infringement of one rule: things that belong together in thought should stand together in composition. Nothing should be allowed to come between a pronoun, an adjective, an adverb, a correlative, a phrase, or a clause, and the word it modifies. Sometimes other modifiers have to be taken into account: where more than one word or phrase modifies the same word, a trial will have to be made to arrange them so that there shall be no obscurity or absurdity. Keep related ideas together; keep unrelated ideas apart.

The second principle which helps to make the relation of parts clear is parallel construction. **Parallel Construction.** It has already been explained in paragraphs. In sentences the commonest errors are in linking an infinitive with a gerund, a participle with a verb, an active with a passive voice, a phrase with a clause. The result is sentences like the following: —

You cannot persuade him to go and into buying what he does not want.

Thus he spoke, and turning to the door.

The king began to force the collection of duties, and an army was sent by him to execute his wishes.

He was resolved to use patience and that he would often exercise charity.

Such sentences are offensive to the ear; and were they as long as the ones below, they would not be clear.

"You cannot persuade them *to burn* their books of curious science; *to banish* their lawyers from their courts of laws; or *to quench* the lights of their assemblies by refusing to choose those persons who are best read in their privileges."

"For though rebellion is declared, it *is* not *proceeded against* as such, nor *have* any steps *been taken* towards the apprehension or conviction of any individual offender, either on our late or our former Address; but modes of public coercion *have been adopted*, and such as have much more resemblance to a sort of qualified hostility towards an independent power than the punishment of rebellious subjects."

"My Resolutions therefore mean TO ESTABLISH the equity and justice of a taxation of America by grant and not by imposition; TO MARK the legal competency of the colony Assemblies for the support of their government in peace, and for public aids in time of war; TO ACKNOWLEDGE *that this legal competency has had* a dutiful and beneficial exercise; and *that experience has shown* the benefit of their grants, and the futility of Parliamentary taxation as a method of supply."

In the second sentence Burke has used a passive voice when it would certainly be more elegant to change to the active. "Is proceeded against" is surely awkward, but for uniformity and resulting clearness he has retained the passive. In the last sentence the infinitives "to establish," "to mark," and "to acknowledge" are in the same construction; they are objects of "mean." Then comes a change of form to show that the clauses "that this legal competency has had," etc., and "that experience has shown," etc., are in a like relation to the infinitive "to acknowledge." Though the last clause by reason of the punctuation looks correlative with the others, it is not related as object to the verb "mean," as the others are, but it is the object of "to acknowledge." There could hardly be a better example of the value of parallel constructions for the purpose of avoiding confusion, and linking together parts that are related.

Parallel constructions are used in balanced sentences. In balanced sentences one part is balanced against another, — a noun and a noun, an adjective and an adjective, phrase and phrase. Balanced sentences are especially suited to express antithesis, the figure of speech where two ideas are sharply

<small>Balanced Sentences.</small>

opposed to each other. In the following from Newman, the balancing is admirable: "Inebriated with the cup of insanity, and flung upon the stream of recklessness, she dashes down the cataract of nonsense and whirls amid the pools of confusion." This is not antithesis, however; but the following from Macaulay is: "She seems to have written about the Elizabethan age, because she had read much about it; she seems, on the other hand, to have read a little about the age of Addison, because she had determined to write about it."

The danger in the use of balanced sentences is excess. Macaulay is very fond of brilliant contrasts. *But* is a very common word with him. In some cases the reader feels that for the sake of the figure he has forced the truth. Balanced sentences are palpably artificial, and should be used but sparingly.

There is, however, but little danger of overdoing the parallel construction where there is no antithesis. The parts of succeeding sentences do not resemble each other so much in thought that there is great danger of resulting monotony in its expression. However, should the difficulty arise, the monotony may be broken up by a trifling variation. Macaulay has done this well in the sentences quoted on page 186, beginning with the words, "For his sake empires had risen, and flourished, and decayed," and continuing to the end of the paragraph.

The third method of securing coherence in a sentence is by the use of connectives. The skillful use of prepositions and conjunctions indicates a master of words. The use of connectives has been discussed when treating of emphasis secured by subdual of unimportant details. Such parts are connected, and in a very definite way. The

Use of Connectives.

relations are evident. Two examples will illustrate. The first group of sentences are the fragments of but one of Irving's.

He did not look to the right or left. He did not notice the scene. The scene was of rural wealth. He had often gloated on this scene. He went straight to the stable. He kicked and cuffed his steed several times, and so forth.

Now note the value of prepositions in giving these separate sentences coherence.

"Without looking to the right or left to notice the scene of rural wealth, on which he had so often gloated, he went straight to the stable, and with several hearty cuffs and kicks roused his steed most unceremoniously from the comfortable quarters in which he was soundly sleeping, dreaming of mountains of corn and oats, and whole valleys of timothy and clover."

The next also is from Irving, and shows the skillful use of conjunctions to point out unerringly the relation of the clauses in a sentence.

"What seemed particularly odd to Rip was that, though these folks were evidently amusing themselves, yet they maintained the gravest faces, the most mysterious silence, and were, withal, the most melancholy party of pleasure he had ever witnessed."

Coherence, the principle of structure that surely holds the parts of a sentence together, is of greater importance than Mass. Upon Coherence depends the meaning of a sentence; upon Mass the force with which the meaning is expressed. That the meaning may be clear, it is necessary that the relation of the parts shall be perfectly evident. This lucidity is gained by placing related parts near together, and conversely, by separating unrelated ideas; by using parallel constructions for parallel thoughts; and by indicating relations by the correct use of prepositions and conjunctions.

To summarize, sentences are the elements of discourse. The ability of a sentence to effect with certainty its purpose depends upon Unity, Mass, and Coherence. A sentence must contain all that is needed to express the whole thought, but it must contain no more. A sentence must be arranged so that its important parts shall be prominent. Position and proportion are the means of emphasis in a sentence. By placing the important words near the major marks of punctuation, by arranging the parts in a climax or a period, by forcing words out of the natural order, and by subduing unimportant details, a sentence is massed to give the important elements their relative emphasis. Last, the parts of a sentence should be arranged so that their relations shall be clear and unmistakable. Proximity of related parts, parallel construction for parallel ideas, and connectives are the surest means of securing Coherence in a sentence.

SUGGESTIVE QUESTIONS

SILAS MARNER.
(Riverside Literature Series, No. 83.)

On page 18 put together the sentence beginning "Every man's work," etc., with the next. What connective and what punctuation will you use? What is the difference in effect? What one of the relations of a compound sentence does the second part bear to the first?

On page 26 could you make two sentences of the sentence beginning, "Raveloe lay low among the bushy trees"? Would it be as well? Would it be better?

On page 35 do the three parts of the compound sentence beginning, "He would have liked," etc., belong to one sentence? Which one?

Is it right to say, "He would have liked to spring," or would it be better to say, "He would have liked to have sprung"?

Do you think colons are used too frequently in Silas Marner? Compare their use with their use in Hawthorne's Stories and Irving's Sketches.

In the sentence beginning, "Let him live," etc., at the bottom of page 94, is "a possible state of mind in some possible person not yet forthcoming," a climax or an anti-climax? Why?

At the bottom of page 183 why was it necessary to crowd so much into one sentence?

MACAULAY'S ESSAY ON MILTON.
(Riverside Literature Series, No. 103.)

Re-write the sentence on page 33 beginning, "Of all poets," etc., making it loose. Is it better or worse?

Why does "here" stand first in the next sentence?

What poets with whom you are familiar have philosophized too much?

Is the first sentence of the paragraph beginning in the middle of page 36 periodic or loose?

How many periodic sentences in this paragraph?

In the paragraph on pages 37 and 38 trace the relation of the succeeding sentences.

At the bottom of page 45 what is the reason for putting first in the sentence, "of those principles"? What do you think of the massing of the whole sentence? What has been made emphatic?

Note the last two sentences at the end of the paragraph on page 58. Is their arrangement effective? Change one. What is the effect? (See also the middle of page 64.)

On page 60 why did he not say, "She grovels like a beast, she hisses like a serpent, she stings like a scorpion"?

What arrangement of clauses in the first sentence in the paragraph beginning at the bottom of page 66? Does it add clearness?

In the same paragraph find a balanced sentence.

What advantage is there in the short sentences on page 68?

In the first sentence of the paragraph, beginning on page 71, read one of the clauses, "by whom king, church, and aristocracy were trampled down." What is the effect of the change?

Is the parallel construction in the last sentence beginning on page 77 good? Is it good in the last sentence of this paragraph?

In the next paragraph, why is Macaulay's way better than this: "He was neither Puritan, free-thinker, nor royalist"?

When a sentence is introduced by a participial phrase or a dependent clause it is in part or wholly periodic. Does Macaulay frequently use this introduction? What is the effect upon his style?

Can you find examples of sentences beginning with a loose structure, and having within them examples of the periodic structure?

In the paragraph filling pages 79 and 80 there are many examples of periodic and parallel structure. Contrast this paragraph with some of Lamb's paragraphs.

What is the effect of position upon the phrase, "Even in his hands," on page 67?

When Macaulay inverts the order of a sentence does he usually do it for emphasis or to secure coherence?

Does he use many pronouns and conjunctions?

Does he repeat words?

BURKE'S SPEECH ON CONCILIATION WITH THE COLONIES.

(Riverside Literature Series, No. 100.)

How many sentences in the first paragraph are periodic?

What kind of sentences in paragraph 10?

What is the effect of this paragraph?

Notice the arrangement of loose and periodic clauses in the last sentence in paragraph 12. Make this sentence entirely loose.

In the long sentence in paragraph 25 do the he's and him's all refer to the same person?

What would you say of Burke's use of pronouns?

Find examples of balanced sentences in this oration.

Are you ever astray regarding Burke's meaning?

What has he done to gain clearness?

For what purpose does he frequently use questions?

WEBSTER'S BUNKER HILL ORATION.

(Riverside Literature Series, No. 56.)

What relation has the second sentence of paragraph 1 to the first?

Is the last sentence in paragraph 3 clear? How has he made it so?

Compare this sentence with the one beginning at the bottom of page 12.

In the last sentence of paragraph 6 where does loose structure change to the periodic?

In paragraph 7 why would it be a blemish to write, "That we may keep alive similar sentiments"?

Why does he repeat "We wish" so many times? Why did he not substitute synonyms?

In paragraph 18 why has he used the word "interest" more than once? If the thought is to be repeated, why not some other word?

In the eighth sentence of paragraph 21 is the structure periodic or loose?

Reverse the order of clauses in the last sentence of paragraph 28. What is the effect?

CHAPTER IX

WORDS

A WORD is the sign of an idea. Whether the idea be an object, a quality, an action, simple existence, or a relation, if it be communicated to another, it must have some sign; in language these signs are words. Infinitely varied are the ideas man has to express. Each day, each moment, has its new combination of circumstances; yet by the common person the effect of the novel situation is described as "horrid" or "awful" or "perfectly lovely." Three adjectives to describe all creation! No wonder that people are constantly misunderstood; that others do not get their ideas. How can they? Do the best the master can, the thought will not pass from him to his reader without considerable deflection. He cannot say exactly what he would. His words do not hold the same meaning for him as for others. "Mother" to him is a dear woman with a gentle voice, always dressed in black, sitting by the window of home; to another she is a shrieking termagant, whose phrases are punctuated by blows. There is not a word that means exactly the same to two persons; yet with words men must express their thoughts, their feelings, their hopes, their purposes, — always changing, ever new, — and for all this shall they use but a few score of words? Words are the last, least elements of language; without these least elements, these atoms of language, no sentence, however simple, can be made; by means of them, the master drives mobs to frenzy or soothes the pain of eternal loss. The calm and peace which Emerson knew, we know; the perpetual benediction of past years which Wordsworth felt, all may feel. These thoughts masters have expressed in words, but not in three words. Thousands are not enough accurately to transfer their visions of this changing universe from them to us. Ideas infinite in their variety demand for their expression all the means which our language has placed at the disposal of the master. For this true expression the whole dictionary with its thousands of words is all too small.

Whoever hopes to be understood must acquire a full, rich vocabulary. However clearly he may think, however much he may feel, until he has words, the thought, the emotion, must remain his alone. To get a vocabulary, then, is a person's business. He who has it can command him who has it not. Not in literature alone, but in business,— in medicine, in law, behind the accountant's desk or the salesman's counter,— he is master who can say what he means so that the person to whom he speaks must know just what he means. Now it is a singular truth that when we read any great author, the words which we do not understand are remarkably few. Even in Shakespeare there are not many; and the few are unknown by reason of a constantly changing vocabulary. It was probably true then, as it would certainly be to-day, that the large majority of audiences lost not a word of his fifteen thousand, while they themselves used less than eight hundred. We know what others say; yet we say nothing ourselves. What a vocabulary one could accumulate, if from six to eighteen he added only two words a day! Twelve years, and each year more than seven hundred words! It does not look a difficult task. Children do more, an never realize the superiority of their achievement. Nine thousand words at eighteen! Shakespeare alone used more. Macaulay needed scarcely six thousand.

How shall a vocabulary be accumulated? One method is by the use of a dictionary; and many persons find it a source of great pleasure. *Dictionary.* The genealogy and biography of words are as fascinating to a devoted philologist as stamps to a philatelist or cathedrals to an architect. "Canteen" is quite an unassuming little word. Yet imperious Cæsar knew it in its childhood. The Roman camp was laid out like a small city, with regular streets and avenues. On one of these streets called the "Via Quintana" all the supplies were kept. When the word passed into the Italian, it became "cantina;" and cantinas may be found among all nations who have drawn their language from the Latin. There is this difference, however: that whereas eatables were to be had in the Roman quintana, only drinkables can be found in the Italian cantina. When the English adopted the word, the middle meaning, a place where wines are stored, a wine-cellar, came to be a small flask especially fitted for the rough usage of a soldier's life, in which a necessary supply of some sort of liquid may be carried. So the name of a street has become the much-berated canteen of the sutler and the much needed canteen of the soldier. The dictionary is full of such fascinating biographies. Still its fascination is not the reason why most people study the dictionary: it is because such a study is necessary for the person who hopes for an accurate knowledge of the words he reads. It is not impossible to know "pretty nearly what it means" from the context; but no master uses words without knowing exactly what they mean. Certainty of meaning precedes frequency of use; and this necessary confidence is gained from a study of the dictionary. In a general way we know all the words of Macaulay's vocabulary; but the average man uses only eight hundred of them. His knowledge of words is no more than an indistinct, mumbling knowledge. To lift each word out of its context, to make it a distinct, living entity, capable of serving, the definition must be studied. Then the student knows just what service the word is fitted for, and finds a pleasure in being competent to command that service. The dictionary is a necessity to the person who hopes to use words.

Yet the knowledge of words that the student derives from the dictionary is not sufficient. **Study of Literature.** When one hears an educated foreigner speak, he detects little errors in his use of words, — errors which are not the fault of definition, but errors in the idiomatic use of words. This use cannot be learned from a dictionary, where words are studied individually, but only by studying them in combination with other words where the influence of one word upon another may be noted. There is little difference in the size of a pile of stones, whether we say a great pile of stones or a large pile of stones; but a great man is of much more consequence than a large man. A dictionary could hardly have told a foreigner this. A man may pursue or chase a robber, as the author wishes; but he may not chase a course. Prepositions are especially liable to be misused, and their correct use comes from a study of literature, not of the dictionary. The nice and discriminating refinements in the use of words are learned by careful reading. When a phrase is met, such as "the steep and solitary eastern heaven," where each word has been born to a new beauty; or this, "And the sweet city with her dreaming spires," where the adjectives "sweet" and "dreaming" have a richer content, they should be regarded with great care and greeted with even more delight than words entirely new. How to read that we may gain this complete mastery of words, Mr. Ruskin has best told us in "Sesame and Lilies." Every person should know "Of Kings' Treasuries" by reading and re-reading. Literature, the way masters have used words, will furnish a knowledge of the nicer discriminations in their use.

The dictionary and literature are the sources of a full and refined vocabulary. But the vocabulary which may be perfectly understood is not entirely in one's possession until it is used. Seek the first opportunity to use the newly acquired word. It will be hard to utter it; you will feel an effort in getting it out. Only once, however; after that it rises as easily as any old familiar word. Because the companion with whom you speak is always "just as mad as" she can be, is no reason why you may not at times be vexed, annoyed, aggravated, exasperated, or angry. Men are not always either "perfectly lovely" or "awful;" neither are all ladies "jewels." There are degrees of villainy and nobility; and all jewels have not the same lustre. Know what you want to say, and find the one word that will exactly say it. This costs work, it is true; but what is there worth having which has not cost some one work? Do the work; search for the word; then use it. In this way a vocabulary becomes a real possession.

The words which a person may use are generally described as reputable, national, and present. Words must be reputable; that is, sanctioned by the authority of the creators of English literature. They must be national; words that are the property of the mass of the people, not of a clique or a district. And they must be of the present; Chaucer's vocabulary, though it be the source of English, will not satisfy the conditions of to-day.

First, words must be of reputable use. No person would consider vulgarisms reputable. When a person says "I hain't got none," he has reached about the acme of vulgarisms, the language of the illiterate. Grammar has been disregarded; a word has been used which is not a word; and another word has no reason for its appearance in the sentence. Yet sometimes this expression is heard; seldom seen written. It is always set down to the account of an illiterate home; for no one can reach a high school without knowing its grammatical errors. The unerring use of *don't, me, I, lie, lay, set,* and *sit,* is not so assured that the list can be omitted. Adjectives are used for adverbs; "real good" is not yet forgotten. Nouns are called upon to do the work of verbs. This is the language of the illiterate, and it should be avoided; for vulgarisms are not reputable.

Vulgarisms are not reputable.

Neither is slang reputable. He would be a prude who would not recognize that slang is sometimes right to the point; and that many of our strongest idioms were originally slang. Still, although many phrases which to-day are called slang were at one time reputable, the fact of their respectable birth cannot save them from the slight imputation that now they are slang. Notwithstanding the fact that we owe some of our strongest idioms to slang, the free use of slang always vulgarizes. It generally is called upon to supply a deficiency either in thought or in the power of expression. People too lazy to think, too indolent to read, with little to say, and but a few slang phrases to say it with, may be allowed to practice this vulgarity; but cultured persons in cultured conversation will eschew all acquaint-

Slang is not reputable.

ance with it. To find it in the serious composition of educated persons always raises a question of their refinement. It is the stock in trade of the lazy and the uncultured. It is used to divert attention from poverty of thought and a threadbare vocabulary. It is unnecessary for the complete expression of thought by the scholar and man of refinement.

It is a real misfortune that many good words have been tarnished by the handling of the illiterate. "Awful," "horrid," and "lovely" are good words; but they have been sullied by common use. So common have they become that they approach slang. They may be rescued from that charge in each person's writing, if he shows by accurate use of them that he is master of their secret strength.

Milton wrote: —

"No! let us rather choose,
Armed with Hell-flames and fury, all at once
O'er Heav'n's high towers to force resistless way,
Turning our tortures into *horrid* arms
Against the Torturer."

Lord Lytton makes Richelieu exclaim: —

"Look where she stands! Around her form I draw
The *awful* circle of our solemn church."

And in the New Testament we read: —

"Finally, brethren, whatsoever things are true, whatsoever things are honest, whatsoever things are just, whatsoever things are pure, whatsoever things are *lovely*, whatsoever things are of good report; if there be any virtue, and if there be any praise, think on these things."

There is no question here of the words; they have all the freshness and vigor of their youth. Do not hesitate to use such words exactly. When the thought calls for them, they say with certainty what can be expressed only doubtfully by other words.

Second, words must be of national use. They cannot be words confined to a locality. When Morris talks of a house that has been "gammoned," he deprives a large number of readers of his meaning. "Gums" and "brasses" may be good in certain districts of England, but in literature they should not be used, for they would not generally be understood. For the same reason much of the common conversation of the South is foreign to a native of New York. Whoever employs the language of a locality limits his circle of readers to that locality. To write for all he must use the language of all; he must avoid provincialisms.

Words must be national. Provincialisms.

Like words that are used by a small region are words which are understood by a clique of persons. Scholars are inclined to use a scholarly vocabulary. The biologist has one; the chemist another; the philosopher a third. This technical vocabulary may be a necessity at times; but when a specialist addresses the public, his words must be the words which an average cultured man can understand. Such words can be found if the writer will look for them; if he does not, his work can scarcely be called literature. Technical words and bookish terms are not words of national use.

Technical and Bookish Words.

The following by Josiah Royce illustrates how clearly a most abstruse topic can be handled by a man willing to take the trouble : —

"If you ask what sort of thing this substance is, the first answer is, that it is something eternal ; and that means, not that it lasts a good while, but that no possible temporal view of it could exhaust its nature. All things that happen result from the one substance. This surely means that what happens now and what happened millions of years ago are, for the substance, equally present and necessary results. To illustrate once more in my own way: A spider creeping back and forth across a circle could, if she were geometrically disposed, measure out in temporal succession first this diameter, and then that. Crawling first over one diameter, she would say, 'I now find this so long.' Afterwards examining another diameter, she would say, 'It has now happened that what I have just measured proves to be precisely as long as what I measured some time since, and no longer.' The toil of such a spider might last many hours, and be full of such successive measurements, each marked by a spun thread of web. But the true circle itself within which the web was spun, the circle in actual space as the geometer knows it, would its nature be thus a series of events, a mere succession of spun threads? No, the true circle would be timeless, a truth founded in the nature of space, outlasting, preceding, determining all the weary web-spinning of this time-worn spider. Even so we, spinning our web of experience in all its dreary complications in the midst of the eternal nature of the world-embracing substance, imagine that our lives somehow contain true novelty, discover for the substance what it never knew before, invent new forms of being. We fancy our past wholly past, and our future wholly unmade. We think that where we have yet spun no web, there is nothing, and that what we long ago spun has vanished, broken by the winds of time into nothingness. It is not so. For the eternal substance there is no before and after; all truth is truth. 'Far and forgot to me is near,' it says. In the unvarying precision of its mathematical universe, all is eternally written.

> 'Not all your piety nor wit
> Can lure it back to cancel half a line,
> Nor all your tears wash out one word of it.'"

Words and phrases from a foreign language should be used only as a last resort. *Bon mot, sine qua non,* and *dolce far niente* are all very apt, and to a person like Mr. Lowell, who was intimately

<small>Foreign Words.</small>

acquainted with many languages, they may come as soon as their English equivalents. In the case of such a person, the reason why they should not be used is that the reader cannot understand them. But when a young smatterer uses them to advertise his calling acquaintance with a language, he is but proclaiming his own lack of good taste. In his composition they are as ineffective to make it respectable as a large diamond on a gamester's finger to make him an honored gentleman. Use the English language when writing for English-speaking people. It has the fullest, richest vocabulary in the world. It will not be found unequal to the task of expressing your thoughts.

Third, words should be in present use. Words may be so new that people do not know them they may have passed out of use after years of good service. Of new words, but little can be said. The language constantly changes. New discoveries and inventions demand new words. What ones will be more than temporary cannot be prophesied. "Blizzard" and "mugwump" were new but a short time ago: the latter is dying from disuse, the former has come to stay. In this uncertainty one thing can be said, however. No word which has not secured recognition should be used by a young person, if by reputable words already in the language he can express his meaning. And just as he should not be the first to take up an untried word, so the young writer should not be the last to drop a dead one. There is at present a sort of fad for old English. A large number of words that have been resting quietly in their graves for centuries have been called forth. Some may enjoy a second life; most of them will feel only the weakness of a second obsolescence. "Foreword" and "inwit" were good once; but "preface" and "con-

Words in Present Use.

science" mean as much and have the advantage of being alive. To be understood use the words of the present.

Use words in their present signification. Not only has language cast out many words; it has changed many others so that they are hardly recognized. When Chaucer wrote,

Words in their Meaning.

> "Ther may no man Mercury mortify
> But hit be with his brother knowleching,"

"mortify" meant to make dead, to kill. To-day a lady may say she was mortified to death; but that is hyperbole. In "Paradise Lost" Satan may

> "Through the palpable obscure find out
> His uncouth way."

But a person to-day is not justified in using "uncouth" for "unknown." The works of Shakespeare and Milton abound in words whose life has been prolonged to the present, but whose signification has been changed. The writer who seeks to use words with these old meanings is standing in his own light. Such use always attracts attention to the words themselves, and by so much subtracts attention from the thought.

Words that are in good use have been divided into two classes, as they have been drawn from two sources. Some differences between Anglo-Saxon and Latin words are marked. Saxon words are generally short; Latin words long. The first are the words of home and are concerned with the necessities of life; the second are the words of the court and the adornments of polite society. The former made the foundation of our language and gave to it its idiomatic strength; the latter came later, and added to the strength of the language its grace and refinement.

Words of Anglo-Saxon Origin.

In our speech there can be no doubt that short words are used when the purpose is to be understood quickly, even harshly, while the longer words are frequently employed for saying unpleasant things pleasantly. Euphemism, the choice of words not harsh for harsh ideas, has its uses. It is not always wrong to say, "He was taken away" for "He was killed." But when the plain truth is to be spoken, when, as in most composition, the object is to be understood, the words should be chosen which exactly express the thought, be those words Latin or Saxon. For any one to say, "Was launched into eternity" for "Was hanged," or "When the fatal noose was adjusted about the neck of the unfortunate victim of his own unbridled passions" for "When the halter was put around his neck," is a useless parade of vocabulary.[1] One knows that such phrases are made by a writer who is ignorant of the value of words, or by a penny-a-liner, willing to sacrifice every effect of language to the immediate needs of his purse. Such writing has no power. The words are dictated by too low a motive to have any force in them. Let a writer go straight to the point as directly as the hindrances of language will allow. Even then his expression will lag behind his thought.

This does not mean that one is to use Saxon words always. It means that one shall use the words that say exactly what is to be said, so that the reader can get the exact thought with the least outlay of attention to the words. Latin words are as common as Saxon words. To search out a Saxon word because it is Saxon and short is as reprehensible as to use the indirection of Latin words where directness is wanted. Latin words have a place; they express the finer distinctions and gradations of thought. In the discussion

---

[1] See Lowell's *Biglow Papers*, Introduction to Second Series.

of any question requiring nice precision of statement Latin words are necessary. In the following from Newman, it would be difficult, perhaps impossible, to substitute words of Anglo-Saxon origin for the words of Latin origin, and could it be done, the passage would not then have the clearness it now has from his use of common words, though they be Latin : —

"I mean then by the Supreme Being, one who is simply self-dependent, and the only Being who is such; moreover, that He is without beginning or Eternal, and the only Eternal; that in consequence He has lived a whole eternity by Himself; and hence that He is all-sufficient, sufficient for his own blessedness, and all-blessed, and ever-blessed. Further, I mean a Being who, having these prerogatives, has the Supreme Good, or rather is the Supreme Good, or has all the attributes of good in infinite intenseness; all wisdom, all truth, all justice, all love, all holiness, all beautifulness; who is omnipotent, omniscient, omnipresent; ineffably one, absolutely perfect; and such that what we do not know of Him is far more wonderful than what we do and can."

Latin words, moreover, have a fullness of sound which gives them an added weight and dignity. One would hesitate long before changing one of Milton's big-sounding phrases, even if he were not compelled to sacrifice the metre. In Webster's orations there is a dignity, a sublimity, gained by the use of full-mouthed polysyllables. Supposing he had said at the beginning of his eulogy of Adams and Jefferson, "This is a new sight" instead of "This is an unaccustomed spectacle," the whole effect of dignified utterance commensurate with the occasion would have been lost. The oration abounds in examples of reverberating cadences. Milton's sentences are a stately procession of gorgeous words: the dignified pomp of the advance is occasioned by the wealth of essential beauty and historical association in the individual words : —

> " That proud honor claimed
> Azazel as his right, a Cherube tall :
> Who forthwith from the glittering staff unfurl'd
> Th' imperial ensign, which, full high advanc't
> Shon like a meteor streaming to the wind,
> With gemms and golden lustre rich emblaz'd
> Seraphic arms and trophies ; all the while
> Sonorous metall blowing martial sounds :
> At which the universal host up-sent
> A shout that tore Hell's concave, and beyond
> Frighted the reign of Chaos and old Night.
> All in a moment through the gloom were seen
> Ten thousand banners rise into the air,
> With orient colours waving ; with them rose
> A forrest huge of spears ; and thronging helms
> Appear'd, and serried shields in thick array
> Of depth immeasurable."

The choice of words does not depend on whether they are of Latin or of Saxon origin. In use it will be found that short words, like short sentences, give more directness and force to the composition ; while long words have a dignified elegance and refinement of discrimination not the property of monosyllables. No one should think, however, that short words cause the force or long words cause the dignity. These qualities belong to the thought ; the completeness of its expression is approached by a choice in words. Choose words for their fitness to say what you think, or feel, or purpose, having no regard for their origin.

Words are also classified as general and specific. *General specific* By a general word is meant a word common to or denoting a large number of ideas. By specific is meant a word that denotes or specifies a

WORDS 249

single idea. "Man," "move," "bad," are general and denote a large number of ideas; while "Whittier," "glide," "thieving," are specific, denoting but one man, one movement, one kind of badness. "Man" denotes the whole human race, while it implies a feeling, thinking, speaking, willing animal. "Whittier" denotes but a single person, but beside all the common qualities implied by the word "man," "Whittier" suggests, among other things, a homely face, serious and kind, a poet, and an anti-slavery worker.

As a principle in composition, it may be said that the more a word or phrase can be made to imply or suggest, while at the same time expressing all that the writer wishes to say, the more valuable does that word or phrase become. Yet it should be remembered that words may be so specific that they do not include all that the author wishes to include. For instance, if instead of "Blessed are the peacemakers," the beatitude should be made to read "Blessed are the Quakers," though this organized body of persons labor for the blessings of peace, the meaning would be restricted by the limited denotation of the term. It does not include enough. So of almost all of Emerson's writing, it would not be possible to express his entire thought with more specific words. Therefore regard must always be had for the thought, — that it may be expressed in its perfect fulness and entirety. Keeping this full expression in mind, those words are strongest, truest, richest, which suggest most. To say of a person that he is a bad man is one thing; that he is a traitor is quite another; but when one writes that he is a veritable Judas, words fail to keep pace with suggestions, and reason yields to emotion. Specific words, if they denote the whole idea, are as much better than general terms as their suggestion exceeds the suggestion of general terms.

Those Words that suggest most.

Much of the force of figures of speech is derived from the suggestive quality of the specific words employed. When a man calls another a dog, he has used a metaphor. He has availed himself of a term that gathers up all the snarling qualities of the worst of the dog species. The figure has high suggestive power. Synecdoche, too, that figure of speech in which a part is used for the whole or the whole for a part, employs a term of higher suggestive power for one of lower connoting force. "All hands took hold" is better than "All persons went to work." Metonymy is the substitution of the name of one thing for that of another to which the former bears a known and close relation. The most common of these known and close relations are those of cause and its effects, of container and the thing contained, and of sign and the thing signified. "He has read Shakespeare," "He was addicted to the use of the bottle," "All patriots fight for the flag," are examples of metonymy. All these figures depend in large degree for their power upon the greater suggestiveness of specific words; and their use gives to composition an efficiency and directness commensurate with the greater connoting value of the specific words.

<small>Synecdoche, Metonymy</small>

A writer should keep in mind the fact that the same word may mean widely different things to two persons. For this reason the specific word that appeals to him most may be of no value in addressing others. "Free silver" means to one set of men the withdrawal of money from investment, consequent stagnation in business, followed by the closing of factories and penury among laborers. To others it means three dollars a day for unskilled labor, fire, clothes, and something to eat. Again, if one wished to present the horrors of devastating dis-

<small>Care in Choice of Words.</small>

ease, in the South he would mention yellow fever, in the North smallpox; but to a lady who saw six little brothers and sisters dead from it in one week, three carried to the graveyard on the hillside one chill November morning, all the terrors of contagious disease are suggested by the word "diphtheria." Words are weighted with our experiences. They are laden with what we have lived into them. As persons have different experiences, each word carries to each person a different meaning. The wise writer chooses those specific words which suggest most to the men he addresses, — in general, to the average man.

There are many words that carry some of the same suggestions to all. These words are connected with the common things of life: such words as "home," "death," "mother," and the many more that have been with all people from childhood. They are simple little words crowded with experiences. Such words carry a weight of suggestion not found in strange new words. It is for this reason that simple language goes straight to the heart; it is so loaded with life. Of two expressions that convey the thought with equal accuracy, always choose the simpler.

The following poems — one by Tennyson, steeped in pain, perfect in its phrasing; the other by Kipling, rising to a conception of a true artist's work, never before so simply expressed — are both written in home words, little words, but words all know, words that carry to all a common meaning: —

> "Tears, idle tears, I know not what they mean:
> Tears from the depth of some divine despair
> Rise in the heart and gather to the eyes,
> In looking on the happy autumn fields,
> And thinking of the days that are no more.

"Fresh as the first beam glittering on a sail
  That brings our friends up from the underworld;
  Sad as the last which reddens over one
  That sinks with all we love below the verge;
  So sad, so fresh, the days that are no more.

"Ah! sad and strange as in dark summer dawns
  The earliest pipe of half-awakened birds
  To dying ears, when unto dying eyes
  The casement slowly grows a glimmering square;
  So sad, so strange, the days that are no more.

"Dear as remembered kisses after death,
  And sweet as those by hopeless fancy feigned
  On lips that are for others; deep as love,
  Deep as first love, and wild with all regret;
  O Death in Life, the days that are no more!"

L'ENVOI.[1]

"When Earth's last picture is painted and the tubes are twisted and dried,
When the oldest colors have faded, and the youngest critic has died,
We shall rest, and, faith, we shall need it — lie down for an æon or two,
Till the Master of All Good Workmen shall put us to work anew!

"And those that were good shall be happy: they shall sit in a golden chair;
They shall splash at a ten-league canvas with brushes of comets' hair;
They shall find real saints to draw from — Magdalene, Peter, and Paul;
They shall work for an age at a sitting and never be tired at all!

[1] From *The Seven Seas*, published by D. Appleton & Co., New York. Copyright, 1896, by Rudyard Kipling.

"And only the Master shall praise us, and only the Master
  shall blame;
And no one shall work for money, and no one shall work
  for fame;
But each for the joy of the working, and each, in his sepa-
  rate star,
Shall draw the Thing as he sees It for the God of Things as
  They Are!"

Much like general terms, which mean something or nothing, are expressions that have become trite and hackneyed. At some time they were accurate phrases, saying just what was needed. By being used for all sorts of purposes, they have lost the original thought of which they were the accurate expression. They have no freshness. The sounding phrases repeated in the pulpit, or the equally empty phrases of the scientist, however good they were at their inception, are, in the writing of many persons, but theological and scientific cant relied upon by ignorant people to cover up the vacuity of their thought. One's own expression, even though it be not so elegant and graceful, is better than any worn-out, hackneyed phrase. Think for yourself; then say what you have thought in the best language you can find yourself. *Hackneyed Phrases.*

"Fine writing," the subjection of noble words to ignoble service, is to be avoided. Mr. Micawber was addicted to this pomposity of language; and Dickens, by the creation of this character, has done literature a real service, by showing how absurd it is, how valueless for anything more than humor. "'Under the impression,' said Mr. Micawber, 'that your peregrinations in this metropolis have not as yet been extensive, and that you might have some difficulty in penetrating the arcana of the Modern Babylon in the direction of the City Road — in short,' *"Fine Writing."*

said Mr. Micawber, in another burst of confidence, 'that you might lose yourself — I shall be happy to call this evening, and install you in the knowledge of the nearest way.'" Here are great words in profusion to dress out a little thought. "Fine writing is as much out of taste as over-dressing. When the thought calls for noble expression, then all one's energies should be bent to finding noble phrases; but for common things common expressions are the only ones in good taste.

<small>In Prose a Poetical Words.</small> Much like "fine writing" is the use of poetical words in prose. *Enow, erstwhile, besprent, methinks, agone,* and *thine* are examples of a large class of words which, though in perfectly good taste in poetry, are in extremely poor taste in prose. They are out of place; and so attract attention to themselves, not to the thought they express. When writing prose, avoid poetical words.

All of this comes at last to one rule : be exact, be accurate in the choice of words. Not a word that half expresses the thought, not even one that is pretty near, but the only word that exactly expresses the meaning, that word must be used. It is not a question of long or short, of Latin or Saxon, of general or specific it is a question of accuracy or inaccuracy, the whole or a part, the whole or too much, of just right or about right. No one would entirely misunderstand the following sentence; and just as certainly no one would derive from these words the impression the author had when he wrote it. He has phrased it as follows "Another direction in which free education is most valuable to society, is the way in which it removes the gulf affixed between the rich and poor." The boy wanted the opening sentence to sound big, and forgot that the first use of words is accurately to express the thought. In this sentence are the commonest errors in the choice of words. "Most valuable" says more than truth; "direction" says less than truth; and "affixed" does not say anything. Had the boy studied the dictionary, had he been familiar with the Bible, had he carefully considered the figure he introduced with the word "gulf," he would not have written this incongruous sentence; he would not have been inaccurate. Spare no pains in your effort to be exact. Search through the words of your own vocabulary; if these fall short, find others in the dictionary. Get the word that exactly expresses the thought. Let no fine-sounding or high-born word trick you into saying what you do not mean. Be master of your words; never let fine expressions enslave you. In a word, be accurate.

Such painstaking labor has its reward not alone in the increased power of expression; there is also a corresponding growth in the ability to observe accurately and to think clearly. No man can write such descriptions as Ruskin and Stevenson have written without seeing accurately; nor can a man speak with the definite certainty of Burke without thinking clearly. The desire to be accurate in expression drives a writer to be accurate in thinking. To think is the highest that man can hope from education. Anything that contributes to this highest attainment should be undertaken with joy. Whether planning a story or constructing an argument; whether excluding irrelevant matter or including what contributes to the perfection of the whole; whether massing the material so that all the parts shall receive their due emphasis; whether relating the parts so that the thought advances steadily and there can be no misunderstanding,—in all this the student will find arduous labor. Yet after all this is done, — when the theme, the paragraphs, and the sentences contain exactly what is needed, are properly massed, and are set in perfect order, — then comes the long labor of revision, which does not stop until the exact word is hunted out. For upon words, at last, we are dependent for the expression of our observation and thought. He is most entirely master of his thoughts who can accurately express them : clearly, that he cannot be misunderstood ; forcefully, that he will not be unread and elegantly, that he give the reader joy. And this mastery he evinces in a finely discriminating choice of words.

APPENDIX

A. SUGGESTIONS TO TEACHERS.

The Course of Study given on pages xx-xxvi contemplates five days a week to be given to English. During the first two years, three of these days should be devoted to the study of literature, and two to the study of composition. In practice I have found it best to have the study of literature occupy three consecutive days, — for example, Tuesday, Wednesday, and Thursday. This arrangement leaves Monday and Friday for composition. Friday is used for the study of the text-book and for general criticism and suggestion. On Monday the compositions should be written in the classroom. To have them so written is, at least during the first year, distinctly better. The first draft of the composition should be brought to class ready for amendment and copying. During the writing the teacher should be among the pupils offering assistance, and insisting upon good penmanship. Care at the beginning will form a habit of neatness, and keep the penmanship up to a high standard. For both pupil and instructor it is worth all it costs.

The arrangement suggested is only one plan. This works well. Many others may be adopted. But no plan should be accepted which makes the number of essays fewer than one a week; nor should the number of days given to literature be smaller than three a week.

During the second year, if the instructor thinks it can be done without loss, the compositions may be written outside of school hours and brought to class on a definite day. A pupil should not be allowed to put off the writing of a composition any more than a lesson in geometry. On Monday of each week a composition should be handed in; irregularity only makes the work displeasing and leads to shirking. Writing out of school gives more time for criticism and study of composition, and during the second year this extra time is much needed.

By the third year the pupils certainly can do the work out of school. As the compositions increase in length, more time will be necessary for their preparation. The teacher should, however, know exactly what progress has been made each week; and by individual criticisms and by wise suggestions she should help the pupil to meet the difficulties of his special case.

In order that the instructor may have time for individual criticism, she should have two periods each day vacant in which to meet pupils for consultation. To make this clear, suppose that a teacher of English has one hundred pupils in her classes. She should have no more, for one hundred essays a week are enough for any person to correct. If there be six recitation periods daily, place twenty-five pupils in each of four sections for the study of literature, composition, and general criticism. This leaves two periods each day to meet individuals, giving ten pupils for each period. These should come on scheduled days, with the same regularity as for class recitation. The pupil's work should have been handed in on the second day before he comes up for consultation, in order that the teacher may be competent to give criticisms of any value. The inspiration of the first reading cannot be depended upon to suggest any help, nor is there time for such a reading during the recitation.

There will be need of class recitation in argument. Ten days or two weeks are all that is necessary for text-book work. This should be done before pupils read the "Conciliation." In the reading constantly keep before the pupils the methods of the author.

Every teacher should be able to do what she asks of the pupils. No person would dare to offer herself as a teacher of Latin or algebra until she could write all the translations of the one and solve all the problems of the other. Yet there are persons who have the audacity to offer their services as teachers of English, when they cannot write a letter correctly, to say nothing of a more formal piece of composition.

If an instructor in physics, who had asked his pupils to solve a problem in electricity, should say to each unfortunate person as he handed in his solution, "No, that isn't right; you'll have to try again," without offering any help or suggestion, and should continue this discouraging process until some bright pupil worked it out, or perhaps some one guessed it, we should say that such a person was no instructor at all. We might go so far as to question his intellectual competency. We certainly should think him quite deserving of dismissal. Still many teachers of English do nothing more than say, "It isn't right. Make it so." If the teacher does not know how to do the thing she asks the pupils to do, she should not be teaching. And even when she can do it, she will often benefit herself and the pupils by actually writing the composition. In this way not only does she gain command of her own powers of expression, but she finds out the difficulties with which the pupils have to contend. Every teacher of English composition should be able to do some creditable work in English; and every teacher of English should put this talent into actual use.

Numerous examples of correct paragraphs, well-made sentences, and apt words have not been included in the text. They have been omitted because they can be found in the literature study. It is better for pupils to find these for themselves. It will put them in the way of reading with the senses always alert for something good; and all good paragraphs and sentences lose something of their beautiful adaptation when torn from the place of their birth and growth.

So, too, there are no long lists of errors. One hundred pupils in a term make enough to fill a volume. When a teacher knows that Sentences is to be her next subject she should begin three months in advance to get a good collection of specimens. These should be classified so that they may be most usable. By the time the class comes to the study of Sentences some new, live material will be on hand for illustration.

In the pupils' exercises each week those errors should be singled out and dwelt upon which are the special subject of text-book work. If the pupils are studying Coherence in sentence structure, select all violations of this principle in the week's exercises, and by means of them nail that one principle down instead of trying to lay down the whole set of principles given in the chapter on Sentences. Alongside of this collection of mistakes in Coherence of sentences show the pupils the best examples of tight-jointed sentences to be found in the literature they are studying. Point out how these sentences have been made to hold together, and how their own shambling creations can be corrected.

Some teachers will fear the amount of literature required. It may seem large, especially in the first two years. It certainly would be quite impossible to read aloud in class all of this. However, that is not intended. There would be but sorry progress either in the course of study or in the power to analyze literature if the class time were taken up with oral reading of narration and description. The whole of a short story or one or two chapters of a novel are not too much for a lesson. The discussion of the meaning and the method of the author should take up the largest part of the time. Then such portions should be read aloud as are especially suited to an exercise in oral reading. In this way the apparently large list will be easily covered within the time.

Moreover, there is distinct gain in reading much. If only three or four pages be given for a lesson, the study of literature degenerates into a study of words. A study of words is necessary, but it is only a part of the study of literature. Such a method of study gives the pupil no sense of values. He does not get out into the wide spaces of the author's thought, but is eternally hedged about by the dwarfing barriers of etymology and grammar.

B. THE FORM OF A COMPOSITION.

THE MARGIN. It is the custom to leave a margin of about an inch at the left side of the page. In this margin the corrections should be written, not in the composition. There should be no margin at the right. The device of writing incomplete lines, or of making each sentence a paragraph, is sometimes adopted by young persons in the hope of deceiving the teacher as to the length of the composition. Remember that pages do not count for literature any more than yards of hideous advertising boards count as art. Write a full page with a straight-lined margin at the left.

INDENTION. To designate the beginning of a new paragraph, it is customary to have the first line begin an inch farther in than the other lines. This indention of the margin and the incomplete line at the end mark the visible limits of the paragraph.

THE HEADING. The heading or title of the composition should be written about an inch and a half from the top of the page, and well placed in the middle from left to right. There should be a blank line between the title and the beginning of the composition. Some persons prefer, in addition to the title, the name of the writer and the date of writing, — an unnecessary addition, it seems to me. If they are to appear, the name should be at the left and the date at the right, both on one line. The title will be on the next line below.

Jay Phillips.   *Jan. 27, 1900.*

The Circus-Man's Story.

"There was once an old man whom they called a wizard, and who lived in a great cave by the sea and raised dragons. Now when I was a very little boy, I had read a great deal about this old man and felt as if he were quite a friend of mine. I had planned for a long time to pay him a visit, although I had not decided *just when I should start. But the day Jim White's father brought him that camel, I was crazy to be after my dragon at once.*

"When bedtime came, I had made all my plans; and scarcely had Nurse turned her back when I was on my way. It was really very far, but I traveled so swiftly that I arrived in a remarkably short time at the wizard's house. When I rapped, he opened the door and asked me in.

"'I came to see if you had any dragons left,' I told him. 'I should like a very good, gentle dragon,' I added, 'that would not scare Nurse; and if it is n't too much trouble, I should want one that I could ride.'"

THE INDORSEMENT. When the composition is finished, it should be folded but once up and down the middle of the page. The indorsement upon the back is generally written toward the edges of the leaves, not toward the folded edge. I prefer the other way, however; and for this reason. If in a bunch of essays a teacher is searching for a particular one, she generally holds them in the left hand and with the fingers of the right lifts one essay after another. Indorsing toward the folded edge insures lifting a whole essay every time; while if the edges of the leaves be toward the right hand, too many or too few may be lifted.

The indorsement should contain: first, the name of the writer; second, the term and period of his recitation; third, the title of the essay; and fourth, the date. In describing the class and period, it is well to use a Roman numeral for the term, counting two terms in each year, and an Arabic numeral to denote the period of his recitation.

> *Jay Phillips.*
>
> II, 3.
>
> *The Circus-Man's Story.*
>
> *Jan. 27, 1900.*

PENMANSHIP. The penmanship should be neat and legible. Not all persons can write elegantly; but all can write so that their work can be easily read, and all can make a clean page. Scribbling is due to carelessness. A scribbled page points to a scribbling mind; clean-cut handwriting, perhaps not Spencerian, but a clear, legible handwriting is not only an indication of clear-cut thinking but a means and promoter of accurate thought. Moreover, as a business proposition, one cannot afford to become a slovenly penman. Every composition should be a lesson in penmanship, and by so much improve one's chances in the business world. And last, the teacher who has to read and correct the compositions of from one hundred to two hundred persons each week demands some consideration. No one but a teacher knows the drudgery of this work; it can be much lightened if each pupil writes so that the composition can be read without difficulty. By doing this, the pupil is sure of better criticism; for the teacher can give all her attention to the composition, none being demanded for the penmanship.

C. MARKS FOR CORRECTION OF COMPOSITIONS.

In correcting compositions certain abbreviations will save a teacher much time. Some of the common ones are given below. Underscore the element that needs correcting, and put the abbreviation in the margin. In case the whole paragraph needs remodeling, draw a line at its side and note the correction in the margin.

Cap. Use a capital letter.
l. c. Use a small letter.
D. See the dictionary for the correct use of the word.
Sp. Spelling.
Gr. A mistake in grammatical use of language.
Cnst. The construction of the sentence is awkward or unidiomatic.

Cl.	Not clear. The remedy may be suggested by reference to certain pages of the text.
W.	Weak. As above, point out the trouble by a page reference.
Rep.	Repetition is monotonous; or it may be necessary for clearness.
p.	Punctuation.
Cond.	Condense.
Exp.	Expand.
Tr.	Transpose.
?	Some fault not designated. It is well to use page reference.
¶	Make a new paragraph.
No ¶	Unite into one paragraph.
δ	Cut out.
∧	There is something omitted.

In addition to the above very common corrections, many others should be made. Instead of abbreviations, it will be better to refer the pupil to the page of the book which treats of the special fault. For instance, if there be an unexpected change of construction, underscore it, and write in the margin "226;" on this page is found "parallel construction" of sentences. It may be well to use the letters U., C., and M., in connection with the page numbers to indicate that the fault is in the unity, coherence, or mass of the element to be corrected. The constant reference to the fuller statement of the principles violated will serve to fix them in the mind.

D. PUNCTUATION.

Punctuation seeks to do for written composition what inflections and pauses accomplish in vocal expression. It makes clear what kind of an expression the whole sentence is: whether declarative, exclamatory, or interrogative. And it assists in indicating the relations of the different parts within a sentence. While there is practically uniformity in the method of punctuation at the end of a sentence, within a sentence punctuation shows much variety of method. Where one person uses a comma, another inserts a semicolon; and where one finds a semicolon sufficient, another requires a colon. It should be remembered that the parts of a sentence have not equal rank; and that the difference in rank should, as far as possible, be indicated by the marks of punctuation. Keeping in mind, also, the fact that the internal marks of punctuation, — the colon, the semicolon, and the comma, — have a rank in the order mentioned, from the greatest to the least, a writer will use the stronger marks when the rank of the parts of a sentence demands them, and the weaker marks to separate the lesser elements of the sentence. The sentences below illustrate the variety which may be practiced, and the use of punctuation to show the relation and rank of the elements of a sentence.

1. Internal punctuation is largely a matter of taste, but there are definite rules for final punctuation.

2. Internal punctuation is largely a matter of taste; there are, however, definite rules for final punctuation.

3. Internal punctuation, the purpose of which is to group phrases and clauses which belong together and to separate those which do not belong together, and to indicate the relative rank of the parts separated, is, to a great extent, a matter of taste: on the other hand, there are definite rules for final punctuation, the object of which is to separate sentences, and also to assist in telling what kind of a sentence precedes it; that is, whether it be declarative, interrogative, or exclamatory.

Looking at the first sentence, we find two elements of equal rank separated by a comma. Some authors would prefer no punctuation at all in a sentence as short as this. Again, if one wished to make the two elements very independent, he would use a semicolon. There would be but little difference in meaning between no punctuation and a comma; but there is a wide difference in meaning between no punctuation and a semicolon. The independence caused by the use of the semicolon is felt in the second sentence, where the words are the same except one. In this sentence a colon might be used; and one might go so far as to make two sentences of it. Notice that in these two sentences the question is how independent you wish the elements to be, and it is also a question of taste. In the third sentence, there are elements of different rank. To indicate the rank, punctuation of different value must be introduced. The two independent elements are separated by a colon. A semicolon might be used, if a semicolon were not used within the second independent element. This renders the greater mark necessary. Look at the commas in the first independent element. The assertion is that "internal punctuation is a matter of taste." This is too sweeping. It is modified by an explanatory phrase, "to a large extent;" and this phrase is inclosed by commas. Moreover, the long clause indicating the purpose of internal punctuation is inclosed by commas. The use of a semicolon in the second part falls under the third rule for the semicolon. If one should substitute for this semicolon a comma and a dash, he could use a semicolon instead of a colon for separating the two main divisions of the sentence. However, the method in which they are first punctuated is in accord with the rules generally accepted. The simplest of these rules are given below; but one must never be surprised to find a piece of literature in which the internal punctuation is at variance with these rules.

CAPITAL LETTERS.

1. A capital letter begins every new sentence.
2. A capital letter begins every line of poetry.
3. All names of Deity begin with a capital letter.
4. All proper names begin with capital letters.
5. All adjectives derived from proper nouns begin with capital letters.
6. The first word of every direct quotation begins with a capital letter.
7. Most abbreviations use capital letters.

COMMAS.

8. A series of words or a series of phrases, performing

similar functions in a sentence, are separated from each other by commas, unless all the connectives are expressed.

> "Her voice was ever soft,
> Gentle, and low, — an excellent thing in woman."

> "Good my lord,
> You have begot me, bred me, loved me: I
> Return those duties back as are right fit,
> Obey you, love you, and most honor you."

But, "shining and tall and fair and straight," because all the connectives are expressed.

9. Words out of their natural order are separated from the rest of the sentence by commas.

"To the unlearned, punctuation is a matter of chance."

10. Words and phrases, either explanatory or slightly parenthetical, are separated from the rest of the sentence by commas.

> "Then poor Cordelia!
> And yet not so; since, I am sure, my love's
> More richer than my tongue."

However when phrases and clauses are quite parenthetic, they are separated from the remainder of the sentence by parentheses, or by commas and dashes. The comma and dash is more common, and generally indicates a lesser independence of the inclosed element.

"The Miss Gunns smiled stiffly, and thought what a pity it was that these rich country people, who could afford to buy such good clothes (really Miss Nancy's lace and silk were very costly), should be brought up in utter ignorance and vulgarity."

11. The nominative of direct address, and phrases in the nominative absolute construction are cut off by commas.

> "Goneril,
> Our eldest born, speak first."

"The ridges being taken, the troops advanced a thousand yards."

12. Appositive words and phrases are separated from the remainder of the sentence by commas.

"In the early years of this century, such a linen weaver, named Silas Marner, worked at his vocation, in a stone cottage that stood among the nutty hedgerows near the village of Raveloe, and not far from the edge of a deserted stone-pit."

13. When words are omitted, the omission is indicated by the use of a comma.

> "Fairest Cordelia, that art most rich, being poor;
> Most choice, forsaken; and most loved, despis'd!"

14. A comma is used before a short and informal quotation.

> "In the bitterness of his wounded spirit, he said to himself, '*She* will cast me off too.'"

15. A comma is used to separate the independent clauses of a compound sentence sufficiently involved to necessitate some mark of punctuation, and yet not involved enough to require marks of different ranks.

> "But about the Christmas of the fifteenth year a second great change came over Marner's life, and his history became blent in a singular manner with the life of his neighbors."

16. Small groups of more closely related words are inclosed by commas to indicate their near relation and to separate them from words they might otherwise be thought to modify.

> "In this strange world, made a hopeless riddle to him, he might, if he had had a less intense nature, have sat weaving, weaving — looking towards the end of his pattern, or towards the end of his web, till he forgot the riddle, and everything else but his immediate sensations; but the money had come to mark off his weaving into periods, and the money not only grew, but it remained with him."

SEMICOLONS.

17. A semicolon is used to separate the parts of a compound sentence if they are involved, or contain commas. It is also used to give independence to the members of a compound sentence when not very complex.

> "The meadow was searched in vain; and he got over the stile into the next field, looking with dying hope towards a small pond which was now reduced to its summer shallowness, so as to leave a wide margin of good adhesive mud."

> "As for the child, he would see that it was cared for; he would never forsake it; he would do everything but own it."

18. Semicolons are used to separate a series of clauses in

much the same way as commas are used to separate a series of words.

> "I love you more than words can wield the matter;
> Dearer than eyesight, space, and liberty;
> Beyond what can be valued, rich or rare;
> No less than life, with grace, health, beauty, honor;
> As much as child e'er loved, or father found;
> A love that makes breath poor, and speech unable;
> Beyond all manner of so much I love thee."

19. A semicolon is generally used to introduce a clause of repetition, a clause stating the obverse, and a clause stating an inference.

(Many examples of the last two rules will be found in the discussion of compound sentences on pages 202, 203.)

COLONS.

20. A colon is used to introduce a formal quotation. It is frequently followed by a dash.

> "Under date of November 28, 1860, she wrote to a friend: —
> "'I am engaged now in writing a story — the idea of which came to me after our arrival in this house, and which has thrust itself between me and the other book I was meditating. It is Silas Marner, the Weaver of Raveloe.'"
> "On the last day of the same year she wrote: 'I am writing a story which came across my other plans by a sudden inspiration, etc.'"

21. A colon is used to introduce a series of particulars, either appositional or explanatory, which the reader has been led to expect by the first clause of the sentence. These particulars are separated from each other by semicolons.

> "The study of the principles of composition should include the following subjects: a study of words as to their origin and meaning; a study of the structure of the sentence and of the larger elements of discourse — in other words, of concrete logic; a study of the principles of effective literary composition, as illustrated in the various divisions of literature; and also a study of the æsthetics of literature."
> "What John Morley once said of literature as a whole is even more accurate when applied to fiction alone: its purpose is 'to bring sunshine into our hearts and to drive moonshine out of our heads.'"

22. A colon is used to separate the major parts of a very

complex and involved sentence, if the major parts, or either of them, contain within themselves semicolons.

"For four years he had thought of Nancy Lammeter, and wooed her with a tacit patient worship, as the woman who made him think of the future with joy: she would be his wife, and would make home lovely to him, as his father's home had never been; and it would be easy, when she was always near, to shake off those foolish habits that were no pleasures, but only a feverish way of annulling vacancy."

23. A colon is sometimes used to mark a strong independence in the parts of a compound sentence.

"He did n't want to give Godfrey that pleasure: he preferred that Master Godfrey should be vexed."

THE DASH.

24. A dash is frequently used with a colon to introduce a formal quotation. The quotation then begins a new paragraph.

(Example under colon.)

25. A dash is used alone or with a comma to inclose a phrase or clause which is parenthetic or explanatory.

"'But as for being ugly, look at me, child, in this silver-colored silk — I told you how it 'ud be — I look as yallow as a daffadil.'"

(Example under comma.)

26. A dash is used to denote a sudden turn of the thought.

"'I 've no opinion of the men, Miss Gunn — I don't know what *you* have.'"

"'It does make her look funny, though — partly like a short-necked bottle wi' a long quill in it.'"

27. A dash is frequently used when the composition should be interrupted to indicate the intensity of the emotion.

"'No — no — I can't part with it, I can't let it go,' said Silas abruptly. 'It 's come to me — I 've a right to keep it.'"

"And my poor fool is hang'd! No, no, no life!
Why should a dog, a horse, a rat, have life,
And thou no breath at all? Thou 'lt come no more,
Never, never, never, never, never! —
Pray you, undo this button: — thank you, sir. —
Do you see this? Look on her, — look, — her lips, —
Look there, look there!" —

28. A dash is sometimes used alone before an appositive phrase or clause.

"For the first time he determined to try the coal-hole — a small closet near the hearth."

PERIOD, EXCLAMATION POINT, INTERROGATION MARK.

29. A period closes every declarative sentence.

30. A period is used after abbreviations.

31. An exclamation point follows an expression of strong emotion.

32. An interrogation mark follows a direct question.

33. An interrogation mark is sometimes used in the body of a sentence, when the writer wishes to make the assertion forceful and uses a rhetorical question for the purpose.

"The shepherd's dog barked fiercely when one of these alien-looking men appeared on the upland, dark against the early winter sunset; for what dog likes a figure bent under a heavy bag? — and these pale men rarely stirred abroad without that mysterious burden."

34. Quotation marks inclose every quotation of the exact words of another. When one quotation is made within another, the inner or secondary quotation is inclosed with single marks, the main or outer quotation is included within the double marks.

(Examples of both may be found above.)

SUGGESTIONS FOR TEACHING PUNCTUATION.

At the time the pupils are studying the rules for punctuation they are reading Hawthorne or some other author equally careful of his punctuation. In his writing they will find numerous examples of the rules for punctuation. Let them take five rules for the comma, finding all the examples in five pages of text. In the same way furnish semicolons, colons, and dashes. When the rules have all been learned, they should be able to give the reason for every mark they find in literature. Next place upon the board paragraphs not punctuated, and have the pupils punctuate them. Remember that there is not absolute uniformity in the use of the comma, semicolon, and colon; though in each author there is unwavering adherence to the principles he adopts. Punctuation should be consistent. Insist that the pupil punctuates his written work consistently.

E. SUPPLEMENTARY LIST OF LITERATURE.[1]

Hawthorne	A Wonder-Book for Girls and Boys.
Tennyson	Enoch Arden.
Longfellow	Tales of a Wayside Inn.
Whittier	The Tent on the Beach.
Macaulay	Lays of Ancient Rome.
Dickens	A Christmas Carol.
Kipling	Wee Willie Winkie, and Other Stories.
Kipling	The Jungle Books.
Hawthorne	Twice-Told Tales.
Hawthorne	Mosses from an Old Manse.
Dickens	The Cricket on the Hearth.
Brown	Rab and his Friends.
Ouida	A Dog of Flanders.
Hale	The Man without a Country.
Defoe	Robinson Crusoe.
Poe	The Gold-Bug.
Scott	Marmion.
Scott	The Lady of the Lake.
Browning	Hervé Riel, an Incident of the French Camp, and other Narrative Poems.
Franklin	Autobiography.
Cooper	The Last of the Mohicans.
Longfellow	Evangeline.
Longfellow	Miles Standish.
Davis	Gallegher, and Other Stories.
Maupassant	Number Thirteen.
Miss Wilkins	Short Stories.
Miss Jewett	Short Stories.
Pope	The Iliad.
Aldrich	Marjorie Daw.
Lowell	The Vision of Sir Launfal, and Other Poems.

[1] See p. xix.

IRVING	Tales of a Traveller.
IRVING	The Sketch Book.
POE	The Fall of the House of Usher.
WHITTIER	Snow-Bound.
BURROUGHS	Sharp Eyes; Birds and Bees; Pepacton.
GOLDSMITH	The Deserted Village.
SCOTT	Ivauhoe.
DICKENS	David Copperfield.
SHAKESPEARE	Julius Cæsar.
SHAKESPEARE	The Merchant of Venice.
IRVING	Rip Van Winkle.
IRVING	The Legend of Sleepy Hollow.
BRYANT	Selected Poems.
GRAY	An Elegy in a Country Churchyard.
TENNYSON	The Princess; Idylls of the King.
DICKENS	The Pickwick Papers.
BURNS	Selected Poems.
DRYDEN	Alexander's Feast.
BYRON	Childe Harold.
GEORGE ELIOT	Silas Marner.
COLERIDGE	The Rime of the Ancient Mariner.
MACAULAY	Essay on Milton.
RUSKIN	Sesame and Lilies.
EMERSON	Friendship; Self-Reliance; Fortune of the Republic; The American Scholar.
ARNOLD	On the Study of Poetry; Wordsworth and Keats.
LOWELL	Emerson, the Lecturer; Milton; Books and Libraries.
HOLMES	The Autocrat of the Breakfast-Table.
ADDISON	The Sir Roger de Coverley Papers.
WORDSWORTH	Intimations of Immortality, and Other Poems.
KEATS	Selected Poems.
SHELLEY	Selected Poems.
SHAKESPEARE	Macbeth.
SHAKESPEARE	A Midsummer Night's Dream.
SHAKESPEARE	As You Like It.
WEBSTER	Bunker Hill Monument Oration; Adams and Jefferson.

GOLDSMITH	The Vicar of Wakefield.
MILTON	L'Allegro; Il Penseroso; Comus; Lycidas.
DE QUINCEY	Confessions of an English Opium Eater, and Other Papers.
JOHN HENRY NEWMAN	Selected Essays.
THACKERAY	Henry Esmond.
STEVENSON	Virginibus Puerisque.
STEVENSON	Memories and Portraits.
SCHURZ	Abraham Lincoln.
GEORGE WILLIAM CURTIS	Selected Addresses.
CHARLES LAMB	Essays of Elia.
STEVENSON	Travels with a Donkey.
STEVENSON	An Inland Voyage.
BURKE	Conciliation with the Colonies.
LINCOLN	Cooper Union Address; Gettysburg Speech.
CHAUCER	Prologue, and Two Canterbury Tales.
MILTON	Paradise Lost, and Sonnets.
CARLYLE	Essay on Burns.
TENNYSON	In Memoriam, and Lyrics.
BROWNING	Rabbi Ben Ezra; Saul; A Grammarian's Funeral.
THOREAU	Walden.
AUSTEN	Pride and Prejudice.
GEORGE ELIOT	Romola.
SHAKESPEARE	King Lear.
SHAKESPEARE	Hamlet.
MACAULAY	Essay on Johnson.
THACKERAY	Vanity Fair.
LOWELL	Democracy; Lincoln.
STEVENSON	Lantern Bearers; A Humble Remonstrance; Gossip about Romance.

The Riverside Press
Electrotyped and printed by H. O. Houghton & Co.
Cambridge, Mass, U. S. A.

ADVERTISEMENTS OF THE LITERATURE CALLED FOR BY THE COURSE OF STUDY GIVEN IN WEBSTER'S ENGLISH: COMPOSITION AND LITERATURE THAT IS PUBLISHED BY HOUGHTON, MIFFLIN & CO.

NOTE: R. L. S. stands for the Riverside Literature Series. Rolfe stands for Rolfe's Students' Series. Prices are net, postpaid, to teachers.

Narration

(*See Webster's English, page* xxi.)

The Great Stone Face: Hawthorne. In R. L. S. 40, paper, 15 cents; cloth, 40 cents.

The Gentle Boy; The Gray Champion; Roger Malvin's Burial: Hawthorne. In R. L. S. 145, paper, 15 cents.

Tales of a Wayside Inn: Longfellow. R. L. S. 33, 34, 35, each, paper, 15 cents; the three numbers in one vol. cloth, 50 cents.

The Gold-Bug: Poe. In R. L. S. 120, paper, 15 cents; cloth, 40 cents.

Marmion: Scott. Rolfe 2, cloth, 53 cents.

The Lady of the Lake: Scott. R. L. S. 53 (*Double Number*), paper, 30 cents; Rolfe 1, cloth, 53 cents.

A Christmas Carol: Dickens. R. L. S. 57, paper, 15 cents.

The Cricket on the Hearth: Dickens. R. L. S. 58, paper, 15 cents. Also 57 and 58 in one vol., cloth, 40 cents.

The Vision of Sir Launfal: Lowell. In R. L. S. 30, paper, 15 cents; cloth, 25 cents.

Other Narrative Poems by Lowell can be found in R. L. S. 30 and 15, each, paper, 15 cents. The two numbers, in one vol., cloth, 40 cents.

An Incident of the French Camp; Hervé Riel; The Pied Piper of Hamelin; How they brought the Good News from Ghent to Aix: Browning. In R. L. S. 115, paper, 15 cents.

HOME READING.

The Last of the Mohicans: Cooper. R. L. S. 95, 96, 97, 98, each, paper, 15 cents; the four numbers in one vol., cloth, 60 cents.

Tom Brown's School Days: Hughes. R. L. S. 85 (*Triple Number*), paper, 45 cents; cloth, 50 cents.

Nicholas Nickleby: Dickens. 2 vols.; cloth, $2.55.

Description

(*See Webster's English, page* xxiii.)

The Old Manse; The Old Apple Dealer: Hawthorne. In R. L. S. 69, paper, 15 cents; cloth, 40 cents.

An Indian Summer Reverie; The Oak: Lowell. In R. L. S. 30, paper, 15 cents; cloth, 25 cents.

To the Dandelion: Lowell. In R. L. S. 15, paper, 15 cents; 30 and 15 in one vol., cloth, 40 cents.
>Other Descriptive Poems, Lowell, can be found in R. L. S. 30 and 15 as above.

The Fall of the House of Usher: Poe. In R. L. S. 119, paper, 15 cents; cloth, 40 cents.

The Legend of Sleepy Hollow, and Other Selections from the Sketch Book: Irving. In R. L. S. 51, 52, each, paper, 15 cents; the two numbers in one vol., cloth, 40 cents.

Selections from Childe Harold: Byron. Rolfe 10, cloth, 53 cents.

Silas Marner: George Eliot. R. L. S. 83 (*Double Number*), paper, 30 cents; cloth, 40 cents.

The Deserted Village: Goldsmith. In R. L. S. 68, paper, 15 cents; cloth, 25 cents.

Julius Cæsar: Shakespeare. R. L. S. 67, paper, 25 cents; cloth, 25 cents.

The Merchant of Venice: Shakespeare. R. L. S. 55, paper, 15 cents; cloth, 25 cents. R. L. S. 55 and 67 in one vol.; cloth, 40 cents.

HOME READING

The Sketch Book (Essays from): Irving. R. L. S. 51, 52, each, paper, 15 cents; the two numbers in one vol., cloth, 40 cents.

Ivanhoe: Scott. R. L. S. 86 (*Quadruple Number*), paper, 50 cents; cloth, 60 cents.

The Princess: Tennyson. R. L. S. 111 (*Double Number*), paper, 30 cents; Rolfe 4, cloth, 53 cents.

Pepacton: Burroughs. Cloth, $1.06.

Sharp Eyes: Burroughs. In R. L. S. 36, paper, 15 cents; cloth, 40 cents.

Exposition and Argument

(See Webster's English, page xxv.)

L'Allegro, Il Penseroso, Comus, Lycidas: Milton. In R. L. S. 72, paper, 15 cents; cloth, 25 cents.

Essay on Milton: Macaulay. R. L. S. 103, paper, 15 cents; cloth, 25 cents.

Commemoration Ode: Lowell. In R. L. S. 30, paper, 15 cents; cloth, 25 cents.

Bunker Hill Oration; Adams and Jefferson: D. Webster. R. L. S. 56, paper, 15 cents.

Intimations of Immortality, and Other Poems: Wordsworth. R. L. S. 76, paper, 15 cents.

Of Kings' Treasuries. [From Sesame and Lilies]: Ruskin. In R. L. S. 142, paper, 15 cents

Conciliation with the Colonies: Burke. R. L. S. 100, paper, 15 cents; cloth, 25.

HOME READING

The Sir Roger de Coverley Papers. (Selections from): Addison. R. L. S. 60, 61, each, paper, 15 cents; the two numbers in one vol., cloth, 40 cents.

The Life and Writings of Addison: Macaulay. R. L. S. 104, paper, 15 cents; cloth, 25 cents.

Backlog Studies: Warner. Riverside Aldine Series, cloth, 85 cents.

Abraham Lincoln: Schurz. In R. L. S. 133, paper, 15 cents; cloth, 40 cents.

Difficult Selections

(See Webster's English, page xxvi.)

Paradise Lost. Two Books: Milton. In R. L. S. 94, paper, 15 cents; cloth, 40 cents.

Selected Poems: Burns. In R. L. S. 77, paper, 15 cents.

Essay on Burns: Carlyle. R. L. S. 105, paper, 15 cents; cloth, 25 cents.

In Memoriam: Tennyson. Rolfe 6, cloth, 53 cents.

Selected Poems: Tennyson. In R. L. S. 73, paper, 15 cents; cloth, 25 cents. In R. L. S. 99, paper, 15 cents. In Rolfe 5, 7, 8, 9, cloth, 53 cents.

The Lost Leader; Rabbi Ben Ezra; A Grammarian's Funeral: Browning. In R. L. S. 115, paper, 15 cents.

Friendship; Self-Reliance: Emerson. Cambridge Classics, cloth, 85 cents.

Short History of English Literature. *In preparation.*

HOME READING

The Autocrat of the Breakfast-Table: Holmes. R. L. S. 81 (*Triple Number*), paper, 45 cents; cloth, 50 cents.

Our Old Home: Hawthorne. Little Classics Edition, cloth, 85 cents.

Walden: Thoreau. Cambridge Classics, cloth, 85 cents.

Cambridge Thirty Years Ago: Lowell. In Fireside Travels, Cambridge Classics, cloth, 85 cents.

Emerson; Keats; Don Quixote: Lowell. In R. L. S. 39, paper, 15 cents.

On a Certain Condescension in Foreigners: Lowell. In R. L. S. 123, paper, 15 cents. Nos. 39 and 123 in one vol., cloth, 40 cents.

On the Threshold: Munger. Cloth, $1.06.

MINIMUM LIST PRICES*

OF BOOKS CALLED FOR BY THE COURSE OF STUDY

Narration: $1.65. Description: $2.18. Exposition and Argument: $1.20. Difficult Selections: $2.13. Webster's English: Composition and Literature: 90 cents.

* Exclusive of Palgrave's Golden Treasury, a Short History of English Literature, and the works suggested for Home Reading. In cases of alternatives the cheapest have been computed here.

Descriptive Circulars of the Riverside Literature Series, Rolfe's Students' Series, and Modern Classics sent on application. Correspondence solicited.

HOUGHTON, MIFFLIN & CO.

4 Park St., Boston; 11 E. 17th St., New York
378-388 Wabash Ave., Chicago

AUG 10 1983

**PLEASE DO NOT REMOVE
CARDS OR SLIPS FROM THIS POCKET**

UNIVERSITY OF TORONTO LIBRARY

Made in the USA
Middletown, DE
10 September 2015